SIMON FRASER UNIVERSITY
W.A.C. BENNETT LIBRARY

Author Chronologies

General Editor: **Norman Page**, Emeritus Professor of Modern English
Literature, University of Nottingham

Published titles include:

J.L. Bradley
A RUSKIN CHRONOLOGY

Michael G. Brennan and Noel J. Kinnamon
A SIDNEY CHRONOLOGY 1554–1654

Gordon Campbell
A MILTON CHRONOLOGY

Edward Chitham
A BRONTË FAMILY CHRONOLOGY

Martin Garrett
A BROWNING CHRONOLOGY:
ELIZABETH BARRETT BROWNING AND ROBERT BROWNING

A MARY SHELLEY CHRONOLOGY

A.M. Gibbs
A BERNARD SHAW CHRONOLOGY

Graham Handley
AN ELIZABETH GASKELL CHRONOLOGY

J. R. Hammond
A ROBERT LOUIS STEVENSON CHRONOLOGY
AN EDGAR ALLAN POE CHRONOLOGY
AN H.G. WELLS CHRONOLOGY
A GEORGE ORWELL CHRONOLOGY

Edgar F. Harden
A WILLIAM MAKEPEACE THACKERAY CHRONOLOGY
A HENRY JAMES CHRONOLOGY

John Kelly
A W.B. YEATS CHRONOLOGY

John McDermott
A HOPKINS CHRONOLOGY

Roger Norburn
A JAMES JOYCE CHRONOLOGY

Norman Page
AN EVELYN WAUGH CHRONOLOGY
AN OSCAR WILDE CHRONOLOGY

Peter Preston
A D.H. LAWRENCE CHRONOLOGY

Nicholas von Maltzahn
AN ANDREW MARVELL CHRONOLOGY

Author Chronologies Series
Series Standing Order ISBN 0–333–71484–9
(*outside North America only*)

You can receive future titles in this series as they are published by placing a standing order.
Please contact your bookseller or, in case of difficulty, write to us at the address below with
your name and address, the title of the series and the ISBN quoted above.
Customer Services Department, Macmillan Distribution Ltd, Houndmills, Basingstoke,
Hampshire RG21 6XS, England

A Christopher Marlowe Chronology

Lisa Hopkins
Sheffield Hallam University

palgrave
macmillan

First published 2005 by
PALGRAVE MACMILLAN
Houndmills, Basingstoke, Hampshire RG21 6XS and
175 Fifth Avenue, New York, N. Y. 10010
Companies and representatives throughout the world

PALGRAVE MACMILLAN is the global academic imprint of the Palgrave
Macmillan division of St. Martin's Press, LLC and of Palgrave Macmillan Ltd.
Macmillan® is a registered trademark in the United States, United Kingdom
and other countries. Palgrave is a registered trademark in the European
Union and other countries.

ISBN-13: 978-1-4039-3815-2
ISBN-10: 1-4039-3815-6

This book is printed on paper suitable for recycling and made from fully
managed and sustained forest sources.

A catalogue record for this book is available from the British Library.

Library of Congress Cataloging-in-Publication Data
Hopkins, Lisa, 1962-
  A Christopher Marlowe chronology / Lisa Hopkins.
    p. cm. – (Author chronologies)
  Includes bibliographical references and index.
  ISBN 1-4039-3815-6
    1. Marlowe, Christopher, 1564-1593–Chronology. 2. Dramatists,
English–Early modern, 1500-1700–Chronology. I. Title. II. Author chronolo-
gies (Palgrave Macmillan (Firm))

PR2673.H593 2005
822'.3–dc22
[B]

2005050867

10 9 8 7 6 5 4 3 2 1
14 13 12 11 10 09 08 07 06 05

Printed and bound in Great Britain by
Antony Rowe Ltd, Chippenham and Eastbourne

Contents

General Editor's Preface

Most biographies are ill-adapted to serve as works of reference – not surprisingly so, since the biographer is likely to regard his function as the devising of a continuous and readable narrative, with excursions into interpretation and speculation, rather than a bald recital of facts. There are times, however, when anyone reading for business or pleasure needs to check a point quickly or to obtain a rapid overview of part of an author's life or career; and at such moments turning over the pages of a biography can be a time-consuming and frustrating occupation. The present series of volumes aims at providing a means whereby the chronological facts of an author's life and career, rather than needing to be prised out of the narrative in which they are (if they appear at all) securely embedded, can be seen at a glance. Moreover, whereas biographies are often, and quite understandably, vague over matters of fact (since it makes for tediousness to be forever enumerating details of dates and places), a chronology can be precise whenever it is possible to be precise.

Thanks to the survival, sometimes in very large quantities, of letters, diaries, notebooks and other documents, as well as to thoroughly researched biographies and bibliographies, this material now exists in abundance for many major authors. In the case of, for example, Dickens, we can often ascertain what he was doing in each month and week, and almost on each day, of his prodigiously active working life; and the student of, say, *David Copperfield* is likely to find it fascinating as well as useful to know just when Dickens was at work on each part of that novel, what other literary enterprises he was engaged in at the same time, whom he was meeting, what places he was visiting, and what were the relevant circumstances of his personal and professional life. Such a chronology is not, of course, a substitute for a biography; but its arrangement, in combination with its index, makes it a much more convenient tool for this kind of purpose; and it may be acceptable as a form of 'alternative' biography, with its own distinctive advantages as well as its obvious limitations.

Since information relating to an author's early years is usually scanty and chronologically imprecise, the opening section of some volumes in this series groups together the years of childhood and adolescence. Thereafter each year, and usually each month, is dealt with separately.

Information not readily assignable to a specific month or day is given as a general note under the relevant year or month. The first entry for each month carries an indication of the day of the week, so that when necessary this can be readily calculated for other dates. Each volume also contains a bibliography of the principal sources of information. In the chronology itself, the sources of many of the more specific items, including quotations, are identified in order that the reader who wishes to do so may consult the original contexts.

NORMAN PAGE

Acknowledgements

As always, work on this project has been made immeasurably much easier than it might have been by the support and collegiality of my colleagues in the English department at Sheffield Hallam. Special thanks are due to Matthew Steggle, most long-suffering and patient of office-sharers, and to Ian Baker. Thanks too to the inter-library loan staff of the Mary Badland Library and, again as always, to my husband and son.

I owe a great debt to the extraordinary kindness of Susan Cerasano and David Riggs for sending me copies of their work, and in the case of David Riggs of his own working chronology. Susan Cerasano and Patrick Cheney both very generously read the entire manuscript and caught many errors and omissions, and Michael Frohnsdorff graciously sent me a copy of his *Christopher Marlowe: The Local Connection and New Research*. Charles Nicholl has consistently been a source of help and encouragement in matters Marlovian. The anonymous reader for Palgrave did an exceptionally thorough job of going through the manuscript and made many astute suggestions. All remaining errors and infelicities are of course entirely my own.

Introduction

Christopher Marlowe is an unusually difficult subject for a book of this kind because so little evidence survives about his life. To be able to say with precision where he was on any one day, or what he was doing, is the exception rather than the norm. Consequently, this attempt at a chronology will seem disappointingly vague when it comes to providing concrete information about Marlowe's activities and whereabouts, and I make no pretence to be able to fill in any of the many gaps in what we know about him. Conversely, much of the information which I have been able to provide may seem, at least at first sight, irrelevant because so much of it is about people other than Marlowe. However, everything I have included here relates to one (or more) of the categories which I discuss below, which seem to me the crucial rubrics under which the facts relating to Marlowe's life and works need to be considered. In the interests of economy and clarity, I have keyed the entries to a bibliography, so that a reference in brackets after a item always indicates a book or article which contains significantly more information on the topic for readers with a particular interest in that area. I have also adopted a 'fish-eye lens' approach to the years of Marlowe's actual life, by which I mean that I have noted for these years major festivals, particularly Easter, Accession Day and the principal fair held in the city in which he was then living or might be expected to be found in the summer. These events may or may not have been of any interest to Marlowe himself, but they will have shaped the experiences of those around him, and will have affected the range of activities available at those particular times. On the same principle, I have recorded striking natural phenomena such as earthquakes and comets, which will have attracted widespread comment at the time and which everyone will have been aware of. I have taken a similar approach to the theatrical entrepreneur Philip Henslowe's diary: when Marlowe was alive, I have noted all performances, to give a sense of the nature of the other plays on the London theatrical scene with which his works were in competition and dialogue; after his death, I have noted only those of Marlowe's own plays.

The kinds of information found here, then, fall broadly into the following categories.

Significant dates in Marlowe's life and in the lives of his family

This is the simplest and most straightforward category, but also, alas, the smallest. Marlowe is elusive even by the standards of Elizabethans, as will indeed be apparent when the number of entries directly about his doings is compared with the number on other people who we know or assume to have been involved in intelligence work.

The bare facts of his life are these. He was christened at St George's Church, Canterbury, on Saturday, 26 February 1564, and normal Elizabethan customs for the baptism of babies would suggest that he was no more than a few days old at the time. He was the second child and first son of John Marlowe, a relatively recent newcomer to busy commercial Canterbury from the quieter Kent town of Ospringe, and of John's wife Katherine, who was originally from Dover. 1564 was also the year in which William Shakespeare was born (he was christened at Holy Trinity Church, Stratford-upon-Avon, on 26 April 1564), but although Marlowe and Shakespeare were to grow up as unquestionably the two greatest dramatists of the time, and despite the persistent speculation that they collaborated on the *Henry VI* plays, there is no proof that they ever met. Nevertheless, their works were undoubtedly in dialogue; Shakespeare's *Venus and Adonis*, for instance, forms a natural pair with Marlowe's *Hero and Leander*, and Shakespeare's *Richard II* with Marlowe's *Edward II*, even if the precise chronological sequence – and hence which is responding to which – cannot always be established. There are not many dates directly relevant to Shakespeare to be found in this edition (not least because his where-abouts during these years are even more shrouded in mystery than Marlowe's); however, I have tried to provide dates for, or in connection with, all those of Shakespeare's works which show signs of this literary dialogue.

For much of Marlowe's early life, little more is known than when his various siblings were born and died and the occasions on which his quarrelsome father got himself involved in lawsuits or other legal dealings. Not until December 1578 does Marlowe's life begin to take concrete shape, for in that month he was enrolled as a scholar at the King's School, Canterbury. Since fourteen was unusually late for an Elizabethan boy to start attending grammar school, it seems likely that he was already a student either there or elsewhere, but there is no record of this. He did not stay at the King's School long, because by December 1580 he had arrived as a scholar at Corpus Christi College,

Cambridge to study divinity. He was the beneficiary of a scholarship set up by Archbishop Matthew Parker, which was bestowed on students who were considered likely to study divinity and take Holy Orders. This suggests that at this stage of his life Marlowe must either have believed in God or must have been prepared to act a part.

Marlowe's time at Cambridge passed, as far as is known, without either incident or any particular academic distinction until some time in the early summer of 1587, for on Thursday, 29 June of that year the Privy Council drafted a minute to the Cambridge authorities ordering them to stop making difficulties in the matter of conferring Marlowe's degree. This extraordinary document, which I have reproduced in full within the Chronology, unfortunately suggests more than it explains, but two things seem to be relatively clear. The first is that the authorities were reluctant to allow Marlowe to proceed to the degree because he had been absent, hence presumably failing to fulfil the university's strict residence requirements. The draft wording of the Privy Council's minute (which is all that survives) says that 'it was reported that Christopher Morley was determined to have gone beyond the sea to Reames and there to remain'. Unfortunately, as generations of scholars have discovered to their cost after poring over this in vain, this is about the least helpful formulation that could possibly have been found. Does it mean that Marlowe had never in fact gone to 'Reames' (i.e. the French city of Rheims) at all? Or does it mean that he had gone there, but had not intended to stay?

Fortunately there is not much doubt about what Marlowe would have been doing in Rheims if he had in fact gone there, and that gives us a pretty good clue to what this was all about. Since 1578, Rheims had been the home of the seminary to which English Catholics could go in secret to train for the priesthood, which they were forbidden to do in Protestant England. An atmosphere of paranoia about Catholic plots had prevailed in England after the Pope had excommunicated Elizabeth I in 1570 and thus effectively given Catholics a licence to kill her. In such a climate, to go to Rheims was a treasonable act. Presumably the implication of the Privy Council's letter is that it had been erroneously rumoured that Marlowe was one of these young men.

Since we have the Privy Council's word for it that this was not in fact the case, two possibilities remain open: first, that the entire Rheims story was a red herring and that Marlowe had actually been somewhere else entirely; and second, that Marlowe had in fact been to Rheims, but for completely the opposite purpose to that rumoured – not because he himself was a Catholic, but because he was spying on Catholics.

Because this has generally been accepted by Marlowe scholars as the more likely possibility, I have included in the Chronology a lot of information about others known to have been involved in the Elizabethan secret service, even though in so doing I have been particularly struck by the fact that no entries recording payment to Marlowe for this kind of work have ever been traced. I have no explanation for this, but one possibility might conceivably be that we should be looking for an alias for him – or, of course, that we need to revisit the hypothesis that he was indeed in long-term government employment after 1587. I have also widened the focus to include not just those members of the intelligence service whose careers are known to have intersected at some stage with Marlowe's, such as Robert Poley, the known agent who was in the room when Marlowe was killed, but also other people who may or may not have been directly or indirectly involved with him, most notably the Earl of Essex, who launched a rival intelligence service after the death of Sir Francis Walsingham and whom many Marlowe scholars have suspected of being in one way or another implicated in Marlowe's death.

After his degree had duly been awarded, Marlowe left Cambridge and appeared almost immediately in London, where his play *Tamburlaine the Great* became an overnight success, to be followed in quick succession by *Tamburlaine the Great*, Part Two, *Doctor Faustus*, *The Jew of Malta*, *The Massacre at Paris* and *Edward II*, as well as the great poem *Hero and Leander*. For the six remaining years of Marlowe's life after he left Cambridge, I have concentrated on three kinds of information: information about the London theatrical and literary scene, of which he was so prominent a part; information about the various kinds of legal difficulties in which Marlowe found himself from time to time during these years (he was arrested on 18 September 1589 for his part in the killing of William Bradley by his friend Thomas Watson; on 26 January 1592 he was arrested for coining in Flushing; on 9 May 1592 he was bound over in the sum of £20 to keep the peace towards Allen Nicholls, Constable of Holywell Street, Shoreditch, and Nicholas Helliott, beadle, and to appear at the General Sessions in October; and on 15 September 1592 he was arrested for fighting in the streets of Canterbury with a tailor named William Corkine); and lastly, information about any events which may possibly have a bearing on the circumstances surrounding his mysterious death at Deptford on Wednesday, 30 May 1593.

In recent years, principally as a result of Charles Nicholl's magisterial *The Reckoning: The Murder of Christopher Marlowe*, interest in Marlowe's death has in fact outweighed interest in his life. This interest was first sparked when Leslie Hotson uncovered the coroner's report on Marlowe's death in 1925. (I have reproduced this in full in the Chronology in the entry for 30 May 1593.) Many aspects of the story it tells do not seem to make much sense, not least the fact that the wound it describes, if it was indeed in the precise location which the report claims, would not have proved mortal. Moreover, it seems very strange that Marlowe was in the room with three other men – Ingram Frizer, Nicholas Skeres and Robert Poley – but that when he allegedly turned violent, two of them were no more than passive bystanders in the ensuing scene. Consequently, many scholars have suspected either a cover-up or a conspiracy of some kind, and a lot of names and events have been adduced in connection with this. I have given information about as many of these as I can, including the previous histories and subsequent careers of the three other men in the room at the time of Marlowe's death, though I have not pursued the lunatic fringe theory that he was not in fact killed at all but smuggled abroad to write the works of Shakespeare, while another body (in some versions that of John Penry, author of the Martin Marprelate tracts, who had been executed the day before) was substituted for his.

Finally, I have tried to trace something at least of the afterlife, in both the popular and literary imaginations, of Marlowe himself and also of his works. This is why the Chronology continues long after his death in 1593 to trace his continuing and indeed escalating impact on the development of English literature and drama.

Dates of events which are dramatised in Marlowe's works

Apart from *Dido, Queen of Carthage* and *Hero and Leander*, both of which are set in the mythic past, the events described and dramatised in Marlowe's works are almost always precisely datable. I have included information on those events both because this illustrates the remarkable chronological range of Marlowe's attention and interests, which spread from the wars of ancient Rome to figures who were his contemporaries, and also because it allows for comparison between the real chronology of events and Marlowe's fictionalised representations of it. This, along with the attention to his sources discussed in the next section, does produce the initially odd-seeming effect of a Chronology of Christopher Marlowe's life that starts hundreds of years before he was even born, but my hope is that it facilitates a clearer understanding of both the scope of Marlowe's achievement and the nature of his dramaturgy, particularly the sharp, cynical, almost Hollywood-style cutting with which he likes to segue between events, as in *Tamburlaine the Great*, Part One where Mycetes runs off the stage, only for the news of his death to be coolly reported seconds later, while his erstwhile favourite Meander passes smoothly into the service of his probable killer. To organise the information related to Marlowe's life and works chronologically does also throw up some interesting facts and conjunctions. It is striking, for instance, how little time separates the death of Edward II from the birth of Timur Leng, the model for Tamburlaine, although the plays based on their respective figures seem to belong to such very different worlds. Focusing on history in this way also makes starkly visible just how much of the available life history of Timur Marlowe used in Part One, and hence the reasons why he had to rely on invention and anachronistic material in Part Two.

Dates of Marlowe's sources

Marlowe used a significant number of sources for his work, which have been magisterially documented by Vivien Thomas and William Tydeman in *Christopher Marlowe: The Plays and Their Sources* (London: Routledge, 1994). I have noted dates of both first publication (where known) and also of significant re-publication (especially where new material has been included). I have been particularly careful to track anything bearing on what is perhaps the most important of the many unsolved puzzles of Marlowe's career, the dating of *Doctor Faustus*, which is divergently ascribed by Marlowe critics to either *c.* 1588 or *c.* 1592/3. This may seem an infinitesimal difference, but not only do these two possible dates represent the two poles of Marlowe's literary career, they would also have given very different contexts for the first performances of the play. 1588 was the year in which the Spanish Armada sailed; Englishmen, including Marlowe's father, were training for military service and expecting an imminent invasion, and in such a context Faustus's call for defiance of the Prince of Parma, prospective leader of the invasion forces, would have been a sharply urgent and contemporary one, whereas by 1592, four years after the Armada had been dispersed by storms, it would have had merely historical interest. (By 1591, for instance, the Canterbury records note that John Marlowe no longer possessed any of the military equipment he had had at the time of the Armada.) Many critics (myself included) think that *Doctor Faustus* 'feels' early, and its references to Spain and the Prince of Parma would certainly have made it a far more topical and exciting play in

Armada year than it would have been four or five years later. The insuperable objection to the 'early date' theory appears to be the lack of proof that there was any edition of the *English Faust Book*, Marlowe's principal source, before 1592. However, the bibliographical and archival evidence on this issue is by no means conclusive, and recently uncovered evidence makes the possibility of an early edition seem ever more real, so I have tried to provide a clear enough guide to the maze for the reader at least to understand the issues, even if they feel that a definitive conclusion is presently impossible to reach.

Landmarks on the literary scene

Marlowe wrote a number of different kinds of work. Some of these conform fairly well to Elizabethan generic rules and expectations – *Edward II* is easily recognisable as a history play, and *Hero and Leander* as an epyllion (a short, mock-epic, comic poem on love) – but others are much less readily classifiable: *Tamburlaine the Great*, for instance, claims to be a tragedy, but ends with a marriage. Some are entries in a crowded field – translations of the classics, in particular, were very much in vogue – but in other instances Marlowe proves surprisingly reluctant to imitate contemporary fashion: I think we might well be surprised, for example, that as far as we can tell he never wrote a Petrarchan sonnet, a genre at which virtually all his major contemporaries tried their hand. I have tried to give an indication of what other kinds of work were current when he was writing, both to show when he is in line with convention and when he departs from it, and also to give some sense of the extent and immediacy of his influence.

Information about Marlowe's known or probable circle

Although Marlowe himself is so difficult to track down, there is a surprising amount of information available about many of the people with whom he was certainly or probably associated or acquainted, particularly about Ingram Frizer, Nicholas Skeres and Robert Poley, the three men who were in the room when he died, and Richard Baines, whose path crossed his on a number of occasions, most notably when both were arrested for coining in Flushing and when Baines submitted to the Privy Council a 'Note' listing Marlowe's alleged blasphemies. I have therefore recorded information about these men, about others with whom Marlowe is said to have been linked, and also about the various Catholic priests and exiles who are particularly likely to have attracted the interest of the intelligence services during the years when Marlowe was perhaps associated with them. It is unfortunately inevitable that this should produce a somewhat tangled web, in which loyalties and motivations are often entirely unclear. This was simply the nature of the Elizabethan intelligence world, particularly when the success of so many projects depended on men with one set of loyalties being able to pretend convincingly to subscribe to quite another. Often they were so successful that it is no longer possible (if it ever was) to see which is the pretence and which the truth, as in the case of John Cecil, who appears to have been either an improbably accident-prone Catholic priest or an improbably conspicuous government plant. Consequently, the inclusion of details of these men's careers may at times seem more to blur the overall picture than to clarify it, but this is likely to have been exactly what would have been experienced by anyone associated with espionage or counter-espionage in this period.

Material of unknown relevance

It will be apparent from the last few pages of the chronology that a number of really significant discoveries about Marlowe's life (the Dutch shilling incident, the name of his assassin, his role in the Hog Lane fracas) have all been made within the last hundred years or so. I hope that more may follow and that parts of his life which are still mysterious to us, such as the sources of his income, his whereabouts at times when they are currently unknown, and the reasons for his death, may one day become clearer. I have, therefore, included here some pieces of information even though I am unsure what their significance might be, or even whether they are significant at all, for the simple reason that they have proved hard to unearth, and my instinct is that they are better recorded where any future researcher on Marlowe will be easily able to retrieve them. On something of the same principle, I have also included details of the dates when these later discoveries about Marlowe's life were made. Anyone interested in the reception of Marlowe's life and works can thus easily reconstruct whether someone writing about him at a particular time did or did not have access to a particular piece of evidence or information about him.

Places where Marlowe definitely wasn't

Negative evidence is always much less exciting than positive evidence, but it is valuable nevertheless. Marlowe studies have been too long bedevilled by men with similar names. I have tried to make it plain where a mention of a 'Mr Morley' definitely cannot refer to Marlowe, and I have also listed his absences from college as recorded by the Corpus Buttery book. On the same principle, I have tried to make clear to what extent the various Richard Baineses who muddy the waters can or cannot be securely distinguished.

America

One place where Marlowe definitely wasn't, but about which I have nevertheless included considerable information, is America. This is because the single most startling thing about Marlowe to his contemporaries, and the thing on which they most often commented, was his alleged atheism, which the Baines Note links directly to Thomas Hariot's observation 'That the Indians, and many authors of antiquity, have assuredly written of above 16 thousand years agone, whereas Adam is proved to have lived within six thousand years'. Hariot, whom Marlowe knew, went to America with the Grenville expedition in 1585, and his *A Brief and True Report of the new-found Land of Virginia* appeared in 1588. It is a commonplace that Columbus's discovery of America had rocked Renaissance Europe, not least because it called into question the authority of the Bible, which failed to mention America. Marlowe, who was fascinated by geography (see Seaton, 'Marlowe's Map'), will have been interested in this New World, not just for its own sake but also because its discovery prompted the rush to colonise it, and colonisation is something looked at in a number of Marlowe's plays, whether in connection with the marauding Tamburlaine or in relation to Aeneas, whose journey from Troy to Africa and thence to Rome made him in a sense the first of all colonisers. Moreover, Sir Walter Ralegh, the principal impetus behind English voyages to America, is another of the shadowy figures who may well have had some connection with Marlowe's death. As with other areas of focus in this Chronology, then, America may have had no direct connection with Marlowe, but attention to what was going on there does, I think, help us understand more clearly the contexts in which he lived and wrote.

As will be apparent from all this, I have consistently erred on the side of possible over-inclusiveness rather than of omission. I have also assumed that readers are more likely to dip into this book for information about specific dates and events rather than to read it cover from cover, so I have also erred on the side of repeating information about individuals and their relevance to Marlowe rather than risk baffling the reader who has skipped over the first explanation of it.

Note on quotations

For documents directly relating to Marlowe's life, the most comprehensive and readily available source is A. D. Wraight and Virginia F. Stern, *In Search of Christopher Marlowe*. Unless stated otherwise, this is the source of all such quotations.

Note on dates

On Saturday, 24 February 1582, Pope Gregory XIII issued a Papal Bull which instated the Gregorian Calendar and displaced the Julian one. The 'New Style' was ten days ahead of the old, but was not adopted in England until the eighteenth century. After 1582, dates given below therefore continue to be Old Style unless indicated otherwise, but I have also noted the separate Gregorian Easter Sunday for all subsequent years when Marlowe was alive, and have indicated when people writing from the Continent are clearly using the New Style. In some cases, most notably of Englishmen writing from abroad or in the immediate aftermath of the change, it is not clear which is meant, so I have therefore given both possible days of the week.

Chronology

70 BC

Birth of Virgil (Publius Vergilius Maro), whose epic poem *The Aeneid* was the major source of Marlowe's *Dido, Queen of Carthage*. Some of the lines in Marlowe's play are direct translations from Virgil, though in one or two places Marlowe gives his material a contemporary twist.

19 BC

Death of Virgil.

49 BC

The march of Caesar from Gaul towards Rome. This is the main event of the First Book of Lucan's epic poem the *Pharsalia*, which Marlowe later translated.

48 BC

Battle of Pharsalus, after which the *Pharsalia* is named.

43 BC

Birth of Ovid (Publius Ovidius Naso), whose risqué poem *Amores* Marlowe was the first to translate into English. Banished from Rome for reasons which the Renaissance believed to be connected with the sexual indiscretions of the Emperor Augustus's daughter Julia, Ovid acquired a reputation as the most daring and erotic of the major classical poets. On the implications of Marlowe's choice of his *Amores* to translate, see Cheney, *Counterfeit Profession*.

AD 17

Death of Ovid.

39

Birth of Lucan (Marcus Annaeus Lucanus), author of the *Pharsalia*. Lucan was the grandson of Seneca the Elder, a rhetorician, and nephew of Seneca the Younger, whose closet tragedies were very influential in Renaissance England. Lucan's is the only epic not to include machinery (i.e. direct intervention by the gods), which may have made it attractive to Marlowe. It also has a republican bias, and indeed in the seventeenth century translating Lucan was to become effectively an affirmation of republicanism, as in the case of the poet and playwright Thomas May (see Cheney, *Cambridge Companion*, 15–17).

65

Lucan commits suicide, aged 26, after the discovery of his role in a conspiracy to overthrow the Emperor Nero.

597

St Augustine arrives in Canterbury, which is henceforth the premier spiritual site in England. Growing up there and attending a school in the shadow of the cathedral will certainly have been an important influence on Marlowe's view of religion and its ceremonies; it may explain his apparent preference for elaborate ceremonial, as reported in the Baines Note, and *The Jew of Malta* contains a reference to a Dark Entry, which clearly recalls the one at Canterbury.

1174

July
12 (Fri.)   Henry II walks barefoot and weeping through Canterbury to do penance for the murder of Thomas à Becket. This celebrated episode makes Canterbury a symbol of the tensions between spiritual and secular power in England. Becket's magnificent shrine will dominate the cathedral until its destruction in the reign of Henry VIII. There would be people alive in Canterbury when Marlowe was a boy who would have remembered the shrine and its destruction.

1240

Birth of Abraham Abulafia of Zaragoza, founder of the practical Cabbala, who will later become the first known Jewish inhabitant of the Maltese islands (see Roth, 191–2). It is just conceivable that this might form part of the network of ideas and associations activated by the title of Marlowe's play *The Jew of Malta*.

1284

April
25 (Tues.) The future Edward II, hero of Marlowe's play *Edward II*, is born at Caernarfon Castle, Wales, son of Edward I and Eleanor of Castile.

1288

Abraham Abulafia is by now living on the tiny Maltese islet of Comino, where he composes his Book of the Sign.

1298

Piers Gaveston is made one of ten royal wards and official companions of the future Edward II.

July
22 (Tues.) Edward I utterly defeats the army of the Scots, led by William Wallace, at the Battle of Falkirk. This is only one of the many military successes of his reign, with which his son's was to prove such an unfortunate contrast.

1299

Betrothal of the future Edward II, aged fifteen, to Isabella of France, aged eight.

1305

June
14 (Mon.) The future Edward II is banished from court after a quarrel with his father's favourite minister, Walter Langton, Bishop of Coventry and Lichfield. The cause of the disagreement appears to have been Langton's anger at detecting Edward, along with Piers Gaveston and others, poaching his deer. Edward and Gaveston are separated. One of those who provided the prince with financial support during this period was Sir Hugh Despenser the elder, father of his second favourite (Bingham, 43–5).

October
Edward is pardoned and allowed to return to court.

1307

Winter
A fresh disagreement breaks out between the future Edward II and his father over the prince's desire to have Gaveston named Count of Ponthieu. Gaveston is ordered to leave England by the end of April.

July
7 (Fri.)   Death of Edward I of England and accession of Edward II. This is the point at which Marlowe's play *Edward II* opens.

October
13 (Fri.)   Piers Gaveston marries Edward II's niece, Margaret de Clare, heiress of the Earl of Gloucester. Margaret is shown looking forward to this marriage in III, ii of Marlowe's play.

1308

January
25 (Thurs.) Edward II marries Isabella of France at Boulogne. Gaveston is left as regent of the kingdom during his absence.

February
25 (Sun.)   Edward's coronation. Gaveston appears in purple sewn with pearls. He has also been given the pick of Isabella's jewels.

April
Parliament, led by the Earls of Lincoln, Lancaster, Warwick, Hereford, Pembroke and Surrey, demands Gaveston's banishment and sets a deadline of 25 June for him to leave the country. Virtually the only support for Edward comes from Sir Hugh Despenser the Elder (see Bingham, 58–9).

1309

Summer
Gaveston is recalled from Ireland.

October
The Earls of Lancaster, Hereford, Warwick, Oxford and Arundel, whom Gaveston has once again alienated, refuse to attend a council called by the King at York on the grounds of Gaveston's presence at it.

1310

February
Parliament meets at Westminster. Edward sends Gaveston north to ensure his safety.

1311

September
27 (Mon.) The disaffected nobles, who have now banded together as the Lords Ordainers, announce their demands at Paul's Cross. These include stripping Gaveston of all his titles and sending him into perpetual exile.

November
3 (Wed.) Gaveston officially goes into exile, but is openly back at court by Christmas.

1312

In the early part of the year Edward and Gaveston flee north, first to Tynemouth and then to Scarborough.

May
9 (Tues.) Gaveston surrenders Scarborough Castle to the Earls of Pembroke and Surrey and Henry Percy.

June
9 (Fri.) The Earl of Pembroke, wishing to visit his wife, leaves Gaveston at the rectory at Deddington, ten miles south of Banbury, Oxfordshire.
10 (Sat.) Gaveston is captured at the rectory by the Earl of Warwick and imprisoned in Warwick Castle.
19 (Mon.) Gaveston is beheaded on Blacklow Hill, near Warwick.

November

13 (Mon.) Edward's queen, Isabella, gives birth to the future Edward III.

1313

October

14 (Sun.) Edward pardons the Earl of Lancaster for Gaveston's murder at a ceremony in Westminster Hall.

1314

June

23 (Sun.) Battle of Bannockburn, at which Edward's army is utterly defeated by the Scots king, Robert the Bruce.

1321

August

19 (Fri.) Parliament sentences both Despensers to banishment. The younger Despenser, whom Edward had married to the heiress Eleanor de Clare (sister of Gaveston's wife), had been increasingly emerging as a favourite of the King.

1322

January

The Despensers return to England after Edward repeals the decree of banishment and takes the field against the barons. After this, the younger Despenser becomes decisively established as the King's new favourite and the Queen's *bête noire*.

March

17 (Wed.) The Earl of Lancaster, leader of the baronial opposition, surrenders to Edward's forces.

March

22 (Mon.) Lancaster is executed.

May

22 (Sat.) Parliament meets and proves entirely compliant to all the King's requests.

1323

Autumn
The new King of France, Charles IV, brother of Queen Isabella, informs Edward that the homage he owes for his lands in France is overdue. Roger Mortimer of Wigmore, who was imprisoned in the Tower after the failure of Lancaster's rebellion, escapes and flees to France. This is the Mortimer Junior of Marlowe's play.

1325

March
Queen Isabella leaves for France to try to resolve the dispute with her brother. There she liaises with Roger Mortimer. Prince Edward is sent to join his mother towards the end of the year.

1326

September
23 (Tues.) Isabella sails from Dordrecht to invade England.

October
26 (Sun.) The Earl of Winchester (the elder Despenser) surrenders Bristol to Isabella.
27 (Mon.) Winchester is sentenced to death.

November
16 (Sun.) Edward, along with the younger Despenser and his follower Baldock, is captured at Neath Abbey.
24 (Mon.) The younger Despenser is tried at Hereford, sentenced to death and executed immediately.

1327

January
15 (Thurs.) Parliament declares the King deposed.

February
15 (Sun.) Coronation of Edward III.

September
22 (Tues.) Edward II is killed on the orders of his wife, Isabella of France, and her lover, Roger Mortimer.

1330

October

Edward III assumes power. Mortimer is executed and Isabella imprisoned until her death in 1358. This is the point at which *Edward II* ends.

c.1336

Birth of Timur the Lame (also known as Tamerlane or Timur Leng), later to be the subject of Marlowe's *Tamburlaine the Great*, Parts One and Two.

1347

Birth of the future Sultan Beyajid I (Marlowe's Bajazeth), principal antagonist of Tamburlaine in *Tamburlaine the Great*, Part One.

1369

By this date, Timur the Lame is in total control of what is now known as Turkistan.

1387

Timur the Lame is now in control of all land east of the Euphrates.

1389

Sultan Amurath I is assassinated by a Serb after the Battle of Kosovo. Beyajid succeeds to the Turkish throne as Beyajid I.

1392

Timur the Lame advances beyond the Euphrates.

1395

Timur the Lame conquers and sacks the Russian cities of Astrakhan, Sarai and Bolgar.

1398

Timur the Lame invades India.

1400

Timur the Lame captures Aleppo and Baghdad.

1402

July
20 (Thurs.) Timur the Lame captures Sultan Beyajid I at Angora.

1403

Death of Beyajid I. This is roughly the point at which *Tamburlaine the Great*, Part One ends.

1405

January
19 (Mon.) Death of Timur the Lame. He is buried at Samarkand. This is the point at which *Tamburlaine the Great*, Part Two ends.

1414

William Morle, fuller, admitted freeman of the city of Canterbury. This is the first mention of a Marlowe in the Canterbury records. It used to be thought that this was an ancestor of Marlowe's, but recent research has shown that Marlowe's father John in fact came from Ospringe in Kent, and there is no evidence for any previous connection of his family with Canterbury.

1415

Council of Constance, after which the heretic John Hus is burned by order of the Emperor Sigismund, who appears in *Tamburlaine the Great*, Part Two. Roy Battenhouse, in 'Protestant Apologetics', suggests that it was Sigismund's involvement with this episode which lies behind the unfavourable portrayal of him in Marlowe's play.

1438

Simon Morle, vintner, admitted freeman of the city of Canterbury. As with William Morle, Simon used to be identified as a probable ancestor of Marlowe's, but there is now no reason to suppose this.

1444

November

10 (Tues.)   Battle of Varna. Bonfinius' account of this in his Latin chronicle of Hungary was the source of the Sigismund–Orcanes story in *Tamburlaine the Great*, Part Two (see Battenhouse, 'Protestant Apologetics'). Obviously, this is well after the death of the historical Timur/Tamburlaine, but Marlowe had used up so much of the available source material in Part One that he really had no choice but to look to different sources and even different periods for material for Part Two. This might suggest that he had not originally planned a second part of the play, and wrote it solely as a response to the runaway success of Part One (and that the drama was therefore originally intended to end not with Tamburlaine's death but with his triumph).

1453

May

29 (Tues.)   Fall of Constantinople to Sultan Mohammed II. From now on, Ottoman power advances ever deeper and more menacingly into Europe. This is the situation underlying the depiction of Turkish aggression in *Tamburlaine the Great*, in which Bajazet declares that the activities of Tamburlaine are distracting him from the siege of Constantinople, and in *The Jew of Malta* (see Vella Bonavita).

1459

Thomas Morle, fuller, son of William Morle, fuller, admitted freeman of the city of Canterbury. This is the first sign of Morleys/Marlowes being resident in Canterbury and it used therefore to be suggested that this was an ancestor of Marlowe's, but it is now clear that that is not the case.

1467

John Marley, tanner, admitted freeman of the city of Canterbury. This may well be the John Marley whose son Richard made a will in 1521 referring to his son Christopher, a minor. It used to be thought that this Christopher must be the grandfather of Christopher Marlowe the playwright, but recent research has disproved that.

1475

Publication of Geoffrey Chaucer's *The Canterbury Tales* puts Canterbury on the literary map.

1478

Thomas Marlow, roper, admitted freeman of the city of Canterbury. Again, there now seems no reason to suppose a connection with the family of Christopher Marlowe, though this had been posited in the past.

1484

Date of the first traceable printing of Musaeus' late fifth-century Greek poem *Hero and Leander*, the major source of Marlowe's poem *Hero and Leander*.

1486

Birth of Heinrich Cornelius Agrippa, who was to become widely sus-pected of necromancy and is mentioned in *Doctor Faustus*.
Publication of the *Malleus Maleficarum* by the Dominican friars Hein-rich Kramer and James Sprenger. This rapidly became used both as evidence for the actual existence of witches and as a guide to their behaviour. In *Doctor Faustus*, Faustus is technically a witch (see West, 'The Impatient Magic of Dr. Faustus', 226–7, and Traister, *Heavenly Necromancers*, 90).
Publication of Giovanni Pico della Mirandola, *Oration on the Dignity of Man*, a founding text of neo-platonic theory which offered a way of thinking about magic as not necessarily demonic. The contrasting per-spectives offered by Pico della Mirandola and the *Malleus Maleficarum*, ironically originating in the same year, can be seen as jostling for supremacy in *Doctor Faustus*.

1487

Papal condemnation of Pico della Mirandola, who was forced to retract thirteen of his propositions.

1492

May
31 (Sat.)   The decision to expel all Jews from Malta, then subject to the Spanish Crown, is secretly communicated to the authorities. Marlowe's *The Jew of Malta*, set in 1565, shows Jews on the island, but they are threatened with expulsion if they will not part with half their wealth.

June
18 (Mon.)   The expulsion of the Jews from Malta is publicly proclaimed.

September
18 (Tues.)   Deadline for departure of all Jews from Malta (though this was subsequently extended).

1493

Pico della Mirandola absolved by Pope Alexander VI (Rodrigo Borgia).

June
12 (Wed.)   Final deadline for expulsion of all Jews from Malta.

1494

Birth of Süleyman the Magnificent. It was under Süleyman that the Turks besieged Malta, as depicted in Marlowe's *The Jew of Malta*, and his power and the magnificence of his court made him a figure of legend in the west.

1507

The German necromancer George Sabellicus is reported as terming himself 'the younger Faust'.

1509

Publication of Heinrich Cornelius Agrippa, *De nobilitate et praecellentia foeminei sexus* ('Of the Nobility and Excellence of the Female Sex'). Theoretical debate on the nature and roles of the sexes was a popular intellectual pursuit. One might wish to compare the value placed by Faustus on Helen with Agrippa's praise for women.

1512

March

5 (Fri.)   Christening of Gerard Kremer, subsequently to be known as Gerard Mercator, cartographer and friend of both John Dee and Abraham Ortelius.

1517

The Aldine Press in Venice brings out an edition of Musaeus' *Hero and Leander*, accompanied by a Latin translation. This launches the story's popularity and forms the basis for most subsequent editions during the course of the century.

1518

Publication of Orwin Gratius, *Lamentationes obscurorum virorum* ('Lamentations of Obscure Men'), in which one 'Georgius Subbun-culator', who may be George Sabellicus, is said to be in correspondence with 'Agrippa Stygianus' ('Agrippa from the River Styx', the classical gateway to the underworld), i.e. Heinrich Cornelius Agrippa (see Baron, 11–39). This is an indication of the notoriety of both men.

1520

Publication of Martin Luther, *Open Letter to the Christian Nobility of the German Nation*, in which the faith-breaking of Sigismund at Varna is mentioned (see Battenhouse, 'Protestant Apologetics').
Süleyman the Magnificent becomes Sultan of the Ottoman Empire on the death of his father Selim I.

1521

Publication of Oronce Finé, *De mundi sphaera, sive cosmographia.*
Marlowe's apparent ignorance of the Copernican idea of the universe is
much debated; Finé was one of the older authors on whom he might
have been relying (see Johnson).

Richard Marley, tanner, son of John Marley, tanner, dies leaving a will
in favour of his only son Christopher, a minor. It used to be thought
that this child was probably the grandfather of Christopher Marlowe,
and though recent research has disproved the idea of this direct
descent, there might perhaps have been a collateral link. Certainly
some of Richard Marley's property is leased from Sir John Ffyneux, and
it will later be a 'Mr Fineux of Dover' whom Christopher Marlowe is
said to have converted to atheism.

1522

The Knights of St John are driven out of Rhodes by the Turks. An international event, mentioned in Holinshed's *Chronicles*, this has widespread repercussions. The Knights begin a quest for a new home which
will eventually take them to Malta.

Birth of William Allen, later to be Cardinal Allen and a key figure in
the history of Richard Baines, who was the author of the 'Baines Note'
and Marlowe's prime accuser.

1524

Alessandro Pazzi writes an Italian play on Dido, *Dido in Cartagine.* This
will be one of the first of many indications of the growing popularity
of her story in the sixteenth century.

1527

John Rightwise's Latin play on Dido performed before Cardinal
Wolsey.

1529

Publication of Andreas Cambinus, *Libro ... della origine de Turchi et
imperio delli Ottomanni* ('Book ... on the origin of the Turks and of the
Ottoman Empire'), which Thomas and Tydeman include in their

Christopher Marlowe: The plays and their sources (126) as a possible source of material for *Tamburlaine the Great*. The same year saw the publication of Martin Luther, *On War Against the Turk*, indicating the general topicality of matters Turkish.

1530

First publication of Heinrich Cornelius Agrippa, *Of the Vanitie and uncertaintie of Artes and Sciences.*

The Knights of St John take up residence on Malta after being granted it by the Emperor Charles V.

Either in this year or the preceding one, Richard Rose or Rouse poisoned the porridge of the Bishop of Rochester's household, which Thomas and Tydeman see as a possible source for *The Jew of Malta*.

1531

Publication of the first emblem book, Andrea Alciati's *Emblemata cum commentaris* ('Emblems with Commentaries'), which includes an emblem on the fate of Actaeon. The episode of the horning of Benvolio in *Doctor Faustus* clearly relies on the story of Actaeon. The emblematic mode, which pairs text and images to convey a message or moral, becomes increasingly influential and can be seen as lying behind many of the stage pictures created in Marlowe's plays (see Diehl).

Publication of Sir Thomas Elyot, *The Boke Called the Governour*, an important text of Renaissance political theory, and a significant salvo in the debate about right ways of ruling to which *Tamburlaine the Great* can later be seen as a contribution.

1532

Georgius Sabellicus is referred to in the city records of Nuremberg as a 'great sodomite and necromancer' (see Keefer, *Christopher Marlowe's Doctor Faustus*, xxvi). On the question of Dr Faustus's sexuality, and whether anything analogous to this is suggested in Marlowe's play, see Findlay.

1533

Publication of Heinrich Cornelius Agrippa, *De occulta philosophia* ('Of Occult Philosophy').

1534

Sabellicus, by now known as Georgius Sabellicus Faustus, is invited to prepare a prediction for the German explorer Philip von Hutten's expedition to Venezuela. This might be compared with the interest of Marlowe's Doctor Faustus in the gold of the Indies.

1535

Death of Heinrich Cornelius Agrippa.

1536

Pierre de la Ramée, better known as Peter Ramus, receives his MA from the Collège de Navarre in Paris. Ramus was extremely influential on the teaching of Aristotelian theory in both England and France, and his death forms a key scene in Marlowe's *The Massacre at Paris*.

Publication at Lyons of Johannes Quintinus Haedus' *Descriptio Melitensi Insula* ('Description of the Island of Malta'; the author is generally referred to as either Quintinus or Jean Quintin). This shows that there were accounts of Malta to which Marlowe could have turned for background reading for *The Jew of Malta*.

Probable year of birth of Marlowe's father, John Marlowe, at Ospringe near Faversham. Kent (Urry, 12–13).

1537

Probable year of death of Georgius Sabellicus.

The Italian poet Torquato Tasso translates Musaeus' *Hero and Leander* into Italian.

1538

September

The shrine of St Thomas à Becket at Canterbury is dismantled by order of Lord Protector Cromwell and his bones ordered to be burned. On the continuing place of Becket and other martyrs in Canterbury culture, see Kuriyama, *Christopher Marlowe*, 34–5.

1540

Death of Christopher Marley of Canterbury. He left one daughter and a pregnant wife, and stipulated that if the child was a boy he was to inherit the house and the adjoining 'Old Hall'. It used to be supposed that this posthumous child must have been John Marley or Marlowe, father of Christopher the dramatist, but Constance Kuriyama has argued cogently against this (*Christopher Marlowe*, 10). The testator, Christopher Marley, may have been the child Christopher referred to in the 1521 will of Richard Marley.

Publication at Seville of Pedro Mexía, *Silva de Varia Lección* ('The Wood of Varied Reading'), a principal source for Marlowe's *Tamburlaine*.

George Rheticus circulates the first mention of Copernicus' theory that the earth revolves round the sun, rather than, as had been previously supposed, the sun round the earth.

1541

Publication of Clément Marot's translation of Musaeus' *Hero and Leander*, which says of Hero, 'Estoit nonnain, à Vénus dediée' ('She was a nun, dedicated to Venus'), a phrase which recurs in Marlowe's *Hero and Leander*.

Giambattista Giraldi Cinthio writes an Italian play on Dido, *Didone*.

Henry VIII endows the King's School, Canterbury, which Marlowe will later attend.

1542

Publication at London in English translation of Heinrich Cornelius Agrippa, *Of the nobilitie and excellencie of womankynde*.

1543

Bonfinius' Latin chronicle of Hungary, *Antonii Bonfinii Rerum Ungaricarum decades tres* ('Antonius Bonfinus' Three Decades of Hungarian Affairs'), published at Frankfurt. This was a source for Marlowe's *Tamburlaine*.

First publication of Ramus' *Dialecticae institutiones*, which had a major influence on the university curriculum in England.

First publication of Andreas Vesalius' *De Humani Corporis Fabrica* ('On the Fabric of the Human Body', which Matthew Greenfield sees as an influence on Marlowe's understanding of the human body (see Greenfield, 'Christopher Marlowe's Wound Knowledge').

First publication of Copernicus' *De Revolutionibus Orbium Coelestium* ('On the Revolutions of the Heavenly Bodies'). Copernicus dies in the same year. The complete absence of any mention of this theory in Marlowe's works appears to be an extremely surprising lacuna given how well informed he was generally.

1544

March
10 (Mon.) François I of France issues a decree suppressing Ramus' books and forbidding him to teach reformed Aristotelianism.
Matthew Parker appointed Master of Corpus Christi College, Cambridge.

1545

Publication of John Seton, *Dialectica* ('Dialectic'), an important textbook for Cambridge students during Marlowe's time there (see Jardine).

1547

Lodovico Dolce writes an Italian play on Dido, *Didone*, which Marlowe may have known (see Thomas and Tydeman, 17).
João Micques, later known as Nassi and a possible analogue for Barabas in *The Jew of Malta* (see Thomas and Tydeman, 298), leads a group of 500 Jews from Venice to Constantinople. Nassi, who became known as 'The Great Jew', was ultimately to be made Duke of Naxos, by Sultan Selim II, and the only Jewish duke in Europe.

January
28 (Fri.)   Death of Henry VIII and accession of Edward VI.

June
John Dee, the famous English 'magician' whom some have seen as an analogue for Doctor Faustus and who was extensively involved in formulating theories of empire and advising on exploration, visits Gerard Mercator in Louvain (see Crane, 164–5).

1548

December
27 (Thurs.) Death of Francis Spira, whose despair of the possibility of his salvation became internationally famous and who is a possible precedent for Marlowe's conception of Doctor Faustus (see Campbell).
28 (Fri.)   This is the date incorrectly recorded in the parish register of St George's, Canterbury for the christening of Marlowe's sister Margaret, because a loose sheet has been misplaced.

1549

Publication in Basle of an account of the death of Francis Spira, with a preface by Calvin (see Campbell, 229).
Publication of John Proctor, *The Fal of the Late Arrian*. When Marlowe's former roommate Thomas Kyd was arrested in 1593, a copy of part of this treatise, which he said belonged to Marlowe, was found in his rooms and he was therefore deemed to be in possession of dangerous and heretical material (see Briggs).

1550

Re-publication (possibly in Geneva) of the account of the death of Francis Spira. Also in this year Georgio Siculo's *Epistola ... alli citadini di Riva di Trento contra il mendatio di F. Spira, & falso dottrina di Protestanti* (Letter ... to the citizens of the Trento river-bank against the lie of Francis Spira, and the false doctrine of the Protestants) was published at Bologna, and an English translation by Edward Aglionby of Matteo Garibaldi's account of the death of Spira was published in Worcester.
Calvin's *De scandalis* ('Of Scandals') denounces Heinrich Cornelius Agrippa as an atheist.
William Allen, later Cardinal Allen and prominent in the Baines story, receives his BA from Oriel College, Oxford, and is elected Fellow.

1551

Publication of Thomas Wilson, *The Rule of Reason*, the first textbook of logic written in English.
Thomas Arden of Faversham is murdered by his wife, Alice. This famous local scandal will eventually form the basis of the anonymous Elizabethan play *Arden of Faversham*, of which Marlowe has occasionally been proposed as the author.
Nicolas de Nicolay, geographer to Charles IX of France, accompanies the Baron d'Aramont, French Ambassador to the Sublime Porte, to Malta. The Turks attack while he is there and carry off a large part of the population of the neighbouring island of Gozo. Nicolay's subsequent work will be a source for Marlowe's *The Jew of Malta*.
Publication of Paulus Jovius (Paolo Giovio), *Elogia virorum bellica virtute illustrium* ('In Praise of Famous Men of Warlike Courage'), containing an account of Tamburlaine (see Thomas and Tydeman, 132), and two books by Ramus, who is a character in *The Massacre at Paris* (see Bakeless, 62).

1552

Publication of Claude Gruget, *Les Diverses Leçons de Pierre Messie* ('The Varied Readings of Pedro Mexía'), a translation of Mexía later used by Thomas Fortescue in his own 1571 translation into English, and thus a possible source for Marlowe's *Tamburlaine* (Thomas and Tydeman, 74). Birth of Sir Walter Ralegh.
Traditional year of birth of Edmund Spenser.

1553

Machiavelli's *The Prince* (first published in 1532) is translated into French and dedicated to the Earl of Arran. Debate still surrounds the extent of Marlowe's acquaintance with the writings of Machiavelli, who appears as a character in *The Jew of Malta*; this may represent a route by which Marlowe could have encountered Machiavelli's text.
Matthew Parker leaves his post as Master of Corpus Christi College, Cambridge.
The Muscovy Company is floated. Richard Wilson argues, in 'Invisible Bullets', that the affairs of the Company were an important subtext of *Tamburlaine*.
Publication of Petrus Perondinus, *Magni Tamerlanis Scythiarum Imperatoris Vita* ('Life of Tamburlaine the Great, Emperor of Scythia'), a translation of one of the principal sources for *Tamburlaine*.
Gavin Douglas translates the *Aeneid* into Scottish verse. This is part of the vogue for translations of the classics into the vernacular to which Marlowe will later contribute with his translations of *All Ovids Elegies* and the first book of Lucan's *Pharsalia*, and arguably with *Dido, Queen of Carthage*, since it depends so closely on Virgil's *Aeneid*.

July
6 (Thurs.)   Death of Edward VI and accession of Mary I. Catholicism again becomes the official religion of England.

1554

William Allen receives his MA from Oriel College, Oxford.
The Earl of Surrey translates Book II of the *Aeneid* into English, another indication of the vogue for Virgil of which *Dido, Queen of Carthage* will form part.

April

17 (Tues.)   Stephen Gosson, later to become the period's most virulent
ant-theatrical writer, baptised at St George's, Canterbury.

1555

John Lyly, the future dramatist and author of *Euphues His England* and
Euphues' Golden Legacy, is baptised in Canterbury. In many ways
Marlowe's literary project can be seen as antithetical to Lyly's and
indeed as a reaction against it.

1556

Publication of Laonicus Chalcocondylas, *De origine et rebus gestis
Turcorum* ... ('Of the Origin and Deeds of the Turks'), translated by
Conrad Clauderus (see Thomas and Tydeman 142).
Birth of Marlowe's friend Thomas Watson.
William Allen is chosen Principal of St Mary's Hall, Oxford.
Probable year of arrival of Marlowe's father John in Canterbury (Urry,
10). It used to be supposed that Christopher Marlowe came of a long-
established Canterbury family, possessed of property and financial
security; the recent research into John Marlowe's background has dis-
pelled that idea and has shown that the position of the Marlowes was
actually much more precarious than that.

February

5 (Wed.)   Birth of Philip Henslowe, the future theatrical entrepreneur
who will be extensively involved in staging Marlowe's plays
(see Cerasano, 'Philip Henslowe', 153).

1557

Publication of Tottel, *Songs and Sonnets*, inaugurating the vogue for
verse miscellanies like that in which Marlowe's 'The Passionate
Shepherd to his Love' will later appear.
The Earl of Surrey translates Book IV of the *Aeneid*.

1558

Birth of John Cecil, later to be a Catholic priest and possible double
agent. Marlowe's apparent involvement in government service is likely

to have entailed the pursuit of men like Cecil, and perhaps undercover collaboration too.

Matthew Parker appointed Archbishop of Canterbury.

Publication of Thomas Phaer's translation of the first seven books of the *Aeneid*, which may have influenced *Dido, Queen of Carthage* (see Thomas and Tydeman, 18).

November
6 (Sun.)   Thomas Kyd, later Marlowe's roommate, baptised at the church of St Mary Woolnoth, Lombard Street, London.

17 (Thurs.) Death of Mary I and accession of Elizabeth I. After five years of Catholicism, Protestantism again becomes the official religion of England.

1559

Publication of the fourth edition of Robert Fabyan's *The Chronicle of Fabyan* ..., which is the source for the ballad about the defeat of the English at Bannockburn which is quoted in *Edward II* (Thomas and Tydeman, 380).

Probable year of birth of Marlowe's future brother-in-law John Moore, husband of his sister Joan, or Jane, at Ulcombe in Kent.

January
15 (Sat.)   Coronation of Elizabeth I. The date had been selected by the alchemist and astrologer John Dee, who had been consulted to see when would be auspicious.

July
31 (Mon.)   Philip II of Spain obtains from Pope Paul IV authorisation for the foundation of the University of Douai, where a number of English Catholics will eventually go.

1560

First Latin translation of Machiavelli's *The Prince* published.

John Marlowe, father of Christopher, enrolled as an apprentice by Gerard Richardson, shoemaker and freeman of Canterbury.

Publication at London of Joannes Philippson, *A Famous Chronicle of oure time, called Sleidanes Commentaries*, translated by John Daus, which gave an extensive account of the story of Francis Spira.

Births of Thomas Hariot and Gilbert Gifford, both later associates of Marlowe's. Gifford was to be a double agent who was expelled from the seminaries at both Rome and Rheims, and was highly instrumental in the entrapment of Mary, Queen of Scots. Hariot, a celebrated mathematician, sailed to Virginia in 1585, and the Baines Note states Hariot's observations about the Indians to be the source of Marlowe's scepticism about traditional Biblical chronology, as well as quoting Marlowe as saying 'that Moyses was but a Jugler, & that one Heriots being Sir W Raleighs man can do more than he'. Hariot was a close friend of the Earl of Northumberland, to whom Marlowe was later to say he was very well known, and also of Sir Walter Ralegh.

January
6 (Sat.)   Pope Pius IV confirms the establishment of Douai.

1561

A German play about the story of Francis Spira is performed.
William Allen resigns all his offices and leaves England for Louvain.

January
19 (Sun.)   Philip II issues letters patent authorising the establishment
             of the University of Douai.

May
22 (Thurs.) Marriage of Marlowe's parents, John Marlowe and Katherine
             Arthur, at the church of St George the Martyr, Canterbury.

1562

The Thirty-Nine Articles set out the fundamental tenets of the English Church.
William Allen returns to England to evangelise.
Loyalty to Catholicism is still so strong in Canterbury that during this year the government has to intervene to ensure that a Protestant mayor is elected (see Urry, xxi).
Publication of John Shute, *Two Commentaries*, a translation of Andreas Cambinus' *Libro ... della origine de Turchi et imperio delli Ottomanni* ('Book ... on the Origin of the Turks and of the Ottoman Empire'), which includes an account of the treachery at Varna, immediately following the story of Tamburlaine.

The family of the future dramatist John Lyly are recorded as living in the parish of St Alphege's, Canterbury.

Antony Jenkinson, factor of the Muscovy Company, surveys Russia for Abraham Ortelius' atlas *Theatrum Orbis Terrarum* and dedicates his map to Sir Henry Sidney, father of Sir Philip Sidney and the leading light of the Muscovy Company. Marlowe is known to have used Ortelius' atlas (see Seaton, 'Marlowe's Map'). This is particularly interesting because Ortelius' atlas was intended to be not only accurate but also an expression of its maker's irenicism and hopes for religious tolerance (see Binding, 15). Amongst other things, the cordiform projection used by Ortelius was intended to signify sincerity and to resonate in the heart: 'So the very projection, determining our reception of the world, is itself irenicist' (Binding, 131).

Loppe de Aguirre murders his daughter Elvira to prevent her falling into enemy hands, a possible source or analogue for the infanticide of Olympia in *Tamburlaine the Great,* Part Two (see Hopkins, *Christopher Marlowe,* 54).

Birth of John Fixer, later a Catholic priest and probable turncoat (see Loomie, 74).

May

21 (Thurs.) Mary, first child of John and Katherine Marlowe, christened at St George's, Canterbury.

October

5 (Mon.)   Inauguration of the University of Douai.

1563

Publication of Johannes Wier, *De praestigiis daemonum* ('Of the Illusions of Demons'), which defended the reputation of his late master Agrippa and attacked the idea of witch-hunting on the grounds that people who thought they were witches were mentally ill rather than diabolically possessed.

Protestants finally secure definitive control of Canterbury local politics (see Urry, xxi). A household survey of Canterbury suggests that there are approximately 900 households in the city (Urry, 2).

March

Birth of Nicholas Skeres, one of the three men present at Marlowe's death.

Birth of Thomas Walsingham, at whose house at Scadbury Marlowe was staying at the time of his death.

May

16 (Sun.)   Baptism of Leonard Sweeting, a future schoolfellow of Marlowe and son of the rector of St George's, Canterbury. A list of Sweeting's books compiled in 1608 included *Hero and Leander*.

November

19 (Fri.)   Birth of Sir Robert Sidney, who was later to interrogate Marlowe after his arrest in Flushing in 1592.

1564

January

13 (Thurs.) Baptism at Henley-on-Thames, Oxfordshire of John Cranford, future husband of Marlowe's sister Ann.

February

26 (Sat.)   Christopher Marlowe christened at St George's Church, Canterbury. The entry in the parish register reads 'The 26th day of ffebruary was Christened Christofer the sonne of John Marlow'. He is likely to have been a few days old at the time.

March

Gerard Richardson, to whom John Marlowe had been apprenticed, dies.

25 (Fri.)   Lady Day. Start of the Elizabethan new year.

April

2 (Sun.)   Easter Sunday.

20 (Thurs.) Marlowe's father John admitted as a freeman of Canterbury, although he had served only a four-year apprenticeship instead of the customary seven. This was probably because plague had created a labour shortage. From now, or from shortly after, John Marlowe has his own shoemaker's shop.

26 (Sun.)   William Shakespeare is christened at Holy Trinity church, Stratford-upon-Avon. Although seemingly a later starter

than Marlowe, Shakespeare is overwhelmingly likely to
have known him in the 1590s. They may have collaborated
on the *Henry VI* plays and Shakespeare's early work shows
clear signs of the influence of Marlowe.

27 (Thurs.) Henry Percy, later 9th Earl of Northumberland, born at
Tynemouth Castle, Northumberland. Marlowe was later to
say that he was 'very well known' to the earl.

Publication at Douai of William Allen, *Certain Brief Reasons
concerning the Catholick Faith*. Allen's activities increase the
pressure for English Catholics not to accept the *status quo*
and thus foment the discontent and covert activity which
eventually become the principal concern of the government's intelligence agents.

August

4–6 (Fri.–Sun.) Canterbury fair held. For some indication of what this
might have been like, see Jonson's *Bartholomew Fair*.

7 (Mon.)   *Dido*, a version of the Dido story written by Edward
Halliwell, formerly Fellow of King's College, Cambridge,
acted before Queen Elizabeth in King's College Chapel. It is
now lost (see Boas, *University Drama*, 52).

September

8 (Fri.)   The dean of Canterbury Cathedral authorises a payment of
shillings to a 'straunger off the contry of Persia', who was
reputed to come from 'Babylond' (see Urry, 7). Though
Marlowe was still less than a year old, he might perhaps
have heard about this later, and it could conceivably represent his first encounter with the territory which was to
become so crucial a part of *Tamburlaine the Great*.

1565

William Allen leaves England and is ordained priest at Mechlin.

Early in the year Marlowe's father John, along with several of
his neighbours, gives evidence when a local girl, Godelif Chapman,
sues a tailor, Laurence Applegate, for claiming to have had sex with
her.

Publication at London of Arthur Golding's hugely influential translation of the first four books of Ovid's *Metamorphoses*. Marlowe too will
later translate Ovid, though his text will be the far more risqué *All*

Ovids Elegies. Golding's translation will bring Ovid to the forefront of the literary scene, and will have a huge impact on Shakespeare in particular.

Publication at Antwerp of William Allen, *A Defense and Declaration of the Catholike Churches Doctrine touching Purgatory and Prayers of the Soules Departed*. The question of purgatory and of the destination of the soul at death was one of the key differences between Protestantism and Catholicism. Protestant disbelief in purgatory was a major source of spiritual anxiety, and its consequences form an important subtext in both *Doctor Faustus* and *Shakespeare's Hamlet*.

March
25 (Sun.)   Lady Day. Start of the Elizabethan new year.

April
22 (Sun.)   Easter Sunday.

May
18 (Fri.)   Turks are sighted from Fort St Angelo and Fort St Elmo, which guard the Grand Harbour of Malta. This heralds the start of the Siege of Malta, which will later form the backdrop to Marlowe's *The Jew of Malta*.
25 (Fri.)   The siege of Fort St Elmo begins.
28 (Mon.)   Bombardment of Fort St Elmo begins.

June
The Piccolo Siccorso ('Small Relief Force'), including Sir Edward Stanley, sails from Sicily to the relief of Malta, arriving shortly after the fall of Fort St Elmo. This is probably the same Sir Edward Stanley as the man of that name who was the uncle of Ferdinando Stanley, Lord Strange, to whom Marlowe later said he was 'very well known'. Marlowe's account of the part of the siege at which Sir Edward was present seems to come closer to the truth than that of the earlier part to which he was not a witness (see Hopkins, *Christopher Marlowe*, 97–9).
23 (Sat.)   Fall of Fort St Elmo.

August
4–6 (Sat.–Mon.) Canterbury fair held.

September
The Turks abandon the siege of Malta and sail away from the island.

October

26 (Fri.)   Thomas Kyd, later to be Marlowe's roommate and another major force on the Elizabethan theatrical scene, enters Merchant Taylors' School.

December

Date on the dedication to Cardinal Hippolito d'Este of *Della Historia di Malta, et successo della guerra seguita tra quei Religiossimi Cavalieri ed il potentissimo gran Turco Sulthan Soliman, l'anno MDLXV* (Of the History of Malta, and of the War between Those Most Religious Knights and the Most Potent Grand Turk Sultan Soliman, the year 1565), by Pierro Gentile de Vendôme (see Vella Bonavita, 1028).

2 (Sun.)   Date given in the records of St George's, Canterbury, for the christening of Marlowe's sister Margaret (but see entry below for 18 December 1566, which appears to be the right one).

11 (Tues.)   Date sometimes cited as being given in the records of St George's, Canterbury, for the christening of Marlowe's sister Margaret (the confusion has arisen because the entry appears as ii December).

1566

Publication of William Painter, *Palace of Pleasure*, an important compilation of narratives much used as a source by Renaissance playwrights.

John Gresshop is appointed headmaster of the King's School, Canterbury.

Publication at Bologna of Pierro Gentile de Vendôme's *Della Historia di Malta* ... This was subsequently pirated by Marino Fracasso in Rome and by Alfonso Ulloa, who incorporated it into his history of the war in Tripoli and the siege of Malta. It was also the source of Caelius Secundus Curio's *Caelii Secundi Curionis de Bello Melitensi a turcis gesto historia nova* ('Caelius Secundus Curio's New History of the War Waged in Malta by the Turks') (see Vella Bonavita, 1028).

George Gascoigne and Francis Kinwelmershe's *Jocasta*, a possible source for *Tamburlaine*, staged at Gray's Inn (see Thomas and Tydeman, 81).

Death of Süleyman the Magnificent. He is succeeded by his son Selim, the Selim-Calymath of *The Jew of Malta*.

Joseph (João) Nassi, formerly João Micques and a possible analogue for Barabas (see Thomas and Tydeman, 298), is created Duke of Naxos by Sultan Selim II.

March

25 (Mon.) Lady Day. Start of the Elizabethan new year.

April

14 (Sun.) Easter Sunday.

August

4–6 (Sun.–Tues.) Canterbury fair held.

18 (Sun.) Philip II orders an *Ommegang* (ritual procession) in Antwerp in which all are to bow their knees to effigies of the Virgin Mary. The largely Protestant Antwerpers are incensed (see Binding, 143).

20 (Tues.) A disturbance in Onze Lieve Vrouwekathedraal, the cathedral of Antwerp, leads to an iconoclastic riot. This is the first real sign of the religious unrest which will eventually bring war to the Netherlands and lead to the English involvement there.

September

1 (Sun.) Birth of Edward Alleyn, who was to become famous as the first actor of almost all Marlowe's heroes.

2 (Mon.) Edward Alleyn christened at St Botolph Bishopsgate, London, where his father, a porter to the Queen, also owned an inn.

9 (Mon.) Nicholas Skeres' father, Nicholas senior, makes his will, and presumably dies shortly after. From this period on Skeres junior lives on his wits, apparently mainly as a confidence trickster.

December

18 (Wed.) Date given in the Bishop's Transcript for the baptism of Marlowe's sister Margaret. Constance Kuriyama is confident that either this or 28 December 1566 is the right date for Margaret's christening and suggests that the unusually long gap between Margaret's birth and Christopher's may be due to his having been breastfed for longer because he was the eldest male (Kuriyama, *Christopher Marlowe*, 16–17). It is of course also possible that Katherine Marlowe had had a miscarriage between Christopher's birth and Margaret's, or had simply not conceived.

1567

Publication at London of Arthur Golding's translation of the complete fifteen books of Ovid's *Metamorphoses*, and publication at London of George Turberville's translation of Ovid's *Heroides*.

The Knights of Malta take a large number of Jewish prisoners after a sea battle, contributing to the island's evil reputation amongst Jewish chroniclers (see Roth, 215).

A local shopkeeper later recalled that there was a severe water shortage in Canterbury this year (see Urry, 4).

Publication at Basle of Caelius Secundus Curio's *Caelii Secundi Curionis de Bello Melitensi a turcis gesto historia nova* ('Caelius Secundus Curio's New History of the Maltese War and the Deeds of the Turks'), translated into German in the same year by Hieronymus Helvecius and published, again at Basle, as *History von Krieg in der Insul Malta, Verteutscht durch M. Hieronynum Helvecium* ('History of the War in the Island of Malta, translated into German by Master Hieronymus Helvecius'). Curio's account was also republished the next year as part of his son Caelius Augustine Curio's *Caelii Augustini Curionis Sarracenicae historiae Libri tres* (Caelius Augustine Curio's Three Books of Saracen History) (see Vella Bonavita, 1028–9). Curio's account is unusual in being written from the perspective of a Reformer. Curio is also famous for having supposedly escaped from prison (to which he had been sent because of his Reformist views) by inserting a wooden leg into the stocks in place of his own (see Vella Bonavita, 1034 n. 55), something which may seem to foreshadow the trick played by Faustus on the horse-courser.

Birth of John Benchkin, whom Constance Kuriyama ('Second Selves', 89) sees as a close friend of Marlowe. Marlowe was later to be present at the witnessing of the will of Katherine Benchkin, John's stepmother.

Thomas Watson, future friend of Marlowe, goes to school at Winchester.

March
25 (Tues.)   Lady Day. Start of the Elizabethan new year.
30 (Sun.)   Easter Sunday.

August
4–6 (Mon.–Wed.) Canterbury fair held.

November
Thomas Nashe, Marlowe's future friend, is born in Lowestoft.

1568

Bonfinius' Latin chronicle of Hungary reissued at Basle.
Publication at Lyons of Nicolas de Nicolay's account of his visit to Malta.

Marlowe's father John takes his first apprentice, Richard Umbarffeld, or Umberfield, whose father seems to have been John Umberfield, a clock-maker and gunsmith.

March
25 (Thurs.) Lady Day. Start of the Elizabethan new year.

April
18 (Sun.) Easter Sunday.

May
Edmund Spenser, future author of *The Faerie Queene*, enters Pembroke Hall, Cambridge as a sizar (a student of limited means, who earned his keep by performing chores).

June
10 (Thurs.) Birth of Audrey Shelton, later to be the wife of Marlowe's
           friend Sir Thomas Walsingham of Scadbury. Audrey is also
           referred to as Etheldred in some records, and appears in the
           records of the parish church at Scadbury as Adrian.

August
4–6 (Wed. Fri.) Canterbury fair held.
28 (Sat.) Burial of Marlowe's elder sister Mary, aged six. This leaves
           Christopher, aged four, as the elder of the two surviving
           Marlowe children.

October
10 (Sun.) Michaelmas. Robert Poley, later to be one of the three men
           present at Marlowe's death, enters Clare College, Cambridge
           as a sizar.
           William Allen begins to gather English Catholics to form at
           English College at Douai.
24 (Sun.) Raffe Typpinge of Hoxton helps search the Portuguese
           ambassador's chapel for recusants. The Tipping family will
           later feature in the tangled web surrounding Marlowe's

arrest and death (see Seaton, 'Marlowe, Poley, and the Tippings', 277).

31 (Sun.)   An unnamed son of John and Katherine Marlowe is christened.

November
Richard Baines, later to be Marlowe's chief accuser in the Baines Note, matriculates as a pensioner at Christ's College, Cambridge.
The English College founded at Douai.

5 (Fri.)   Burial of John and Katherine Marlowe's unnamed infant son.

1569

Edmund Spenser is recorded as carrying despatches from France.
Gerald Mercator publishes a world map which is the first to make use of his new projection (on its effects and significance, see Binding, 200–1).
João Micques, now Nassi, the Portuguese Jew who was created Duke of Naxos by Sultan Selim II, publicly urges the Sultan to break his alliance with Venice and seize Cyprus.
John Ballard, later to be involved in the Babington Plot of 1586, matriculates as a sizar at St Catharine's College, Cambridge.
Catholic families in Canterbury successfully remove Protestants from office (see Urry, xxi).

March
25 (Fri.)   Lady Day. Start of the Elizabethan new year.

April
10 (Sun.)   Easter Sunday.

July
10 (Sun.)   The churchwardens of St George's Church, Canterbury complain of John Marlowe 'for that he commeth not to church as he ought to doe'.

August
4–6 (Thurs.–Sat.) Canterbury fair held.
20 (Sat.)   Marlowe's sister Joan (or Jane) christened. (The name is erroneously recorded in the parish register as John.)

October

23 (Sun.)   Ortelius receives his first licence to print the *Theatrum Orbis Terrarum*.

1570

Second English edition of John Foxe's *Actes and Monuments*, including new material on Bajazet. It was ordered by Convocation to be placed in every cathedral church.

Nassi persuades Sultan Selim to attempt the capture of Cyprus from the Venetians (see Thomas and Tydeman, 298).

Publication of Abraham Ortelius' atlas *Theatrum Orbis Terrarum*, which Marlowe is known to have used (see Seaton, 'Marlowe's Map').

The Papal Bull 'Regnans in Excelsis' is issued by Pius V. It deposes Queen Elizabeth and declares that her subjects owe her no allegiance. It significantly inflames both Catholic resistance and Protestant anxieties.

Edward Aglionby's English translation of Matteo Garibaldi's account of the death of Spira is reissued in London.

January

18 (Wed.)   John Ballard, who is later to be involved in the Babington Plot, is admitted to Caius College, Cambridge.

February

21 (Tues.)   Ortelius receives a second licence for the *Theatrum Orbis Terrarum*.

March

25 (Sat.)   Lady Day. Start of the Elizabethan new year.
26 (Sun.)   Easter Sunday.

April

Richard Umberfield, John Marlowe's apprentice, is accused of having made one Joan Hubbard pregnant and his apprenticeship seems to have been terminated (Urry, 23).

May

20 (Sat.)   Publication of the *Theatrum Orbis Terrarum* (see Binding, 201).

July

26 (Wed.)   Marlowe's brother Thomas, the first of the two to be so named, is christened.

August

4–6 (Fri.–Sun.) Canterbury fair held.

7 (Mon.)   Marlowe's brother Thomas buried.

September

13 (Wed.)   Burial of Edward Alleyn senior, father of the actor.

1571

Battle of Lepanto, in which Venice defeats the Turks. This is now seen as a turning-point in the struggle against Ottoman power, though the Turks remained a very real threat for some considerable time.

Publication at London of Thomas Fortescue, *The Foreste or Collection of Histories* (a translation of Mexia's *Silva de Vario Lecion*, one of the principal sources of *Tamburlaine*).

Richard Edwardes, *Damon and Pithias*. As a play about male friendship, this has been proposed as a model for *Edward II* (see Mills).

Sir Edward Stanley, uncle of Ferdinando Stanley, Lord Strange and probably the same person as the Sir Edward Stanley who was a veteran of the Siege of Malta, is implicated in a plot to rescue Mary, Queen of Scots.

January

20 (Sat.)   Edward Alleyn's mother Margaret remarries. Her husband, Richard Christopher, also known as Richard Grove, becomes Alleyn's first stepfather.

March

25 (Sun.)   Lady Day. Start of the Elizabethan new year.

April

15 (Sun.)   Easter Sunday.

July

14 (Sat.)   Marlowe's sister Ann christened at St George's, Canterbury. She seems to have been a quarrelsome person; in later life, when 55 years old, she fought a neighbour armed with a staff and a dagger, and the following year she assaulted the same neighbour with a sword and a knife. She was also reported to the ecclesiastical authorities in 1603 as a scold and blasphemer.

August
4–6 (Sat.–Mon.) Canterbury fair held.

October
14 (Sun.) Eleanor Whitney marries Richard Bull at St Mary-le-Bow. It will be in her house that Marlowe dies.

November
7 (Wed.) Edmund, son of Humphrey Rowland, christened at St Botolph's, London. Humphrey Rowland will act as one of Marlowe's sureties when he is arrested after a fight in 1589.

1572

Publication at London of Thomas Churchyard's translation of the first three books of Ovid's *Tristia*, another indication of the growing vogue for translating Ovid.

Sir Walter Ralegh's name appears on the register of Oriel College, Oxford for this year.

Nicholas Faunt, native of Canterbury and later an important figure in Walsingham's espionage network, matriculates at Caius College, Cambridge.

March
25 (Tues.) Lady Day. Start of the Elizabethan new year.

April
6 (Sun.) Easter Sunday.

June
9 (Mon.) Death of Jeanne d'Albret, mother of Henri of Navarre (later Henri IV of France). Marlowe stages her death in scene iii of *The Massacre at Paris*.

August
4–6 (Mon.–Wed.) Canterbury fair held.

18 (Mon.) Marriage of Henri of Navarre and Marguerite de Valois, both characters in *A Massacre at Paris*.

22 (Fri.) Admiral Coligny is shot and wounded, precipitating the St Bartholomew's Day Massacre (Marlowe's 'massacre at Paris').

24 (Sun.)   Coligny is murdered in bed while recovering from his injuries.
Execution of Thomas Howard, Duke of Norfolk, for intriguing with Mary, Queen of Scots.

November
11 (Tues.) A new star appears in the constellation Cassiopeia and is much commented on by astronomers, who see it as an omen (Woolley, 147). This kind of event typically causes considerable consternation in Elizabethan England.

1573

The poet and playwright George Gascoigne is recorded as working in the Low Countries with Rowland Yorke, who, along with Sir William Stanley, would later betray the Dutch city of Deventer to the Spanish.
Religious conservatives in Canterbury complain unsuccessfully about Protestant domination of local politics (Urry, xxi).
Publication, probably at London but possibly at Stirling or Edinburgh, of an English translation of François Hotman, *De Furoribus Gallicis*, as *A true and plaine report of the Furious outrages of Fraunce* (see Kocher, 'François Hotman', 350, n. 4). This recounts some of the events which Marlowe would later dramatise in *A Massacre at Paris*.
John Cecil, later to be either a Catholic priest or a government plant, enters Trinity College, Oxford as a scholar.
Nicholas Faunt enters Corpus Christi College, Cambridge as a scholar.
John Marlowe appears to have been acting as a sidesman at St George's (Urry, 28).

March
22 (Sun.)   Easter Sunday.
25 (Wed.)   Lady Day. Start of the Elizabethan new year.

May
20 (Wed.)   A boy called Christopher Mowle is recorded as living in the house of John Roydon, victualler, of Canterbury, and as witnessing an assault alleged to have taken place there on this date. Andrew Butcher suggested that this boy was Christopher Marlowe, although he conceded that the age is wrong – Christopher Mowle's age is given as twelve years, whereas Christopher Marlowe was three months short of his

tenth birthday (Butcher). If the suggestion were accepted, it would mean that Marlowe was living away from his family at this time, which would be interesting in the light of the numerous family conflicts dramatised in his plays. However, the discrepancy in age cannot simply be ignored. As we have seen, there had previously been Christopher Morleys or Morles living in Canterbury; this makes it possible that some of their descendants would have been given that name, so conceivably Christopher Mowle was one of these.

July
John Marlowe sues Leonard Browne for debt.

August
4–6 (Tues.–Thurs.) Canterbury fair held.

September
John Marlowe sues Hugh Jones, landlord of the Chequers tavern, for debt.
3 (Thurs.) The Queen, on progress to Canterbury, enters the city, rides in triumph through it, and is greeted at the cathedral by Archbishop Parker.
7 (Mon.) The Queen celebrates her fortieth birthday at Archbishop Parker's palace.

October
18 (Sun.) Marlowe's sister Dorothy christened.
20 (Tues.) John Marlowe sues Thomas Ovington over a quarrel about a horse, and is awarded damages of 9s 4d.
22 (Thurs.) John Marlowe brings his quarrelsome and litigious summer to an end by telling Michael Shaw, basket-maker, 'Michael Shawe thou art a thief and so I will prove thee to be'. Shaw subsequently sued him for slander.

1574

Birth of Thomas Fineux, whom Marlowe was later alleged to have converted to atheism.
Death of Sultan Selim II, Marlowe's Selim-Calymath.
Publication of an English translation of François Hotman's *De Furoribus Gallicis* as *The Three Partes of Commentaries … of the Ciuill warres of Fraunce* (see Kocher, 'François Hotman').

Publication (at Edinburgh but in French) of Nicholas Barnaud, *Le Reveille-Matin des François* ('The Wake-up Call of the French'), another account of the French wars of religion.
Death of the Cardinal of Lorraine, a key figure in the wars.
John Fixer, subsequently to become a Catholic priest, matriculates at Trinity College, Oxford.

January
John Marlowe enters a plea for debt against Michael Shaw.

March
The new star which had appeared in Cassiopeia in 1572 disappears. Contemporary inability to explain this fuels concerns about celestial phenomena and divine warnings.
John Marlowe enters a plea for debt against Robert Shaw.
25 (Thurs.) Lady Day. Start of the Elizabethan new year.

April
11 (Sun.)   Easter Sunday.

May
3 (Mon.)   Burial of William Sweeting, rector of St George's, Canterbury, and father of Leonard Sweeting, who will attend the King's School, Canterbury and will own a copy of *Hero and Leander* at the time of his death.

June
20 (Sun.)   A 'Dick Baies' is mentioned as having carried messages to Mary, Queen of Scots. This is mistakenly indexed as 'Baines' (suggesting Richard Baines) in the *Calendar of the State Papers Relating to Scotland*, but Constance Kuriyama has argued that since the name Baies or Bayes is common in the area around Sheffield where Mary was being held, 'Baies' is likely to be correct (Kuriyama, 'Marlowe's Nemesis', 350).

August
4–6 (Wed.–Fri.) Canterbury fair held.

November
14–15 (Sun.–Mon.) The Northern Lights are seen over Canterbury, to the alarm of the local population.

1575

Coronation of Henri III of France.

Around about this year the Canterbury gallows are moved and re-erected in the parish in which Marlowe was living (Urry, 7).

Robert Greene, later to denounce Marlowe as an atheist in his preface to *Perimedes the Blacksmith*, matriculates at Cambridge.

Death of Marlowe's grandfather, William Arthur of Dover.

William Allen visits Rome and helps in the founding of the English College there.

Publication of Henri Estienne, *A Marvelous Discourse upon the Life, Deeds, and Behaviors of Katherine de Medicis, Queen Mother*. Catherine is an important character in *The Massacre at Paris*, and Marlowe might have consulted this.

Publication of François de Belleforest, *La cosmographie Universelle de tout le monde ... beaucoup plus augmentée, ornée, et enrichie* ('The Universal Cosmography of the Whole World ... Much Augmented, Adorned, and Enriched'), which includes a version of the Olympia story told in *Tamburlaine the Great*, Part Two. The same year also saw the publication of an English version of Celio Secundo Curione, *Notable History of the Saracens*, translated by Thomas Newton. Milton's nephew Edward Phillips will later think that Newton wrote Marlowe's *Tamburlaine*.

John Ballard graduates BA from King's College, Cambridge.

February
27 (Sun.)   The register of the Middle Temple in London records the presence of Walter Ralegh there.

March
25 (Fri.)   Lady Day. Start of the Elizabethan new year.

April
3 (Sun.)   Easter Sunday.
5 (Tues.)   Matthew Parker, Archbishop of Canterbury, makes his will, setting up a scholarship to be held at Corpus Christi College, Cambridge, by a boy from the King's School, Canterbury. Marlowe will be a future holder of it.
May–August Plague in Canterbury pushes the death toll in these months to twice its normal figure.

May
17 (Tues.) Death of Matthew Parker, Archbishop of Canterbury.

August
4–6 (Thurs–Sat.) Canterbury fair held.

October
Heavy snow in Canterbury.

November
10 (Thurs.) First mention of Lady Arbella Stuart, to whom Marlowe might just conceivably later have acted as tutor. Her precise birthdate is unknown, but a letter from her grandmother on this date refers to her. She had probably been born shortly before.

1576

Publication at Geneva of Innocent Gentillet, *Discours sur les moyens de bien gouverner et maintenir en bonne paix un royaume ou autre principauté. Divisez en trois partis; à savoir, du conseil, de la religion et police que doit tenir un Prince: Contre Nicholas Machiavel Florentin* ('Discourse on the Ways of Ruling Well and of Maintaining in Peace a Kingdom or Other Principality. Divided into Thee Parts, that is, on the Advice, Religion and Policy which a Prince Should Follow: against Niccolò Machiavelli the Florentine'). Known as the *Contre-Machiavel*, this is one possible source for the knowledge of Machiavelli displayed by Marlowe in *The Jew of Malta*.

Walter Ralegh publishes his first poetry.

Publication of Thomas Tymme's translation of Jean de Serres, *The Fourth Part of Commentaries of the Civil Wars in France* ..., discussed by Thomas and Tydeman as a possible souce for *The Massacre at Paris* (see Thomas and Tydeman, 333).

Publication of Jean Bodin, *Six Livres de la république* ('Six Books of the Republic'), which contrasts Tamburlaine with Bajazet and subsequently became the subject of lectures at Cambridge.

Publication at London of Arthur Golding's translation of Jean de Serres' *Lyfe of ... Iasper Colignie Shatilion*. The murder of Coligny was one of the key incidents in the St Bartholomew's Day Massacre.

Anthony Marlowe, who may possibly have been a relation of Christopher Marlowe, begins working as London agent of the Muscovy Company and continues in their employ until 1599 (for some details of his career, see Wilson, 'Visible Bullets').

Marlowe's friend Thomas Watson goes to the English College at Douai.

Second English edition of John Foxe's *Actes and Monuments*, which includes the material on Bajazet, reissued.

The Theatre, probably the first purpose-built theatrical venue in England to be used exclusively for plays, is opened in London by James Burbage, a joiner and an amateur player, whose son Richard will eventually become Shakespeare's leading actor. It is financed largely by James's brother-in-law John Brayne, a grocer, who died before the theatre was completed.

Richard Baines, now a member of Caius, receives his MA.

March
25 (Sun.)   Lady Day. Start of the Elizabethan new year.

April
8 (Sun.)   Probable date of the baptism of Marlowe's brother Thomas (the second of his brothers to be so called, and the youngest of the Marlowe children) at St Andrew's Church, Canterbury.
21 (Sat.)   John Marlowe takes Lactantius Presson as his apprentice, but the two soon fall out. After a fight, Presson leaves and John Marlowe is fined for drawing blood.
22 (Sun.)   Easter Sunday.

May
Heavy storms lead to severe flooding in Canterbury (see Urry, 4).
17 (Thurs.) John Cecil, who is later to be either a Catholic priest or a government double agent, receives his BA from Trinity College, Oxford.

August
4–6 (Sat.–Mon.) Canterbury fair held.

October
15 (Mon.) Thomas Watson leaves Douai for Paris.

November
4 (Sun.)   The 'Spanish Fury' – Spanish soldiers from the citadel devastate and pillage the city of Antwerp. Contemporary accounts suggested that as many as 18,000 people died on this and the subsequent days, though 8,000 is now considered a more likely figure (see Binding, 269–75).

1577

A Thomas Baines of Southwell matriculates at Caius. The coincidence of name and college suggests that this may be Richard Baines's brother, and that if so, Richard Baines came from Southwell.

William Parry, later to be executed for supposedly attempting to assassinate Elizabeth, visits Rome and Siena.

Gentillet's *Contre-Machiavel* is translated into English by Simon Patericke (though this was not published until 1602).

Publication of Pierre de la Primaudauye, *French Academy*, containing an account of Tamburlaine influenced by Perondinus.

First publication of Raphael Holinshed's *Chronicles*, later to be used by Marlowe as a source for *Edward II*.

Publication of *Beautiful Blossoms, gathered by John Bishop, from the best trees of all kinds ...*, cited by Thomas and Tydeman as a possible source for *Tamburlaine* (see Thomas and Tydeman, 139).

January
31 (Thurs.) Gilbert Gifford, future recusant priest, arrives at Douai.

March
12 (Tues.) Abraham Ortelius, whose map *Theatrum Orbis Terrarum* Marlowe will use for *Tamburlaine*, visits John Dee at his home in Mortlake (see Crane, 364).
25 (Mon.) Lady Day. Start of the Elizabethan new year.

April
7 (Sun.)   Easter Sunday.

May
Thomas Watson returns from Paris to Douai.

July
Thomas Watson leaves Douai.

August
4–6 (Sun.–Tues.) Canterbury fair held.
7 (Wed.)   Thomas Watson embarks for England.

November

10 (Sun.)   A comet is seen over Europe and the astrologer John Dee is asked by the Queen to comment on what it portends. It is variously viewed as, amongst other things, being shaped like a Turkish sword and thus foreboding Turkish invasion, and as pointing threateningly towards the Muscovites and Tartars (Woolley, 161–2).

30 (Sat.)   Execution of the Catholic priest Cuthbert Mayne at Launceston in Devon. Mayne has been condemned by Sir Roger Manwood, on whom Marlowe will later write an epitaph, and sentence has been enforced by Sir Richard Grenville, with whom Hariot will later sail to America. This is the first execution of a seminary priest. On the repercussions of Mayne's death, see Kendall, *Christopher Marlowe*, 121–5.

December

13 (Fri.)   Sir Francis Drake sets sail for Plymouth, ostensibly for the Mediterranean but in fact for the Americas (see Bawlf).

1578

England and Turkey open formal trade relations.

John Marlowe is acting as a sidesman at the church of St Andrew, having moved out of the parish of St George.

Publication at Frankfurt of the second edition of Philippus Lonicerus, *Chronicorum Turcicorum tomi duo* ('Two Volumes of the Chronicles of the Turks'), which included *Antonii Bonfinii Rerum Ungaricum decades tres* ('Antonius Bonfinus' Three Decades of Hungarian Affairs') and *Callimachi Experientis de clade Varnensi Epistola* ('The Letter of Callimachus Experiens [Filippo Buonaccorsi] on the defeat at Varna') (see Boas, *Christopher Marlowe*, 88–9). Marlowe drew on the Battle of Varna material in *Tamburlaine the Great*, Part Two.

Publication at London of Gabriel Harvey, *Gratulationum Valdinensium libri quattuor* ('Four Books of Welcome to Saffron Walden'), including an epigram on the image of Machiavelli, which indicates that he was already known about at Cambridge (see Thomas and Tydeman, 335). Gabriel Harvey and his brother Richard were the targets of satirical attacks from a number of those in Marlowe's circle.

February
Heavy snow in Canterbury; snowdrifts block roads (see Urry, 4).

March
The seminary at Douai transfers to Rheims.
9 (Sun.) Burial of Edward Alleyn's first stepfather, Richard Christopher (also known as Grove).
25 (Tues.) Lady Day. Start of the Elizabethan new year.
30 (Sun.) Easter Sunday.

June
The Queen issues a patent to Sir Humphrey Gilbert for 200 leagues of any American coast which he may find unoccupied by a Christian ruler. This is to expire on 11 June 1584 if he has not found and settled any such land by that date.

August
4–6 (Mon.–Wed.) Canterbury fair held.

September
21 (Sun.) Robert Dudley, Earl of Leicester, marries Lettice Knollys, the widow of the 1st Earl of Essex, and thus becomes the step-father of Robert Devereux, 2nd Earl of Essex. The name of Essex is one of the most frequently invoked in speculation about the causes of Marlowe's death, and it was this mar-riage of his mother to Elizabeth I's favourite which paved the way for the earl's subsequent rise to favour.
26 (Fri.) Walter Ralegh and his half-brother Sir Humphrey Gilbert set sail in an attempt to raid the French, Spanish and Portuguese fishing fleets and raise money for New World exploration from the proceeds (see Lacey, 28–9). Storms drive them back to Plymouth.

November
19 (Wed.) Ralegh and Gilbert try again, but once more the weather gets the better of them.

December
Marlowe is enrolled as a scholar of the King's School, Canterbury.
8 (Mon.) Henry Woodward, first husband of Agnes Woodward, wife of the theatrical entrepreneur Philip Henslowe, is buried in the parish of St Saviour's in London.

1579

Thomas Watson is involved with Anne Burnell, who believed herself the daughter of Philip of Spain. Watson seems to have encouraged her in the delusion (see Nicholl, *Reckoning*, 185–6).
Thomas Hariot graduates from Oxford.
Publication of *The School of Abuse*, written by Marlowe's fellow parishioner in Canterbury, Stephen Gosson. This was an 'invective against Poets, Pipers, Plaiers, Jesters and such like', and a milestone in the growing anti-theatrical movement. It was dedicated to Sir Philip Sidney, though Sidney's own *Apologie for Poetrie*, published two years later, suggests that he by no means shared Gosson's views.
Publication of Edmund Spenser, *The Shepheardes Calender.*
Death of Joao Micques, now Nassi.
Publication of *Tocsain contre les Massacres* ('Tocsin against the Massacres'), which mentions Ramus' efforts to buy his life and so was proposed by John Bakeless as a source for *The Massacre at Paris* (see Bakeless, 255).
Prince John Casimir, a Protestant continental leader, meets Philip Sidney in Canterbury.
Robert Greene graduates BA from St John's College, Cambridge.
The printer John Stubbs has his right hand amputated as punishment for having published an attack on the Queen's apparent plan to marry the Catholic Duke of Anjou.

January
11 (Sun.)   Date at the end of the dedication of Thomas Mainwaringe's translation of Caelius Secundus Curio's history of the siege of Malta to the Queen's Champion, Sir Henry Lee. This is the first full account of the siege to appear in English. Mainwaringe notes that he writes from 'my chamber in St. Johns College in Oxforde' (see Vella Bonavita, 1040–1).
14 (Wed.)   Official recording of Christopher Marlowe's enrolment as a scholar of the King's School, Canterbury.

February
Anthony Munday, poet, playwright and secret agent, enrolls at the English College at Rome, where students include Gilbert Gifford and Charles Sledd, who may have been an associate of Richard Baines. Gifford is expelled during the course of the year.
14 (Sat.)   The theatrical entrepreneur Philip Henslowe marries the widowed Agnes Woodward and becomes stepfather to her two daughters, Joan and Elizabeth.

March
25 (Wed.)   Lady Day. Start of the Elizabethan new year.
Marlowe receives his first scholarship payment at the King's School, Canterbury.

April
19 (Sun.)   Easter Sunday.
28 (Tues.) Marlowe's father John acts as a professional bondsman for a couple seeking a marriage licence, offering security of £100. This was a way of supplementing his income. (A bond was given to the court by the groom and would be forfeited if he subsequently failed to marry the bride. The role of the bondsman was to guarantee payment if need be in return for a fee.)

June
15 (Mon.)   Richard Jones, later to print *Tamburlaine* (and not to be confused with the actor of the same name), is fined for unlicensed printing of *A True Copy Of a Letter sent by the Prince of Parma to the generall States of the lowe Countries*. Parma will be mentioned in *Doctor Faustus* and will lend his surname, Farnese, to the Governor in *The Jew of Malta*. On the reputation of Parma in England, and in particular for an argument that he came to be associated with Tamburlaine, see Voss, 166–7 and 170–1.

July
4 (Sat.)   Records of the Rheims seminary record the arrival from England of 'Holmes et Baynes', i.e. Richard Baines.

August
The Duke of Anjou arrives in England to pursue his courtship of Elizabeth.
4–6 (Tues.–Thurs.) Canterbury fair held.

October
21 (Wed.)   Margaret Alleyn, mother of Edward, marries for the third time. Her husband is a haberdasher named John Browne.

November
20 (Fri.)   John Ballard arrives at Rheims.

December

1 (Tues.)   A charter issued to all Canterbury leatherworkers decrees that from now on they are all to be part of one 'Fellowshippe companye crafte and mysterye of shoemakers'.

1580

Raffe Typpinge of Hoxton has his house searched on suspicion of recusancy (see Seaton, 'Marlowe, Poley, and the Tippings', 277).

Thomas Hariot enters the household of Sir Walter Ralegh (see Rukeyser, 6–7).

Probable year of arrival in Canterbury of Marlowe's future brother-in-law John Moore, who, after leaving his birthplace of Ulcombe at the age of fifteen, has spent seven years in Faversham.

John Alleyn, Edward's elder brother, mentioned as a player and as a servant of Lord Sheffield.

Publication of Robert Greene, *Mamillia*, a 'Looking-Glasse for the Ladies of England', which was modelled on Lyly's *Euphues* (see Nicholl, *Cup*, 27).

Death of Raphael Holinshed, author of Holinshed's *Chronicles*, used by Marlowe as one of the sources for *Edward II*.

Publication of John Stow, *Chronicles*, also a source for *Edward II*.

January

Richard Kitchen, later to stand surety for Marlowe, marries Agnes Redman.

February

Death of John Gresshop, Marlowe's first headmaster at the King's School, Canterbury. Nicholas Goldsborough succeeds as headmaster, presumably shortly afterwards.

23 (Tues.)   An inventory is taken of Gresshop's goods (see Urry, 46–7).

March

14 (Mon.)   John Cecil receives his MA from Trinity College, Oxford.

25 (Fri.)   Lady Day. Start of the Elizabethan new year.

April

Possible mention of Richard Baines in the diary of Charles Sledd. The man referred to by Sledd is a Walsingham agent lodging with the Catholic scholar Thomas Court in Paris, and is ejected thence on

Friday, 15 April (see Nicholl, *Reckoning*, 125–7). However, Kendall (*Christopher Marlowe*, 84–5) argues that in fact the reference is to William Wade.

Indenture drawn up between Corpus Christi College, Cambridge, and John Parker, son of Archbishop Matthew Parker, in which John Parker reserves to himself the nomination of the Parker scholars, of whom Marlowe will later be one. It is expected that Parker scholars will go on to take holy orders; Marlowe's acceptance of the scholarship must have meant either that he did originally intend to do this and then changed his mind, or that he was acting a part from the outset.

3 (Sun.)   Easter Sunday.

6 (Wed.)   A two-minute earthquake, apparently centred on Oxford, sets London church bells ringing at 6.10 pm and is felt as far away as France. Like new stars, earthquakes were generally interpreted as portents.

27 (Wed.)   An intelligence report listing 'sundry Englishmen, Papists, presently abiding in Paris' names 'Banes' and two Watsons, of whom one is 'son to the Attorney in London'. Constance Kuriyama suggests that this could be Marlowe's friend Thomas Watson (*Christopher Marlowe*, 86). Also mentioned is William Clitherow, who, on 21 September 1586, will write to 'Gerard Burghet', which may have been an alias of Richard Baines (see Kendall, *Christopher Marlowe*, 101).

Summer
Walter Ralegh sails to Cork in the first of his attempts at 'planting' in Ireland.

July

6 (Wed.)   A meeting of Gresshop's creditors includes John Marlowe, to whom 16s 4d is owed from the headmaster's estate.

13 (Wed.)   Francis Kett resigns as a Fellow of Corpus Christi College, Cambridge, but remains in residence during early 1581. It is sometimes suggested that Kett's subsequent execution for heresy might have been a factor in Marlowe's disillusionment with the Church (if indeed he ever had intended to take holy orders). Adrian Morey calls Kett 'the tutor of Christopher Marlowe' (Morey, 210), but this is conjecture.

23 (Sat.)   John Marlowe enrolls Elias Martin and William Hewes as apprentices.

August

Nicholas Faunt, Canterbury man and spy, whom Constance Kuriyama sees as a friend of Marlowe's, meets Anthony Bacon, the flamboyantly homosexual brother of Francis Bacon, in Paris (see Kuriyama, 'Second Selves', 94).

4–6 (Thurs.–Sat.) Canterbury fair held.

September

Gabriel Harvey informs Edmund Spenser that Turkish affairs are currently the talk of the university.

26 (Mon.) Sir Francis Drake returns from circumnavigating the world and having skirted the American coastline perhaps as far as Vancouver Island (see Bawlf).

October

Thomas Walsingham, at whose house Marlowe seems to have been staying when he died, is recorded as bringing letters for the Queen from the English ambassador in France.

10 (Mon.) A blazing star appears in Pisces. Again this is taken by astrologers as an omen.

November

2 (Wed.) William Parry, later to be executed for allegedly attempting to assassinate Elizabeth, is involved in an altercation in the Inner Temple with Hugh Hare, to whom he owes money, and is subsequently sentenced to death for burglary and attempted murder. This is commuted, but Parry will later be sent to the debtors' prison. The sureties for his release from this included Sir William Drury and Sir Edward Stafford (see *DNB* entry on Parry).

9 (Wed.) Walter Ralegh, serving under Lord Grey of Wilton, participates in the Smerwick massacre in Ireland, which involved the brutal killing of a number of Irish (including pregnant women), as well as Italians and Spanish mercenaries who were helping the Earl of Kildare in his rebellion against the English (see Lacey, 35–7).

December

10 (Sat.) Probable date of Marlowe's arrival at Corpus Christi College, Cambridge, to study divinity. His roommates were Robert

Thexton, a native of Norfolk, studying for his MA; Thomas Lewgar, also from Norfolk, a Parker scholar; and the outgoing holder of his scholarship, Christopher Pashley.

Among the many books in the Corpus library at the time of Marlowe's arrival, there are known to have been copies of Ortelius' *Theatrum Orbis Terrarum* and the works of Paolo Giovio, which he used as sources for *Tamburlaine*.

16 (Fri.)   Michaelmas Term ends.

21 (Wed.)   Christopher Pashley, Marlowe's predecessor in his Parker scholarship, is ordained priest at Ely, and subsequently becomes curate of St Benet's, dying in 1612.

1581

William Perkins, later to be a famous populariser of Calvinism and a theorist of witchcraft, receives his BA (see Pinciss). The importance of both Calvinism and witchcraft in *Doctor Faustus* is still debated. Perkins was one of the Protestant reformers of whom there were later to be portraits in the college founded by Edward Alleyn in Dulwich (Foister, in Reid and Maniura, 54).

Richard Harvey, brother of Marlowe's future antagonist Gabriel, is elected a fellow of Pembroke Hall, Cambridge.

Sir Walter Ralegh starts to rise to favour at court.

Marlowe's father John is appointed 'searcher' (i.e. inspector) of leather, along with Christopher Ashenden.

Publication of Nathaniel Wood's *Conflict of Conscience*, a play based on the story of Francis Spira.

Publication of William Allen, *An Apology for the English Seminaries*. To those concerned with English national security, this will have seemed like a clear sign of the magnitude of the threat posed by seminaries like the one at Rheims.

Publication at London of Thomas Watson's *Antigone*, dedicated to Philip Howard, Earl of Arundel. Watson was later to be a friend of Marlowe and this play shows the importance of classical models for English tragedy, as in Marlowe's own *Dido, Queen of Carthage*.

January

13 (Fri.)   Lent term starts at Cambridge.

February

Pedantius, a satire on Gabriel Harvey, presented at Trinity College, Cambridge.

March
4 (Sat.)   John Ballard ordained at Châlons.
17 (Fri.) Marlowe matriculates at Corpus Christi College, Cambridge.
           Lent term ends.
25 (Sat.) Lady Day. Start of the Elizabethan new year.
           Richard Baines ordained subdeacon by the Bishop of
           Châlons.
26 (Sun.) Easter Sunday.
29 (Wed.) John Ballard sent to England.

April
4 (Tues.) A banquet is held on board the *Golden Hind* to celebrate Sir
           Francis Drake's safe return from circumnavigating the
           world.
5 (Wed.)   Easter term starts at Cambridge.

May
7–11 (Sun.–Thurs.) Marlowe is formally elected to his scholarship at
           Corpus Christi College, Cambridge: 'Marlin electus et admis-
           sus in locum domini Pashly' (Marlin elected and admitted
           in the place of Master [Christopher] Pashly).
8 (Mon.)   Richard Baines ordained deacon by the Bishop of Soissons.

June
Thomas Watson, yeoman of St Helen's Bishopsgate, is recorded as not
going to church, usually though not invariably an indication of
Catholicism. This is probably Marlowe's future friend.
6 (Tues.) John Marlowe acts as bondsman for W. Key of Croydon,
           shoemaker, guaranteeing his appearance at the Sessions.
13 (Tues.) Baptism at Kingsclere in Hampshire of an Ingram Chamber-
           lain, who may perhaps have been a relative of Ingram Frizer
           and may one day provide a clue to Frizer's origins and loy-
           alties, and hence to his possible motivations and rôle in the
           death of Marlowe (see Hopkins, 'New Light on Marlowe's
           Murderer').

July
4 (Tues.) Commencement (the equivalent of graduation) day at
           Cambridge.
7 (Fri.)   End of Easter term. University vacation begins.
17 (Mon.) The famous Catholic priest Edmund Campion is captured
           at Lyford in Berkshire.

27 (Thurs.) Sir Francis Walsingham, who is effectively head of the English secret service, lands at Boulogne.

31 (Mon.) Edmund Campion is tortured on the rack.

August

Thomas Watson is recorded as attending on Sir Francis Walsingham in France.

3 (Thurs.) Alexander Hoghton of Lea Hall near Preston makes his will (as a direct result of Edmund Campion's arrest, knowing he too is likely to be arrested and not to survive), in which he requests his friend and neighbour Sir Thomas Hesketh to be 'ffrendly vnto ffoke gyllome & William Shakshafte now dwellynge with me'. It is conceivable that 'William Shakshafte' was William Shakespeare. If so, Shakespeare would, at any rate at this stage of his life, have been a Catholic and in touch with underground Catholic networks, and is also very likely to have known Lord Strange. The Earl of Southampton, father of Shakespeare's future patron, also makes his will on the same day and for the same reason (see Wilson, 'Torturing Hour').

4–6 (Fri.–Sun.) Canterbury fair held.

September

The Catholic exile Robert Persons reports to Claudius Acquaviva, General of the Jesuits in Rome, that a Catholic priest has succeeded in infiltrating Cambridge University and has already sent seven recruits to Rheims (see Nicholl, *Reckoning*, 97).

21 (Thurs.) Richard Baines ordained as a priest.

October

4 (Wed.)   Richard Baines celebrates his first Mass.

10 (Tues.) Michaelmas Term starts at Cambridge.

29 (Sun.)   Date on a list of students in the class of 'Mr. Johnes, professor lecturae dialecticae' ('Mr Jones, professor of dialectic') at Cambridge, including Marlowe, Thomas Lewgar and Thomas Munday, also Corpus scholars (see Boas, *Christopher Marlowe*, 16).

November

12 (Sun.)   Sir Henry Cobham, English ambassador to France, writes to Sir Francis Walsingham to tell him that his young relative,

Thomas Walsingham, has narrowly escaped being robbed by French soldiers (see Nicholl, *Reckoning*, 116).

21 (Tues.)   Edmund Campion is condemned to death.

December

1 (Fri.)   Edmund Campion is executed at Tyburn.
John Ballard is recorded as staying at the Red Lion in Holborn.

16 (Sat.)   Michaelmas Term ends.

1582

Approximate date of the marriage of Robert Poley, one of the three men who will be in the room with Marlowe when he dies, to 'one Watson's daughter', who may well have been the sister of Marlowe's friend Thomas Watson.

Publication of Richard Hakluyt, *Divers Voyages touching the Discoveries of America*. Marlowe's friend Nashe refers to Hakluyt's *English Discoveries* in his *Lenten Stuff* (Nashe, 398).

Elizabeth I sends an embassy to Sultan Murad II in an attempt to establish closer relations with Turkey.

Printing of the New Testament of the Douai Bible, an English version intended for Catholics.

Peter Frenche, whom Paul Kocher suggested as a possible candidate for the 'P. F.' who is known to have translated the *English Faust Book*, Marlowe's principal source for *Doctor Faustus*, receives his BA from Magdalene College, Cambridge (see Kocher, 'The *English Faust Book*', 99).

Publication at London of T. Styward, *The Pathwaie to Martiall Discipline*. This is typical of the kind of military manual on which Marlowe draws in Tamburlaine's famous advice to his sons.

Publication at London of Thomas Watson, *Ekatompathia*, including a laudatory poem by Matthew Roydon, later to be named as a friend of Marlowe's.

Publication of Richard Stanyhurst's translation of the *Aeneid*, showing the continuing vogue for translations of the classics.

Edward Kelley, who claimed to be able to converse with spirits, meets the conjurer and mathematician John Dee, using the name of Talbot. Kelley was a charlatan, but none the less managed to win the favour of the Emperor Rudolf, rather as Faustus wins that of the Emperor Charles.

Publication in France of Giordano Bruno, *De Umbris Idearum* ('Of the Shadows of Ideas'). Bruno is probably the 'Saxon Bruno' mentioned in the B text of *Doctor Faustus*, and signs of his presence are sometimes suggested elsewhere in Marlowe's *oeuvre* (see Farley-Hills).

During this year the first payments for spying appear in government records (Riggs, 139).

January

6 (Sat.)   Marlowe's friend and fellow-poet Matthew Roydon signs a bond for £40 to a London goldsmith, along with Nicholas Skeres, who was later to be present at Marlowe's death, and his brother Jerome Skeres. The signing of the bond indicates that Roydon has borrowed this sum from them, and reveals that moneylending was one of Skeres' activities.

13 (Sat.)   Lent term starts at Cambridge.

February

24 (Sat.)   Pope Gregory XIII issues a Papal Bull which instates the Gregorian Calendar and displaces the Julian one. The 'New Style' is ten days ahead of the old, and is not adopted in England until 1752. Dates mentioned from now on therefore continue to be Old Style unless indicated otherwise.

March

Henry Percy, later 9th Earl of Northumberland, is in Paris, where he meets Charles Paget. The English ambassador, Sir Henry Cobham, is concerned that Percy might be converted to Catholicism (see Nicholl, *Reckoning*, 197).

Nicholas Faunt returns to England (see Kuriyama, 'Second Selves', 94).

25 (Sun.)   Lady Day. Start of the Elizabethan new year.

April

6 (Fri.)   Lent Term ends.

15 (Sun., Julian calendar) Easter Sunday in England.

18 (Sun. Gregorian calendar) Easter Sunday on the continent.

22 (Sun.)   Marlowe's sister Joan (or Jane) marries John Moore, shoemaker, at St Andrew's Church, Canterbury. Joan is twelve and her husband twenty-three. Given that her first child was born in January of the next year, she may already have been pregnant, unless the baby was born prematurely.

25 (Wed.)   Easter Term begins at Cambridge.

May

2 (Wed. Julian, Sun. Gregorian: in this and the subsequent entries relating to this issue, it is not clear which is meant) An unsigned letter from Paris directed 'To the right honorable Sr ffran: Walsyngham knight Principall Secretary to the Qu: Ma 2' informs him, amongst other things, that '[Richard] Banes has had the strapedo [i.e. has been tortured] and is often tormented', and appears to assume that the name of Baines will be familiar to Walsingham. (see Kendall, 'Richard Baines', 518–19).

3 (Thurs. Julian, Mon. Gregorian) William Allen, by now President of the English College at Rheims, writes to say that he is prepared to give Gilbert Gifford a second chance.

12 (Sat. Julian, Wed. Gregorian) William Allen writes to George Gilbert, 'Mr Tirell writeth that he hath written som what to me before concerning Mr. Banes, for whose troobles I am right sory; but tell him, I pray you, that I have not received his letters' (see Kendall, 'Richard Baines', 527).

21 (Mon., Julian) A Richard Baines is admitted to the Middle Temple. For the reasons why this was not the same man as Marlowe's eventual betrayer, but another of the same name, see particularly Kendall, *Christopher Marlowe*, 32. This Richard Baines will subsequently go to Oxford and is therefore generally known as the Oxford Baines to distinguish him from Marlowe's Cambridge-educated betrayer.

28 (Mon. Julian, Fri. Gregorian) Allen writes in a letter to Alphonso Agazzari, S. J., Rector of the English College in Rome, that Richard Baines has been living at the seminary for four years and secretly spying.

29 (Tues. Julian, Sat. Gregorian) Richard Baines imprisoned for seeking to poison the seminary well. Perhaps makes his first confession (see Kendall, 'Richard Baines', 517). Poisoning wells will be one of the crimes of which Barabas boasts in *The Jew of Malta*.

June

9 (Sat. Julian, Wed. Gregorian) William Clitherow, who may have been corresponding with Baines in 1586, is ordained priest at Soissons.

11 (Mon. Julian, Fri. Gregorian) Allen writes to Agazzari that Baines has told him that the reason for his malice towards him and his seminary was their reluctance to send him to Rome.

23 (Sat. Julian, Wed. Gregorian) Gilbert Gifford arrives at Rheims, but leaves again before September (see Anstruther, 132). On the same day Samuel Kennett, a former schoolfellow of Marlowe, also arrives. A once fervent Puritan, Kennett had been converted to Catholicism by a priest while a prison warder in the Tower of London. He was ordained a priest and eventually died a Benedictine monk. Kennett's story shows something of the fluidity of religious allegiances of the time.

July

John Fixer receives his BA from Trinity College, Oxford.

Marlowe's first recorded absence from Cambridge is in July and August of this year.

3 (Tues.)   Commencement (the equivalent of graduation) day at Cambridge.

6 (Fri.)   Easter Term ends. University vacation begins.

17 (Tues. Julian, Sat. Gregorian) Castelli, Nuncio of France, writes to the Cardinal of Como that Baines had been sent to Rheims to kill Allen.

18 (Wed. Julian, Sun.) Allen tells Agazzari that Baines has declared that the devil has been sent into his heart and mind.

August

4–6 (Sat.–Mon.) Canterbury fair held.

5 (Sun. Julian, Thurs. Gregorian) Allen writes to Agazzari describing Baines' confession.

22 (Wed.) The Ruthven Raid, in which James VI of Scotland is kidnapped by his own lords, anxious to break the influence of his favourite, his uncle Esmé Stuart, Duke of Lennox. The relationship between James and Lennox has often been seen as an influence on Marlowe's portrayal of Edward and Gaveston. Roy Kendall links the subsequent decline in the political importance of Lennox to the imprisonment and recantation of Richard Baines (Kendall, *Christopher Marlowe*, 70–1).

September

18 (Tues.) Baptism at St Mary Northgate, Canterbury, of Dorothy Arthur, daughter of Katherine Marlowe's brother Thomas

and his wife Ursula Moore, whose brother John was probably the husband of Marlowe's sister Jane. All of the Arthur
family except Dorothy would die of the plague in 1593,
after which Dorothy was taken in by John and Katharine
Marlowe.

October
First clear signs of Walter Ralegh's meteoric rise in the Queen's favour
(see Lacey, 46–7).
10 (Wed.)   Michaelmas Term begins at Cambridge.
13 (Sat.)   Thomas Nashe, future friend and possible collaborator of
            Marlowe, matriculates as a sizar at St John's College,
            Cambridge, though he had in fact probably already been at
            the college for some months (see Nicholl, *Cup*, 23).
20 (Sat. Julian, Wed. Gregorian) Allen tells Agazzari that Baines is still
            in chains.

November
30 (Fri.)   Date on the will of James Benchkin, father of John Benchkin.
            Marlowe will later read the will of James Benchkin's widow
            Katherine.

December
16 (Sun.)   Michaelmas Term ends.

1583

Voyage of the Muscovy Company to the Moluccas (see Wilson, 'Visible
Bullets', 50).
The playing company the Queen's Men is formed. On their repertoire
and their influence on the development of English drama and audience tastes, see McMillin and MacLean.
John Whitgift is appointed Archbishop of Canterbury, and inaugurates
the religious policies that will eventually lead to the Martin Marprelate
contoversy.
Publication of Richard Harvey, *Ephemeron*, which praises Ramist logic,
and of his *Astrologicall Discourse*, which predicted imminent catastro-
phe. Also in this year John Harvey, the third of the Harvey brothers,
publishes *Astrological Addition*, and along with it *Iatromathematica*,
which Harvey ascribed to the supposed Egyptian magus and pioneer of
esoteric wisdom Hermes Trismegistus.
The Queen gives Walter Ralegh the use of Durham House.

Robert Greene graduates MA from Cambridge and publishes the second part of his *Mamillia*.

Gabriel Harvey is elected Proctor at Cambridge University.

Robert Poley is in the Marshalsea, perhaps as an informer (see Nicholl, *Reckoning*, 135).

Reissue of John Foxe, *Acts and Monuments*, with new material in which the humiliation of Pope Victor IV resembles that of 'Saxon Bruno' in the B text of *Doctor Faustus*, and in which the account of the Council of Constance mentions Sigismund, Bajazet and Tamburlaine (see Battenhouse, 32–3).

First performance of *Campaspe*, by John Lyly, who had also been to the King's School, Canterbury. For the suggestion that Marlowe's drama to some extent deliberately opposes the ethos of Lyly's, see Connolly.

Thomas Walsingham returns from France to England and takes up residence in Seething Lane, where he is 'attended' by Robert Poley (see Nicholl, *Reckoning*, 116–17).

First mention of Edward Alleyn, now aged seventeen, as acting with the Earl of Worcester's Men.

January

Marlowe's sister Joan (or Jane) bears her first child sometime before the 13th, and dies later in the month.

James's favourite Lennox is banished from Scotland at the behest of James's Protestant lords.

13 (Sun.) Lent Term starts at Cambridge.

The collapse of some scaffolding at Paris Garden during a bear-baiting leaves a number of spectators killed or injured.

14 (Mon.) The Lord Mayor of London writes to Lord Burghley to inform him of the mishap at Paris Garden and to declare that it shows the hand of God at work and registers His anger at the fact of such performances on the Sabbath (see Rutter, 13; and Wyckham, 87).

18 (Fri.) John Moore, husband of Marlowe's sister Joan (or Jane), is enrolled as a freeman of Canterbury on payment of the reduced fee of $11\frac{1}{2}$d due from those married to daughters of freemen (presumably Joan/Jane was still alive at this date).

February

8 (Fri.) The 'Oxford' Baines matriculates at St John's College, Oxford.

March

25 (Mon.) Lady Day. Start of the Elizabethan new year.

28 (Thurs. Julian) The English ambassador in Paris reports that 'Dr Jordano Bruno Nolano, a professor in philosophy, intendeth to pass into England, whose religion I cannot commend' (see Bossy, 13). This is Giordano Bruno, who probably inspired the inclusion of a character called Bruno in *Doctor Faustus* and who is often thought to have been an influence on Marlowe.

22 (Fri.) Lent Term ends.

31 (Sun.) Easter Sunday.

April

Walter Ralegh is given the leases of two estates belonging to All Souls College, Oxford.

10 (Wed.) Easter Term begins at Cambridge.

10 (Sun. Gregorian) Easter Sunday on the continent.

April–June

Marlowe is away from Cambridge again, though so are his roommates (Kuriyama, *Christopher Marlowe*, xv).

April

14 (Sun. Julian, Thurs. Gregorian) Allen tells Agazzari that Baines has been moved to the seminary (perhaps to avoid the expense of keeping him in prison).

The French ambassador, Michel de Castelnau, receives a letter from the Duke of Guise in France exhorting him to continue plotting on behalf of Mary, Queen of Scots.

18, 19 (Thurs., Fri. Julian, Mon., Tues. Gregorian) Dates of first despatches to Sir Francis Walsingham from 'Henry Fagot' (who, John Bossy argues, was really Giordano Bruno), written from the house of the French ambassador Michel de Castelnau. Walsingham received them around the 20th (see Bossy, 15).

18 (Thur.) The Scottish agent William Fowler, an undercover Catholic, visits the French embassy (see Bossy, 15). It is not clear why, but this visit shows how far-reaching the implications of Catholic plots might be.

19 (Fri.) Castelnau receives a letter directed to James of Scotland asking him to be patient a little longer (i.e. implying that the throne of England will soon be his).

End-April   Arrival in England of the Polish magnate the Palatine Albert Laski, who, according to Michel de Castelnau, was there to try to persuade the English to stop selling arms to the Russians (see Bossy, 22). Such sales have been proposed by Richard Wilson as an important subtext of *Tamburlaine* (see Wilson, 'Visible Bullets').

28 (Sun.)   The date identified by Richard Harvey as likely to prove catastrophic. Nothing of note occurred (Nashe, *Cup*, 34).

May

William Parry tells Burghley that he has 'shaken the foundacon of the English semynary in Rheyms and utterly overthrowen the credite of the English pensioners in Rome' (see *DNB* entry on Parry).

4 (Mon.)   Walter Ralegh is given the immensely lucrative farm of wines, which allows him to profit handsomely from all sales of wine (see Lacey, 51–2).

13 (Mon. Julian, Fri. Gregorian) Richard Baines makes a 'recantation'.

26 (Sun. Julian, Thurs. Gregorian) James VI's erstwhile favourite the Earl of Lennox dies in France 'of a sickness contracted for displeasure'.

30 (Thurs. Julian, Mon. Gregorian) Last reference in Allen's letters to Aggazari to Baines' continuing imprisonment. Baines was released at some point between this and the end of the year.

June

Walter Ralegh's half-brother Humphrey Gilbert sails from Plymouth in an attempt to establish a colony in the New World before his charter expires in March 1584.

1 (Sat. Julian, Wed. Gregorian) Date affixed to the end of *A Trve Report of the Late Apprehension and imprisonment of Iohn Nicols Minister, at Roan, and his confession and answers made in the time of his durance there. Wherevnto is added the satisfaction of certaine, that of feare or frailtie haue lately fallen in England.* Printed at Rhemes By Iohn Fogny 1583. This contains the confession of Richard Baines, credited to William Allen.

7 (Fri.)   Worcester's Men, including Edward Alleyn, are paid 26s 8d not to perform in Norwich. This reflects contemporary fears that players spread disease and incited disorder.

12 (Wed. Julian, Sun. Gregorian) The English Catholic George Stransham (alias Potter and Popham, and probably originally a Canterbury man) arrives at Rheims (see Anstruther,

338). George Stransham's brother Robert owned a third of the site of Faversham Abbey, and their father had been a contemporary of Thomas Arden of Faversham on the town council. Roy Kendall adduces this as possible evidence for Marlowe's authorship or part-authorship (he suggests with Kyd) of *Arden of Faversham* (Kendall, *Christopher Marlowe*, 176–7).

Dido, a version of the Dido story written by William Gager of Christ Church, Oxford, is played in the college hall before the Polish prince Albert Laski (see Boas, *University Drama*, 182–3).

15 (Sat.) Laski calls on John Dee, perhaps with Giordano Bruno in the party. Laski and Bruno have certainly been in Oxford together (see Bossy, 23).

30 (Sun.) The Lord Mayor of London replies to a letter from Lord Burghley, who had sought permission for Humphrey Rowland, later to act as a surety for Marlowe after his 1589 fight, to be admitted to the Cutlers' Company. The Lord Mayor describes Rowland as 'a very honest poore man' and 'a maker of Lanterne hornes' (see Boas, *Christopher Marlowe*, 107).

July

Marriage of Dorothy Devereux, sister of the Earl of Essex and later to be the wife of the Earl of Northumberland, to Thomas Perrot. The match was a runaway one because of the much lower status of the bridegroom. Perrot was the half-brother of Lettice Perrot, whose stepson William Vaughan was later to give the most accurate account of Marlowe's death in his *Golden Groue*. Charles Nicholl suggests that Vaughan's superior knowledge may be traceable to this connection (Nicholl, *Reckoning*, 93).

2 (Tues.) University commencement at Cambridge.

3 (Wed.) Elias Martin, formerly apprenticed to Marlowe's father John, admitted as a freeman of the city of Canterbury.

5 (Fri.) Easter Term ends. University vacation begins.

7 (Sun.) Date on the dedicatory epistle of Greene's prose romance *Mamillia*, which he says he is writing 'From my study in Clare Hall'. This Ovidian narrative, being written in Cambridge during the time of his own residence there, would certainly have been of interest to Marlowe if he had known of it.

9 (Tues.) The Queen's Men perform in Cambridge.

August
Castelnau reports to Mary, Queen of Scots that Sir Philip Sidney looks sympathetically on her and on Catholicism (see Bossy, 23). Sidney was one of the most influential writers and literary theorists of his day. He died before Marlowe came down from Cambridge, but Marlowe certainly met Sidney's brother, Sir Robert Sidney, who was also privately a poet, in Flushing, and was almost certainly responsible for the posthumous dedication of Thomas Watson's *Amintae Gaudia* to Sidney's sister.
4–6 (Sun.–Tues.) Canterbury fair held.
13 (Tues. Julian, Sat. Gregorian) John Fixer and George Stransham are sent from Rheims to Rome.
  Gilbert Gifford returns to Rheims. He appears to have been a Walsingham spy placed in the seminary as a replacement for Richard Baines.
14 (Wed. Julian, Sun. Gregorian) John Cecil arrives at Rheims.
22 (Thurs.) Anne, daughter of Robert Poley and perhaps of Thomas Watson's sister, baptised at St Helen's Bishopsgate.

September
Humphrey Gilbert is lost at sea in a storm off the Azores.
13 (Fri.)   Gilbert Gifford arrives at Rheims from Rome after being offered a third chance by William Allen (see Anstruther, 132).
20 (Fri.)   Frances Walsingham, only daughter of Sir Francis Walsingham, marries Sir Philip Sidney.
21 (Sat.)   John Dee, Edward Kelley and their families leave England, possibly on an intelligence mission (Woolley, 228–9).
28 (Sat.)   The Dee party reaches the Dutch coast.

October
1 (Tues. Julian, Sat. Gregorian) John Fixer and George Stransham enter the English College at Rome.
10 (Thurs.) Michaelmas Term starts at Cambridge.
17 (Thurs. Julian, Monday, Gregorian) The Dee party reaches Emden (the town to whose seigniory Faustus aspires).

Autumn
The 8th Earl of Northumberland, father of Marlowe's future acquaintance Henry Percy, 9th Earl, is arrested on suspicion of involvement in the Throckmorton plot and imprisoned in the Tower.

15 (Fri.) The spy William Herle reports to the government a conversation with Fagot about the Throckmorton plot (see Bossy,
28–9).

November
c. 20 (Wed.) Arrest of Francis Throckmorton for plotting with the Spanish
to free Mary, Queen of Scots and overthrow Elizabeth.

December
10 (Mon.) End of Michaelmas Term at Cambridge.

1584

Publication at London of Reginald Scot, *The Discoverie of Witchcraft*,
which followed the lead of Johannes Wier in being sceptical about
witchcraft.
John Cranford, future husband of Marlowe's sister Ann, moves to
Cambridge.
Publication at Antwerp of *Leicester's Commonwealth*, a satirical attack
on the Earl of Leicester, which was counted as seditious. Robert Poley
would be charged with possession of it in April of the following year.
Publication of William Allen, *True Sincere and Modest Defence of English
Catholics*.
Machiavelli's *The Prince* and *The Discourses* printed (in London but in
Italian) by John Wolfe, who was later to print *Hero and Leander*. These
were both unlicensed and bore the false imprint 'Palermo'.
Lonicerus' chronicle of the Turke, containing a description of
Joseph (João) Nassi, reissued. Nassi is also mentioned in Belleforest's
Cosmographie.
Probable date of Robert Wilson's *The Three Ladies of London*, a possible
source for *The Jew of Malta* (see Thomas and Tydeman, 299–300).
The anti-theatrical writer Stephen Gosson is at the English College in
Rome, training to be a Catholic priest (Urry, 10).
Thomas Nashe is enrolled as a scholar of the Lady Margaret foundation
at St John's.
John Penry, later to be a suspected author of the Marprelate tracts and
an associate of Marlowe's Corpus contemporary John Greenwood, takes
his BA from Peterhouse, Cambridge (see Kuriyama, 'Second Selves', 89).
William Perkins, later to be a prominent writer on Calvinism, receives
his MA and is appointed as lecturer at Great St Andrews.
Walter Ralegh is knighted and enters Parliament.

The sixteen-year-old Earl of Essex makes his debut at court under the aegis of his stepfather, the Earl of Leicester.

January

Dr William Parry, who will be executed the following year for attempting to assassinate Elizabeth, lands at Rye.

3 (Tues. Gregorian) William Allen refers in a letter to his secretary Roger Baines. Kendall (*Christopher Marlowe*, 147) suggests that this may have been a relative of Richard Baines whose existence might explain his relatively lenient treatment.

13 (Mon.) Start of Lent Term at Cambridge.

15 (Wed.) Marlowe's aunt and uncle, Thomas and Ursula Arthur, are ordered by the Canterbury court to pay £9, which they are deemed to have wrongfully appropriated from the estate of Ursula's father, Richard Moore.

Lent Term

As is customary, Marlowe is required to appear during this term as respondent in the public schools in order to be awarded his Bachelor of Arts degree. He will have had to debate three propositions with three other students from different colleges, in front of an undergraduate audience, in Latin. Success in this exercise secured the right to sit examinations and subsequently to appear in public again to answer questions from Aristotle's *Prior Analytics* (Wraight and Stern, 84–5).

February/March

Fagot reports again via Herle (see Bossy, 34).

March

Walter Ralegh is given the lucrative licence to export woollen broadcloths (see Lacey, 53).

3 (Tues.) Edward Alleyn and a group of other players (Robert Browne, James Tunstall, William Harrison, Thomas Cook, Richard Jones, Edward Browne and Richard Andrews) attempt to perform in Leicester against the will of the Mayor, leading to a public scene in which the players march through the town playing drums and trumpets. The players eventually apologise and the Mayor duly relents (Cerasano, in Reid and Maniura, 13).

Ash Wednesday Supposed date of the events referred to in Giordano Bruno, *Cena de le Ceneri* ('Ash Wednesday Supper'), which, he says, he spent with John Florio, Matthew Gwynne, and

Fulke Greville. Bruno might be referring either to Wednesday, 4 March (Ash Wednesday in the Julian calendar) or
Wednesday, 5 February (the date in the Julian calendar
which coincided with 15 February Gregorian, the date on
which Easter was observed in the Gregorian calendar: see
Bossy, 43–5). During the week before Ash Wednesday was
observed in England, Marlowe will have been taking his
examinations.

c. 16 (Mon.) Fagot writes directly to the Queen warning her of a plot to
assassinate her (see Bossy, 34–5).

18 (Wed.) Death of Ivan the Terrible, whom Richard Wilson proposes
as a possible model for Tamburlaine (Wilson, 'Visible
Bullets').

25 (Wed.) Lady Day. Start of the Elizabethan new year.
Sir Walter Ralegh, his half-brother Adrian Gilbert and John
Davis are issued with a charter for the exploration of
America, describing them as 'The College of the Fellowship
for the Discovery of the North-West Passage' (see Rukeyser,
139).

April

1 (Sun. Gregorian) Easter Sunday.

10 (Fri.) End of Lent Term.

12 (Sun.) Palm Sunday. Marlowe receives his BA. He comes 199th out
of 231 graduates.

15 (Wed. Julian, Sun.) John Cecil admitted to the English College at
Rome.

19 (Sun.) Easter Sunday.

27 (Mon.) Sir Walter Ralegh despatches Captains Philip Amadas and
Arthur Barlow to look for a suitable place to 'plant' a
colony in North America.

29 (Wed.) Start of Easter Term at Cambridge.

May

? Publication at London of Giordano Bruno, *Cena de le ceneri*.

10 (Sun.) Date on which, Richard Ede said in 1589, Robert Poley was
released from the Marshalsea.

June

10 (Sun. Gregorian, Wed. 30 May Julian) The death of François, Duke
of Alençon, leaves the Protestant Henri of Navarre heir to
the French throne.

11 (Thurs.) Date on which Sir Humphrey Gilbert's patent to land in America was due to expire.

July
? Publication of Giordano Bruno, *De l'infinito universo* ('Of the Infinite Universe').
In mid-July Amadas and Barlow arrive in what will soon be called Virginia.

7 (Tues.)   University commencement.
10 (Fri.)   William the Silent, Prince of Orange, is assassinated, precipitating unrest in the Netherlands.
              Easter Term ends. Start of the university vacation.

July–December
Marlowe is away from Cambridge again. Other students also seem to be away at this time (Kuriyama, *Christopher Marlowe*, xv).

August
4–6 (Tues. –Thurs.) Canterbury fair held.

September
Amadas and Barlow return to England, bringing with them two Indians, Manteo and Wanchese, who are presented to the Queen.
7 (Mon.)   John Ballard and his companion Anthony Tirrell arrive in Rome.

October
10 (Sat.)   Start of Michaelmas Term at Cambridge.

December
John Ballard and Anthony Tirrell cross from Rouen to Southampton.
16 (Wed. Julian, Sun. Gregorian: it is not clear which) John Cecil ordained at the English College at Rome.
16 (Wed.)   End of the Michaelmas Term.

1585

Giordano Bruno writes *De gli eroici furori* ('Of Heroic Passions').
The Act of Association is passed. An attempt to prevent plots against Elizabeth, this was also a sternly anti-Catholic measure.

Gabriel Harvey fails to be appointed to the Mastership of Trinity Hall, Cambridge, and moves to Oxford. In the same year his brother Richard becomes University Praelector in Philosophy.

James VI of Scotland requests Princess Elizabeth of Denmark (elder sister of his eventual wife Anne) as a bride.

Thomas Gradwell, future husband of Marlowe's sister Dorothy, arrives in Canterbury from his birthplace of Preston in Lancashire.

Date on the portrait at Corpus Christi College, Cambridge which is sometimes identified as being that of Marlowe.

Publication at London of Thomas Washington's translation of Nicolas de Nicolay, *The Navigations, Peregrinations and Voyages, Made Into Turkey* ..., which Marlowe used as a source (see Thomas and Tydeman, 301; and Bakeless, 184–5).

Publication at London of Thomas Watson, *Amintas*, dedicated to Henry Noel, as also was Watson's undated *Compendium Memoriae Localis*, which was influenced by Giordano Bruno.

Sir Francis Walsingham licenses the poet Samuel Daniel to travel to France, presumably on intelligence work.

Paul Ive, whose treatise on fortification Marlowe was able to consult in manuscript for *Tamburlaine the Great,* Part Two, sends military intelligence to Sir Francis Walsingham from Gravelines (Nicholl, *Reckoning,* 119).

Peter Frenche (Paul Kocher's candidate for the P. F. who translated the *English Faust Book*) receives his MA from Magdalene College, Cambridge.

Publication of Lercheimer's *Christlich Erinnerung von Zauberei* ('Christian Commentary on Magic'), which John Henry Jones sees as an influence on the German *Faustbuch* (Jones, 5).

Henry Carey, Lord Hunsdon, is appointed Lord Chamberlain. His troupe of players, the Lord Chamberlain's Men, will eventually include Shakespeare.

January

George Stransham and Christopher Bagshaw are expelled from the English College in Rome for their opposition to Jesuit rule (see Anstruther, 338).

13 (Wed.) Start of Lent Term at Cambridge.

February

Queen Elizabeth gives the name 'Virginia' to Sir Walter Ralegh's new colony.

8 (Mon.)   Edmund Neville denounces William Parry as his co-conspir-
           ator in an alleged attempt to assassinate Elizabeth. This
           helps create a heightened climate of fears about national
           security.
9 (Tues.) Sack of Cartagena by Sir Francis Drake. Margo Hendricks
           suggests this as a subtext of *Dido, Queen of Carthage*.
18 (Thurs.) The Commons vote to 'dismember' Parry, that is to bar him
           from his role as MP for Queenborough, in Kent.
25 (Thurs.) Parry is tried in Westminster Hall.

February/March
Fagot resumes writing, this time from Paris and to the English ambassador there, Sir Edward Stafford (see Bossy, 54-5).

March
Robert Poley is in London lodging at the house of one Mistress Browne
(see Nicholl, *Reckoning*, 137).
Philip Henslowe obtains the lease of the land on which the Rose
Theatre will subsequently stand.
2 (Tues.) Execution of William Parry for attempting to assassinate
           the Queen.
9 (Tues. Julian, Sun. Gregorian) Thomas Morgan, agent of Mary, Queen
           of Scots, arrested in Paris.
11 (Thurs.) Sir Edmund Stafford writes to Sir Francis Walsingham
           reporting Morgan's arrest.
15 (Mon. Julian, Fri. Gregorian) Thomas Morgan imprisoned in the
           Bastille.
25 (Thurs) Lady Day. Start of the Elizabethan new year.

Spring
Gilbert Gifford ordained deacon.

April
Robert Poley found in possession of copies of *Leicester's Commonwealth*,
and accused of procuring and dispersing them. Poley protests his innocence to Leicester (see Nicholl, *Reckoning*, 138–9).
2 (Fri.)   End of Lent Term.
5 (Mon. Julian, Fri. Gregorian) Gilbert Gifford ordained deacon.
9 (Fri.)   Sir Richard Grenville sets sail from Plymouth for Virginia
           with a fleet of seven ships, with Thomas Hariot on board.

11 (Sun.)   Easter Sunday. Fagot probably returns to London and resumes residence in the French embassy (see Bossy, 58).

21 (Wed.)   Start of Easter Term at Cambridge.

21 (Sun. Gregorian) Gregorian Easter Sunday.

Mid-April–mid-June

Corpus Christi accounts and buttery book reveal that Marlowe was absent from college during this period. When he is in residence, he spends significantly more money. Most other students are also away at this time (Kuriyama, *Christopher Marlowe*, xiv).

May

23 (Sun. Julian, Thurs. Gregorian) John Cecil leaves the English College at Rome for England, but seems not to have got further than Padua (see Anstruther, 63).

26 (Wed.)   A Riceus Banes is installed as rector of Blanckney in Lincolnshire (see Kendall, *Christopher Marlowe*, 114). This might look interesting in connection with the possibility that the Richard Baines who betrayed Marlowe might have become rector of Waltham, also in Lincolnshire, two years later.

June

Robert Poley despatched to Paris by Christopher Blount to make contact with Thomas Morgan in the Bastille.

21 (Mon.)   The 8th Earl of Northumberland, father of Henry Percy, is found shot through the heart in the Tower. This is rather improbably accepted as suicide. Henry Percy succeeds as 9th Earl.

28 (Mon.)   Circulation of *Leicester's Commonwealth* is prohibited by the Privy Council.

30 (Wed.)   John Benchkin, whom Constance Kuriyama sees as a close friend of Marlowe (see Kuriyama, 'Second Selves'), arrives at Corpus Christi College, Cambridge.

July

Poley returns to England with his mission accomplished and subsequently enters the service of Sir Philip Sidney.

Sir Walter Ralegh is appointed Lord Warden of the Stannaries.

5 (Mon.)   University commencement.

7 (Wed.)   William Fleetwood, recorder of London, mentions in a report to Lord Burghley one Nicholas Skeeres as a member of a band of 'maisterles men & cut-purses, whose practice is to robbe Gentlemen's chambers and Artificers' shoppes in and about London' (Wraight and Stern, 299). Wraight and Stern argue that this must be a different Nicholas Skeres from the one known to have been associated with Marlowe, because Marlowe would not have consorted with such a man, but there is no other evidence for the existence of any other Nicholas Skeres.

8 (Thurs.)   Charles Howard, 2nd Lord Howard of Effingham, is appointed Lord High Admiral. It will be his company of players who put on *Tamburlaine the Great*.

9 (Fri.)   End of Easter Term.

18 (Sun. Julian, Thurs. Gregorian) Thomas Morgan's friend Charles Paget tells Mary, Queen of Scots that Poley is writing to Christopher Blount (see Nicholl, *Reckoning*, 142). Blount would later be the third husband of Lettice Knollys and thus the stepfather of Robert Devereux, 2nd Earl of Essex.

28 (Wed.)   The new French ambassador, Châteauneuf, arrives in London.

Mid-July–mid-September
The Corpus Christi buttery books show Marlowe to have been absent from college again during this time. His roommate Thomas Lewgar is also away for the same period. Kuriyama suggests that Marlowe returned to Canterbury with John Benchkin (*Christopher Marlowe*, xv).

August
Sir Richard Grenville sets sail from Virginia to return to England, leaving the colonists in Roanoke.

4–6 (Wed.–Fri.) Canterbury fair held.

19 (Sun.)   Date on Katherine Benchkin's will, which Marlowe read aloud on a visit back to Canterbury (see Wraight and Stern, 228–9).

20 (Mon.)   Treaty of Nonsuch, which guarantees British military intervention in the Netherlands.

31 (Tues.)   Canterbury corporation rules that John Moore, husband of Marlowe's dead sister Joan (or Jane), should be once again enrolled as a freeman of Canterbury, his previous admission on the grounds that he was married to the daughter of

a freeman having presumably been invalidated by his wife's death. The trouble Moore is thus put to shows that Marlowe's surviving sisters are good matches, since marriage to them secures freeman's status at a reduced rate.

September

Fagot leaves England for France with Castelnau (see Bossy, 61).
Mid-September Marlowe and John Benchkin return to Cambridge.
Sir Walter Ralegh is created Lord Lieutenant of Cornwall.
6 (Mon.) Thomas Watson marries Anne Swift at St Antholin's, Watling Street.
14 (Tues.) John Moore admitted as a freeman of Canterbury on payment of 40s.
21 (Tues. Julian, Sat. Gregorian) George Stransham ordained at Rheims.

October

8 (Fri. Julian, Tues. Gregorian) Gilbert Gifford leaves Rheims.
10 (Sun.) Start of Michaelmas Term at Cambridge.
18 (Mon.) A comet appears in Pisces. It is seen by people as far apart as Hariot in Virginia and by the astronomer Tycho Brahe in Denmark.
Sir Richard Grenville arrives back in Plymouth after transporting Ralegh's colonists to Virginia.
30 (Wed. Gregorian) Lorenzo Bernardo, Venetian Ambassador to the Porte, writes to the Doge and Senate mentioning David Passi, a possible analogue or source for Barabas (see Thomas and Tydeman, 309; NB David Passi needs to be distinguished from João Nassi).

November

Marlowe is away from Cambridge for two weeks in the early part of the month.
10 (Wed.) Sir Philip Sidney departs for the Netherlands. Robert Poley stays in London with Sidney's wife, Frances Walsingham. In the later part of the year Poley is seen at Tutbury, where Mary, Queen of Scots was being held.
15 (Mon.) The English commander Sir Henry Norris defeats the Prince of Parma in a skirmish in Flanders. The event is immediately reported in England (Voss, 181–2).
20 (Sat.) The new comet disappears from Pisces.

25 (Mon. Gregorian) Lorenzo Bernardo writes to the Doge and Senate
   mentioning David Passi, and referring to two Englishmen
   who have passed through Constantinople on their way
   from Ragusa (now Dubrovnik) to Poland, and whom he
   thinks were employed in undercover work, and to a third
   Englishman who has come from Poland, is staying with the
   English Ambassador, and has been 'in constant confer-
   ences' with Passi (see Thomas and Tydeman, 309). These
   men seem not to have been identified, but the episode
   confirms English awareness of Passi.

December
Gilbert Gifford returns to England from Rheims.
6 (Mon.)   The Earl of Leicester leaves Court to lead a force to aid the
           Low Countries.
16 (Thurs.) End of Michaelmas Term.
23 (Thurs.) The Earl of Leicester arrives at Rotterdam.
24 (Fri.)   Mary, Queen of Scots is moved from Tutbury to Chartley.
26 (Thurs. Gregorian) Lorenzo Bernardo, Venetian Ambassador to the
           Porte, writes to the Doge and Senate mentioning David Passi,
           and saying that two Englishmen have just left Constan-
           tinople in company with a Jew from Passi's household.

1586

Publication of *The Choice of Emblems* by Geffrey Whitney, the first
English emblem book.
To this year belong the first known signs of a friendship between
Sir Walter Ralegh and Henry Percy, 9th Earl of Northumberland (see
Stevens, 93).
Marlowe's maternal uncle Thomas Arthur becomes joint bailiff of the
Canterbury suburb of Westgate.
Publication at Paris of the *Journal* of the French explorer René de
Laudonnière, dedicated to Sir Walter Ralegh and describing his explo-
rations of the coast of Florida.
John Henry Jones argues in his edition of the *English Faust Book* that
this was the year of the composition of the German *Faustbuch*, *Historia
von D. Johann Fausten* (Jones, 5), which in translation became Marlowe's
principal source for *Doctor Faustus*.
John Poole, almost certainly the man who taught Marlowe how to
forge money, is involved with the Rheims priest George Stransham,

also known as Potter, in land deals in Ireland with Sir Edward Fitton, an associate of Anthony Babington (see Nicholl, *Reckoning*, 242).

John Cecil sent from the English College at Rome to Sicily to collect money for the English College at Rheims.

John Morley is involved in financial dealings for Lord Burghley with Archibald Douglas. Burghley's association with him on this and subsequent occasions makes it plain that it was to him, rather than to Christopher Marlowe, that Burghley later referred as 'Mr Morley of the Exchequer' (see Nicholl, *Reckoning*, 340).

This was the year of the Babington Plot, the aim of which was to murder Elizabeth and put Mary, Queen of Scots on the throne. Its discovery by Walsingham's agents would lead to the execution of Mary. One of the chief conspirators, John Ballard (alias Captain Fortescue), had studied at Caius College, Cambridge, and been recruited thence to Rheims. John Fingelow, who followed the same trajectory, was also hanged in this year.

Publication at London of Thomas Watson, *Helenae Raptus*, dedicated to the Earl of Northumberland. Watson's work was based on a Latin poem by Colluthus (*c.* AD 500) which Marlowe was later said to have translated into English, though, if he did, it is now lost.

Publication at London of George Whetstone, *The English Mirror*. This is a translation of Mexia's *Silva de Vario Lecion*, one of the principal sources of *Tamburlaine the Great*.

The 'other' Christopher Morley, whose career is sometimes confused with Marlowe's, graduates MA from Cambridge.

Richard Harvey, brother of Gabriel, is appointed rector of Chislehurst in Kent, thus becoming the parish priest of Marlowe's friend Sir Thomas Walsingham.

January

1 (Sat.)   A deputation of the States, the governing body of the Low Countries, offers Leicester the governorship of the United Provinces.

12 (Wed.)   Leicester appoints Essex General of the Horse.

13 (Thurs.)   Start of Lent Term at Cambridge.

18 (Tues. Julian, Sat. Gregorian) Thomas Morgan and Charles Paget write to Robert Poley from Paris asking him to perform various commissions. Paget also recommends Poley to Châteauneuf, the French ambassador to England, as a suitable courier for going to Scotland since he is familiar with the route (see Nicholl, *Reckoning*, 144–5).

25 (Tues.)   Leicester is installed at The Hague as Governor of the United Provinces.

February
Marlowe is away from Cambridge for two weeks at the end of February/ beginning of March. He returns with John Benchkin (Kuriyama, *Christopher Marlowe*, xv).

27 (Sun.)   Mary, wife of Humphrey Rowland, buried at St Botolph's, London. Rowland will later act as a surety for Marlowe when he is imprisoned for his part in the killing of William Bradley.

March
Anthony Babington and John Ballard hold a gathering of conspirators. Ballard then goes to France.
Sir William Stanley, later to be infamous as the betrayer of Deventer, goes to Ireland to recruit a regiment to serve in the Low Countries.

14 (Mon. Julian, Fri. Gregorian) George Stransham leaves Rheims for England.

19 (Sat.)   Châteauneuf is recorded as still trying to find a courier for his packet to Scotland.

21 (Mon. Julian, Fri. Gregorian) Thomas Morgan writes to tell Mary, Queen of Scots that Poley has been to visit the area where she is held.

25 (Fri.)   Lady Day. Start of the Elizabethan new year.
End of Lent Term.
Margaret Clitherow, sister-in-law of the William Clitherow, who may have been corresponding with Richard Baines later in the year, is pressed to death at York.

April–June
Corpus Christi accounts and buttery book reveal that Marlowe was absent from college during this period. His roommate Thomas Lewgar is also away for the same period.

April
3 (Sun. Julian) Easter Sunday in England.
6 (Sun. Gregorian) Easter Sunday on the continent.
10 (Sun. Julian, Thurs. Gregorian) Charles Paget writes to Mary, Queen of Scots of one 'called Poley, a great friend to Christopher Blunt, of whome I suppose your majesty hath harde here

tofore. Morgan and I have had conference with the sayd Poley and hope he is in soch place, being servant to Sir Phillipp Sydney, and thereby remayneth with his Ladye and in house with Secretarye Walsingham, so as he shalbe able to give your majesty advertisement from time to time' (see Boas, *Christopher Marlowe*, 122).

13 (Wed.) Start of Easter Term at Cambridge.

27 (Wed.) George Stransham committed to the Marshalsea under the name of Potter.

May

Ballard returns from France.

2 (Mon.) Sir Richard Grenville sets sail from Devon carrying supplies for the colonists at Roanoke. In the same month Sir Francis Drake destroys the Spanish post at St Augustine, in Florida, which is considered dangerously close to the Roanoke colony.

4 (Wed.) Humphrey Rowland, Marlowe's future guarantor when he is arrested after the death of William Bradley, marries Eve Ashe.

20 (Fri. Julian, Tues. Gregorian) The poet Samuel Daniel writes to Sir Francis Walsingham from the English ambassador's house in Paris.

23 (Mon.) A Richard Baines is assaulted on the highway by John Hartopp of Oxford, gentleman, and has a gelding worth £10 and 15 shillings in money stolen from him (see Kendall, *Christopher Marlowe*, 98). There is no firm indication of whether this is Marlowe's betrayer, the Oxford Baines, or yet a third man, though Kendall suggests reasons why it might have been Marlowe's betrayer.

June

Giordano Bruno leaves France.

7 (Tues.) Date later given by the Privy Council for a meeting of the Babington conspirators.

11 (Sat.) Ralph Lane, governor of Virgina, arranges with Sir Francis Drake to transport some of the colonists who are ill or wounded back to England.

13 (Mon.) A storm blows up off Roanoke island, cutting off Drake and the colonists who have embarked on his ships from the rest of the colony.

16 (Thurs.) The storm clears and Drake's ship, the *Francis*, with many
of the colonists on board, is seen to have set sail. The storm
is interpreted as representing God's anger and the incident
seems to have damaged morale in the colony considerably
(see Lacey, 85–6).

18 (Sat.) All the colonists, including Manteo, request Drake to take
them home in his remaining ships and leave Roanoke.

20 (Mon.) A supply ship sent by Sir Walter Ralegh arrives at Roanoke
and finds it deserted. A small force is left behind to maintain an English presence in the colony.

mid-June The period when Poley later said he first met Sir Anthony
Babington and promised to obtain a passport for him.
Poley subsequently introduces Babington to Sir Francis
Walsingham.

25 (Sat.) Sir Francis Walsingham's agent Maliverny Catlin asks to be
moved from Portsmouth prison to the Marshalsea.

27 (Mon.) Sir Walter Ralegh is granted letters patent allowing him to
colonise Cork and Waterford. He is the head of a group of
'undertakers', who will be offered military protection at no
cost until 1591, and thereafter at half-rate until 1594.
Ralegh does not at this stage go to Ireland himself. Others
of the undertakers are so deterred by the risks that within
two months Ralegh has tripled his own holding of lands
(see Lacey, 107).

July
Babington writes to Mary, Queen of Scots. Maliverny Catlin tells
Walsingham that a priest imprisoned in the Marshalsea had travelled
with Henry Percy, 9th Earl of Northumberland and reports him to be a
Catholic.

4 (Mon.) John Ballard's friend Anthony Tirell arrested and imprisoned
in the Counter in Wood Street, where he incriminates
Ballard and says that the two of them had visited Rome to
obtain papal permission for the assassination of the Queen
(see Anstruther, 19).

5 (Tues.) University commencement.

12 (Tues.) Sir Anthony Babington writes to Mary, Queen of Scots
offering to murder Elizabeth.

13 (Wed.) Mary's secretary, Claude Nau, writes, in response to a query
from Babington about what he thinks of Poley, that Mary
does not yet know enough of him, and asks in turn what
Babington thinks.

15 (Fri.)   End of Easter Term. University vacation begins.

17 (Sun.)   Mary, Queen of Scots replies to Babington accepting his
              offer to murder Elizabeth. Thomas Phelippes, Sir Francis
              Walsingham's chief code-breaker, intercepts the letter,
              draws a gallows on the front and sends it to Walsingham.

25 (Mon.)   Giordano Bruno matriculates at the University of Marburg
              but is turned away by the rector on theological grounds.
              Katherine Benchkin, whose will Marlowe had read aloud, is
              buried at St Mildred's, Canterbury.

27 (Wed.)   Mary, Queen of Scots writes that she has received a letter
              which she assumes to be from Robert Poley.

28 (Thurs.)   Thomas Hariot lands at Portsmouth on his return from
              Virginia.

30 (Sat.)   Robert Poley pays for supper for the Babington conspirators
              at the Castle Inn in London, near the Exchange.

August

Giordano Bruno begins lecturing at the University of Wittenberg.

2 (Tues.)   A spy in the service of Sir Francis Walsingham 'found
              Babington to be in town, and was directed where he and a
              whole knot might have been taken at supper in Poley's
              garden' (see Nicholl, *Reckoning*, 31 and 157).

3 (Wed.)   Francis Milles, in the service of Sir Francis Walsingham,
              notifies him that Babington has moved to new premises near
              Bishopsgate, and that 'Skyeres' – presumably Nicholas Skeres,
              who will be present at Marlowe's death – has been there.

4 (Thurs.)   Robert Poley and Thomas Walsingham meet at Poley's
              lodgings. Shortly afterwards John Ballard is arrested there
              and committed to the Counter in Wood Street. Babington
              appeals to Poley for reassurance that Poley is loyal and
              reliable.

4–6 (Thurs.–Sat.) Canterbury fair held.

6 (Sat.)   Robert Poley's servant Nicholas Dalton committed to the
              Counter in Wood Street (see Seaton, 'Marlowe, Poley, and
              the Tippings', 281). Conceivably, this is an attempt to con-
              vince Babington of Poley's good faith.

14 (Sun.)   Babington arrested. Amongst other things, this can be seen
              as a triumph for Walsingham's intelligence methods over
              Ralegh's (see Lacey, 101).

15 (Mon.)   John Ballard is moved to the Tower.
              Babington is brought to London. The church bells are rung
              for the Queen's safe deliverance from danger.

18 (Thurs.) Robert Poley is committed to the Tower on a charge of treacherous dealing. It is difficult to guess whether the government had genuine suspicions of him or if this was to maintain his cover and perhaps enable him to be used as an informer.

30 (Tues.) Maliverny Catlin reports from the north of England.

September
Humphrey Rowland is granted the lease of a house in East Smithfield by the Barber-Surgeons' Company in exchange for the supply of eighteen shoeing-horns a year.

1 (Thurs.) James Tipping is removed from the Gatehouse to the Tower.

4 (Sun.)   The poet Samuel Daniel returns to England, landing at Rye in Sussex. The same ship bears Julio Martino, also known as Renato, allegedly the assassin of Jeanne of Navarre (the Queen of Navarre in Marlowe's *A Massacre at Paris*; Renato corresponds to the 'Pothecary).

7 (Wed.)   George Stransham is recorded as being at Wisbech Castle, the prison traditionally used for the imprisonment of English Catholics. He remained there for ten years, though at some point before 1593 he escaped and was recaptured; he also escaped in February 1597, and it is not clear if he was recaptured thereafter (see Anstruther, 339).

13 (Tues.) The Babington conspirators are tried at Westminster.

15 (Thurs.) Seven men are charged as co-conspirators in the Babington Plot.

20 (Tues.) Execution of the first seven Babington conspirators.

21 (Wed.)   Execution of the remaining Babington conspirators.
            Father William Clitherow, a Catholic exile in France, writes to Richard Baines, who seems to be using the alias 'Monsieur Gerarde Burghet, French gentleman in London' or to be using a real person of that name as a go-between. The letter principally concerns a scheme by Burghet to arrange a marriage between Arbella Stuart, James's cousin and a potential claimant to the thrones of both England and Scotland, and the son of the Prince of Parma (it is transcribed in full in Kuriyama, *Christopher Marlowe*, 199–200).

22 (Thurs.) Sir Philip Sidney is mortally wounded at Zutphen.

25 (Sun.)   A list of 'Prisoners in ye Towre ... fitt to be further examined' made on this date includes Robert Poley and 'James Typping,

accused by Ballard, his offence triable in Yorkeshere' (see
Seaton, 'Marlowe, Poley, and the Tippings', 278).

October
1 (Sat.)   Gabriel Harvey's brother Richard is appointed to the
benefice of Chislehurst. He will therefore be responsible for
Thomas Walsingham's household at Scadbury, where
Marlowe was staying at the time of his death.
10 (Mon.) Start of Michaelmas Term at Cambridge.
11 (Tues.) Mary, Queen of Scots is tried at Fotheringhay.
17 (Mon.) Death of Sir Philip Sidney.
23 (Sun. Julian, Thurs. Gregorian) Sir William Stanley, an officer
serving in the English army in the Netherlands, captures
Deventer.
29 (Sat.)   Parliament meets and both Houses petition the Queen for
the death of Mary, Queen of Scots.

November
? Sir Edward Stafford receives a letter which may have been from Fagot,
including, among a variety of other things, the information that he
has been talking to Thomas Morgan in the Bastille and thinks he
might be able to turn him (see Bossy, 65–7).
12 (Sat.)   Elizabeth receives the parliamentary deputation requesting
the death of Mary, Queen of Scots.
16 (Wed.) Stafford reports the information about Morgan to Lord
Burghley.
17 (Thurs.) Accession Day. This was a public holiday and no business
was conducted.
18 (Fri.)   Sir Edward Stafford receives a friendly letter to Lord
Burghley from Cardinal Savelli, who had assisted Burghley's
grandson on an unauthorised trip to Rome (see Bossy,
70–1).
Leicester and Essex sail from Dort.
21 (Mon.) Leicester and Essex arrive at Margate.
23 (Wed.) Leicester and Essex arrive at the Court at Richmond.
24 (Thurs.) Elizabeth receives another parliamentary deputation requesting the death of Mary, Queen of Scots.
30 (Wed.) Last appearance in the Tower lists of Richard Creagh,
Archbishop of Armagh, whom Poley was later rumoured to
have poisoned (see Nicholl, *Reckoning*, 164). The Privy
Council resolves that James Tipping's case is to be consid-

ered of, Poley's servant Nicholas Dalton to be released upon bonds, and Poley to be kept in the Tower.

December

Sir Richard Grenville sails into Bideford in Devon, having been too late to prevent the departure of the colonists from Roanoke. Ralegh now begins a determined propaganda operation to convince investors and potential colonists that Roanoke has a future.

6 (Tues.)   Richard Harvey confirmed in the benefice of Chislehurst.
11 (Sun.)   Humphrey Rowland elected a churchwarden of St Botolph's.
16 (Fri.)   End of Michaelmas Term.
23 (Fri.)   Date appointed for the re-examination of some of those allegedly concerned in the Babington Plot, including Thomas Tipping.

1587

A man of the name Richard Baines is installed as rector of Waltham, near Cleethorpes, during this year.

Theodore de Bry visits London to arrange for Jacques Le Moyne to illustrate Laudonnière's *Journal*.

Publication of Robert Greene's *Penelopes Web*.

The copy of Raphael Holinshed's *Chronicles of England, Scotland and Ireland* now in Corpus Christi library bears the date 1587. Holinshed was a source for *Edward II*.

Philip Henslowe, originally a dyer, builds the Rose Playhouse.

It was probably during this year that John Poole, brother-in-law of Sir William Stanley, the future betrayer of Deventer, was imprisoned for coining in Newgate, where he seems to have met Marlowe and taught him how to counterfeit money.

F. Paulinus translates Musaeus' Greek poem *Hero and Leander* into Latin.

Publication of the second, revised edition of Holinshed's *Chronicles*.

William Allen is made a cardinal. John Cecil enters his household and is sent by him to Valladolid, where he remains until at least 1590 (see Anstruther, 63).

Battle of Coutras, at which Henri of Navarre (the future Henri IV, and a character in *The Massacre at Paris*) defeated Henri III.

Publication at London of Barnabe Rich, *A Path-Way to Military practice*, another example of the kind of military advice which Tamburlaine offers to his sons.

Publication of the German *Faustbuch, Historia von D. Johann Fausten,* printed by Johann Spies at Frankfurt am Main. Since it is assumed that Marlowe did not read German, the date of the first English edition of this is crucial for the dating of *Doctor Faustus,* which clearly relies on it.

Francis Walsingham and his brother-in-law George Barne, possibly in collusion with Anthony Marlowe, defraud the Muscovy Company (see Wilson, 'Visible Bullets', 49).

Francis Meres, later to be the author of *Palladis Tamia,* which included an (erroneous) account of Marlowe's death, graduates BA of Pembroke College, Cambridge.

Marlowe's play *Dido, Queen of Carthage* is recorded as being acted at Norwich and Ipswich, 'Played by the Children of Her Majesties Chappell'.

January

The Cambridge university preacher, preaching at St Mary's, warns students about members of the university who were acting as spies for the seminaries at Rheims and Rome (see Nicholl, *Reckoning,* 98).

The spy Michael Moody is imprisoned in the Tower for involvement in the 'Stafford Plot' (see Nicholl, *Reckoning,* 164). He will later be involved in a scheme in Flushing, where Marlowe also had dealings.

7 (Sat.)   Sir Walter Ralegh charters John White and twelve others as governors and assistants of the 'Cittie of Ralegh', the new colony which he proposes to establish a little way north of Roanoke, in Chesapeake Bay.

10 (Tues.) Henslowe signs a deed of partnership in the Rose Theatre with John Cholmley, 'citizen and grocer' (see Chambers, *Elizabethan Stage,* 406; and Rutter, 36–9). (Note that Henslowe dates this 1586 because he followed the contemporary practice of beginning the new year on 25 March.)

13 (Fri.) Start of Lent Term at Cambridge.

24 (Tues.) Thomas Nashe's father is buried at West Harling in Norfolk. This sounds the death-knell of Nashe's university career, and he leaves Cambridge the following year (see Nicholl, *Cup,* 37).

25 (Wed.) An anonymous letter to Sir Francis Walsingham complains about the behaviour of players (see Rutter, 39–40; and Wyckham 90–1).

26 (Thurs.) A letter referring to a new French conspiracy refers to a 'Drury' who, Roy Kendall, suggests may have been Thomas Drury, later to be implicated in the machinations surrounding the death of Marlowe (see Kendall, *Christopher Marlowe,*

241). 'One Moody', presumably the known spy Michael Moody, is also mentioned. The conspiracy referred to appears to be the Stafford Plot.

27 (Fri.)   Sir Walter Ralegh is given a Privy Seal warrant allotting him provisional title to 42,000 acres of cultivable land in Ireland, as well as a considerable quantity of waste land. Together with his Virginia venture, this makes Ralegh vastly the most important holder of lands outside of England. Many of those involved in the Virginia venture, including Hariot, visit or settle in Ralegh's Munster lands (see Lacey, 108–9).

29 (Sun. Julian, Thurs. Gregorian) Sir William Stanley and Sir Rowland Yorke betray the Dutch town of Deventer to the Spanish.

February

1 (Wed.)   Elizabeth signs the warrant for the execution of Mary, Queen of Scots.

8 (Wed.)   Execution of Mary, Queen of Scots.

15 (Wed.) Parliament begins to sit.

16 (Thurs.) Funeral of Sir Philip Sidney.

March

The preacher John Penry, the principal author of the Martin Marprelate tracts, presents Parliament with a supplication deploring the current state of church ministry in Wales. Known as the *Aequity*, this is immediately outlawed by Archbishop Whitgift (see Nicholl, *Cup*, 63).

The estates of Anthony Babington are bestowed upon Sir Walter Ralegh.

14 March (Tues. Julian, Sat. Gregorian) John Fixer and Gilbert Gifford ordained priests at Rheims.

17 (Fri.)   A Thomas Barnes sends a plea for pardon for his part in the Babington Plot, alleging that he was unwittingly inveigled into participating by his cousin Gilbert Gifford. Both Barnes and Gifford were later to be Walsingham spies. P. M. Handover suggested that it was Barnes, not Baines, who was meant in the letter referring to Gerard Burghet of 21 September 1586 (see Kendall, *Christopher Marlowe*, 99).

23 (Thurs.) Parliament breaks up.

25 (Sat.)   Lady Day. Start of the Elizabethan new year.
            End of Lent term.

29 (Sun. Gregorian) Gregorian Easter Sunday.

31 (Fri.)   Marlowe and Thomas Lewgar are granted 'grace' to proceed to the MA.

April
The Muscovy Company refloated as the Russia Company. The Roanoke colonists, with John White as governor, set sail.

16 (Sun.)   Easter Sunday.

19 (Wed.)   An English fleet led by Drake and Essex enters Cadiz harbour and burns the Spanish ships there.

26 (Wed.)   Start of Easter Term. Thomas Fineux of Dover, who may have been the 'Mr Fineux' whom Marlowe was later said to have converted to atheism (the other candidate being his brother John), enters Corpus Christi College as a gentleman pensioner.

May

7 (Sun.)   A Privy Council minute to the Lord Mayor of London suspends playing until after Bartholomew Fair (which is held for ten days, beginning 24 August) on the grounds of the heat and of recent disturbances.

8 (Mon.)   John White and his companions sail from Roanoke on their mission to found a new settlement to be called the 'Cittie of Ralegh'.

18 (Sun.)   Essex is made Master of the Horse.

29 (Thurs.) The Privy Council draft a letter to the Corpus Christi authorities telling them that:

> Whereas it was reported that Christopher Morley was determined to have gone beyond the seas to Reames and there to remain, their Lordships thought good to certify that he had no such intent, but that in all his actions he had behaved himself orderly and discretely, whereby he had done Her Majesty good service, & deserved to be rewarded for his faithful dealing. Their Lordships' request was that the rumour thereof should be allayed by all possible means, and that he should be furthered in the degree he was to take this next Commencement, because it was not Her Majesty's pleasure that anyone employed, as he had been, in matters touching the benefit of his country, should be defamed by those that are ignorant in th'affairs he went about.

July
Paul Ive, whose treatise on fortification is quoted in *Tamburlaine the Great*, Part Two, is in the Low Countries.

20 (Thurs.) The colonists land at Roanoke and decide to stay there, contrary to the plan formed before they left England, and despite the fact that there was no sign of the 18 men whom Sir Richard Grenville had left there the year before.

August
Thomas Morgan is released from the Bastille.
4–6 (Fri.–Sun.) Canterbury fair held.
8 (Tues.)   Anne Burnell of London is examined about her delusion that she is the King of Spain's daughter and implicates Marlowe's future friend Thomas Watson as someone who has encouraged her in the idea (see Nicholl, *Reckoning*, 185–8).
12 (Sat.)   Thomas Watson examined about Anne Burnell.
18 (Thurs.) Virginia Dare, granddaughter of John White and the first European child to be born in North America, born at Roanoke.
22 (Mon.)   The colonists ask White to return to England to request more supplies.
24 (Wed.)   Start of Bartholomew Fair, which ran for ten days.
27 (Sun.)   Finding it difficult to obtain food on the island, White leaves Roanoke to set sail for England in search of help. There will be no further contact with the colony until after Marlowe's death, by which time all the colonists have disappeared without trace.

September
18 (Mon.)   Richard Harvey is licensed to preach.

October
The father of John Poole the coiner, whom Marlowe seems to have met in prison, dines at Knowsley Castle with Lord Strange and his father.
2 (Mon. Julian, Fri. Gregorian) Robert Ardern writes to Lord Burghley from Utrecht mentioning Burghley's messenger 'Mr Morley'. The Morley referred to was apparently working for Burghley in late 1585 or early 1586 and was involved, along with Allen King, servant of the Earl of Northumberland, in some business concerning the revenues from the anchorage at Tynemouth (see Nicholl, *Reckoning*, 339–40). This Morley has occasionally been identified as Marlowe, but the entries below show that it was not.

5 (Thurs.) John Morley writes to Archibald Douglas on behalf of Lord
 Burghley.
16 (Mon.) White lands at Smerwick in Ireland after being driven off
 course by a storm.
29 (Sun.) A Privy Council minute to the Justices of Surrey and
 Middlesex draws their attention to complaints that peform-
 ances have been taking place on Sundays at the Rose (see
 Chambers, *Elizabethan Stage*, 407).

November
Sir Walter Ralegh is appointed to the Council of War charged with
defending England from the Armada.
2 (Thurs.) Lord Burghley writes to the Earl of Essex mentioning
 'Mr Morley of the Exchequer'.
10 (Fri.) Date given by the Corpus Christi *Registrum Parvum* ('Little
 Register' for the election of Jacob Bridgeman as Parker
 Scholar at Corpus Christi '*in locum domini* Marley' ('in the
 place of Master Marley').
16 (Thurs.) Philip Gawdy writes to his father that 'My L. Admyrall his
 men and players having a devyse in ther playe to tye one of
 their fellowes to a poste and so to shoote him to deathe,
 having borrowed their callyvers one of the players handes
 swerved his peece being charged with bullett missed the
 fellowe he aymed at and killed a chyld and a woman great
 with chyld forthwith, and hurt an other man in the head
 very soore.' E. K. Chambers took this to refer to the shooting
 of the Governor of Babylon in 2 *Tamburlaine*, v. 1, and therefore to prove that the second part of *Tamburlaine the Great*
 was already on the stage (*TLS*, 28 August 1930, 684). This idea
 has never been challenged and is now generally accepted.
20 (Mon.) John White writes to Ralegh to tell him what the colony
 needs.

December
19 (Tues. Julian, Sat. Gregorian) Gilbert Gifford is arrested in a Paris
 brothel and imprisoned. Since he seems to have been able
 to continue sending messages to London, Roy Kendall
 speculates that Marlowe might have been acting as his messenger (Kendall, *Christopher Marlowe*, 113), but there is no
 evidence for this.

1588

This was the year in which a number of people (including Gerald Mercator and Melanchthon: see Crane, 215) expected the end of the world to occur. The date was arrived at by adding the seventy-one years of the Jews' Babylonian captivity to the date of Luther's posting of the ninety-five theses.

This year was also that written on the manuscript commendation of *The Faerie Queene* which, D. Allen Carroll has recently argued, can be attributed to Marlowe's friend Thomas Watson. If Carroll is right, this would also serve as evidence that Watson was in prison for at least part of this year, since the commendation is signed 'Upon the Authour / At his bookes of the ffayery Queenes first comeinge to the / presse, written by a prissoner: 1588' (Carroll, 106).

Publication of John Penry, *Exhortation*, which refers to the bishops of the Church of England as 'soule-murtherers' (see Nicholl, *Cup*, 63).

Publication of Thomas Kyd's translation of Torquato Tasso's *House-holders Philosophie*.

Publication of Thomas Hariot's *A Brief and True Report of the new-found Land of Virginia*, the result of his voyage with Grenville. In the Baines Note, Richard Baines claimed that Marlowe's atheism was partly founded on Hariot's conviction that the American Indians had clearly been in existence for much longer than the 6,000 years which biblical scholars had calculated as the span of time since the creation of Adam. For the argument that Doctor Faustus is indebted to the *Brief and True Report*, see Hopkins, '*Doctor Faustus* and the Spanish Netherlands'.

The *Faustbuch* is translated into Danish.

Publication of Jean Boucher, *Histoire tragique et mémorable de Pierre de Gaverston* ('Tragic and Memorable History of Piers Gaveston'). Gaveston will later be an important character in Marlowe's *Edward II*.

Richard Kitchen, later to be a surety for Marlowe after the 1589 fight, is assessed as owing 5 shillings for his land in Great St Bartholomew's parish near Smithfield.

John Cecil is in correspondence with Walsingham (see Anstruther, 63).

Publication at Wittenberg of Giordano Bruno's *Oratio Valedictoria* ('Farewell Speech').

Publication at London of M. Hurault, *A discourse upon the present estate of France*, which Marlowe might have consulted while writing *The Massacre at Paris*.

Date given by John Collier for the entry in the Stationers' Register of the English Faustbook. Collier is known to have forged several of the documents he produced, and no one else claims to have seen this entry or to know of it. However, not all of Collier's discoveries were faked, so there remains a possibility that he was telling the truth. Consequently, this is the earliest possible date for *Doctor Faustus*.

John Lyly's plays *Endymion* and *the Man in the Moon* seem both to be datable to this year.

Publication of *The Wars of Cyrus* and of Thomas Lodge, *Wounds of Civil War* (both argued by Peter Berek to be imitations of *Tamburlaine*, and indicative of the speed and extent of its impact).

Publication of William Perkins, *A Treatise Tending unto a Declaration, Whether a Man Be in the State of Damnation, or in the Estate of Grace*. This expounded Calvinist theology in an accessible style aimed at a popular readership (see Waswo). The extent to which *Doctor Faustus* adopts a Calvinist perspective is much debated.

Publication at Trier of *Concertatio Ecclesiae Catholicae in Anglia Adversus Calvinopapistas et Puritanos* ('The Resistance of the Catholic Church in England to Calvinopapists and Puritans'), containing Baines' written recantation, the 'Palinoda Richardi Bainaci' ('The Recantation of Richard Baines').

Giordano Bruno is teaching at Wittenberg.

February
8 (Thurs.) John Marlowe acts as a professional bondsman for a couple seeking a marriage licence (see Boas, *Christopher Marlowe*, 4)

March
The Privy Council forbids Sir Richard Grenville to sail to the relief of the Roanoke colony on the grounds that the Armada is expected.

25 (Mon.) Lady Day. Start of the Elizabethan new year.

31 (Sun.) Robert Greene's *Perimedes the Blacksmith* entered in the Stationers' Register. The preface speaks of how 'I could not make my verses jet upon the stage in tragical buskins, every word filling the mouth like the fa-burden of Bow Bell, daring God out of heaven with that atheist Tamburlan, or blaspheming with the mad priest of the sun. But let me rather pocket up the ass at Diogenes's hand than wantonly set out such impious instances of intolerable poetry, such mad and scoffing poets that have prophetical spirits as bred of Merlin's race.'

The reference to Tamburlaine and the allusion to Merlin ('Merlin' and 'Marlin' are both found as variants of the name 'Marlowe', along with 'Morley' and 'Marlowe') make it quite clear that it is Marlowe who is meant. The 'mad priest of the sun' is generally supposed to be Giordano Bruno (see Farley-Hills).

April

7 (Sun. Julian) Easter Sunday in England.

16 (Tues.) The shop of the printer Robert Waldegrave is raided, and his equipment destroyed, because of his rôle in publishing the works of John Penry.

17 (Sun. Gregorian) Easter Sunday on the continent.

27 (Sat.) Date given by the Corpus Christi Order Book for the election of Jacob Bridgeman as Marlowe's successor as Parker Scholar at Corpus Christi. The delay in installing a successor is unusual and may be a consequence of the irregularities surrounding Marlowe's departure.

May

First indications of Essex's rise to favour.

22 (Wed.) John White sails back to Devon after having failed to reach Roanoke on an attempted relief expedition.

27 (Mon.) 'Banes, Richard, clerk, M.A.' is admitted to the benefice of Waltham in Lincolnshire.

June

Essex is made Master of the Horse.

10 (Mon.) Stationers' Company wardens raid a house in Kingston in search of Robert Waldegrave and the printing equipment he had salvaged from the destruction of his shop.

July

Essex and Ralegh openly quarrel (see Lacey, 103).

19 (Fri.) The Spanish Armada is sighted in the Channel. Troops march to Tilbury, where the Queen visits them. Countrywide musters of men included that of the Canterbury trained bands, in which Marlowe's father John was recorded as carrying a bow; the bands made cabins of sticks and leaves at their camp at Northbourne. An inventory of arms held by citizens of Canterbury records John Marlowe's house as containing a bow, a headpiece, a sword, a dagger and a brown bill (a halberd-like weapon) (Urry, 30–1).

29 (Mon.) In a decisive engagement, the Armada is finally beaten off.

August

8 (Thurs.)   The Queen, still at Tilbury, learns that the Armada has been entirely dispersed.

24 (Mon.)   St Bartholomew's Day, marking the start of Bartholomew Fair, which ran for ten days.

25 (Sun.)   William Bradley, whom Marlowe's friend Thomas Watson was to kill the following year, bound himself to repay £14 to John Alleyn, brother of Edward, on this date, with a penalty of 40 marks [1 mark = 14s 3d] if he did not do so. He defaulted, and John Alleyn sued him.

September

4 (Wed.)   The Earl of Leicester dies.

19 (Thurs.) Thomas Nashe's *Anatomie of Absurditie* is licensed for publication by Thomas Hackett.

30 (Mon.)   The Comitia (governing council) of the Royal College of Physicians condemns one Paul Fairfax for unlicensed practising and fines him £5. John Henry Jones suggests that this may be the P. F. who translates the *English Faust Book*, which Jones sees as almost certain to have been first published in 1588 (see Jones, 31 and 53).

October

Publication of the *Epistle*, first of the 'Martin Marprelate' tracts (see Nicholl, *Cup*, 64).

Michaelmas (early October) Robert Poley is released from the Tower and goes to lodge with the Yeomans family.

John Mathews, later to be known as Christopher Marler, matriculates at Trinity College, Cambridge (see Boas, *Christopher Marlowe*, 24).

16 (Wed.)   James Tipping is moved from the Tower to the Gatehouse.

November

10 (Sun.)   Robert Poley has William Yeomans, husband of Poley's mistress Joan, committed to the Marshalsea for having failed to act on a warrant issued by Sir Thomas Heneage.

14 (Thurs.) The Martinist tract the *Epistle* is reported to be on sale at Kingston-upon-Thames. On the same day Lord Burghley and Sir Christopher Hatton warn Whitgift about its dangers. By around this date Waldegrave, Penry and the third man involved, John Udall, have moved to the house of Sir Richard Knightley at Fawsley, near Northampton. Udall

will move to Newcastle by December and will play no further part in the pamphleteering (see Nicholl, *Cup*, 64–5).

December

Publication of the second Martinist pamphlet, the *Epitome*.

23 December (Mon. Julian, Fri. Gregorian) Assassination of the Duke of Guise. The prologue to *The Jew of Malta* refers to his death. The Comitia of the Royal College of Physicians drafts a reply to Lord Hunsdon concerning an intervention he has made in the case of Paul Fairfax (see Jones, 32).

27 (Fri.)   Sir Francis Walsingham signs a warrant to pay Robert Poley £15 for a trip to Denmark.

31 (Tues.)   Lord Strange's Men, with whom Marlowe may later have been connected, play at Knowsley, the estate of Lord Strange's father the Earl of Derby; Lord Strange himself returns home the same evening (see George, 230–1).

1589

Marlowe's father John is made warden of the leather company.

Marlowe's younger brother Thomas is listed as one of the choirboys of Canterbury Cathedral. This is the last mention of Thomas, unless he is indeed the Thomas Marlowe of the Faversham records (see Frohnsdorff, and entry below for Saturday, 19 November 1603). William Urry speculates that he might have been the same as the Thomas Marloe recorded as arriving in Virginia in 1624 (Urry, 15), but the lack of any reference to him in his mother's will suggests that he was more probably dead by 1605.

Publication of Jean Boucher, *La vie et faits notables de Henri de Valois* ('The Life and Notable Deeds of Henri of Valois [Henri III]'), which Marlowe may have used as a source for *The Massacre at Paris*. The same year saw the publication of two other possible sources for the play, *Le martyre des deux frères* ('The Martyrdom of the Two Brothers') and *Les cruautés sanguinaires ...* ('The Bloody Cruelties ...') (Thomas and Tydeman, 278, 284 and 286), and also of Anne Dowriche, *The French Historie*, showing the extent of English interest in French history (see also Hillman).

It was during this year, Bess of Hardwick, Countess of Shrewsbury later said, that 'One Morley' began 'reading to' her granddaughter, Arbella Stuart.

Thomas Nashe praises Marlowe's friend Matthew Roydon for his 'most absolute comic inventions' (see Nicholl, *Reckoning*, 257). No works which might be candidates for this description survive. Nashe also provides a preface to Greene's *Menaphon*, which is published in this year and ultimately becomes known as 'Greene's *Arcadia*' (see Nicholl, *Cup*, 48). Another work published this year is Greene's *Tullies Love*, dedicated to Lord Strange.

Richard Hesketh, spy and *agent provocateur*, arrives in Prague, revealing that the theatre of espionage operations was not confined to France, Spain and the Low Countries.

The English College at Valladolid is founded by Cardinal Allen and Father Persons, giving the English security service another location to worry about.

Blanche Parry, keeper of Elizabeth I's jewels, leaves her 'cousin' Eleanor Bull £100 in her will. It is in Mrs Bull's house that Marlowe will later die, and this bequest has sometimes been seen as evidence of a government connection.

Christopher Blount, whose mother was a Poley, marries Lettice Knollys, widow of the Earl of Leicester and mother of the Earl of Essex.

Publication of Paul Ive, *The Practise of Fortification*. Marlowe had used this as a source for *Tamburlaine*, Part Two (see Kocher, 'Marlowe's Art of War').

Publication of Thomas Newton's edition of Leland's *Principium Ac illustrium aliquot & eruditorum in Anglia virorum Encomia* ('In Praise of Princes and of Some Famous and Learned Men of England') (no Stationers' Register entry), in a copy of which Marlowe's friend and possible collaborator Thomas Nashe made the marginal annotations 'Faustus: Che sara sara [what will be will be] deuinynitie adieu' and 'Faustus: studie in indian silke' (see Kocher, 'Some Nashe Marginalia').

Publication of *The Contre-Guyse* (a Huguenot tract), indicating the continuing interest in the Duke of Guise, later to be a key character in *The Massacre at Paris*.

The Taming of A Shrew (the 'bad quarto' version of Shakespeare's play) and George Peele, *The Battle of Alcazar* (both argued by Peter Berek to be imitations of *Tamburlaine*) seem both to date from this year.

January

Summoned to Parliament, Ferdinando Stanley, Lord Strange, arrives in London. He stays there until about July and begins involving himself more actively in the patronage of his theatre company, Lord Strange's Men. From this time or shortly after Lord Strange's Men also begin to associate closely with the Lord Admiral's Men, who include Edward Alleyn's brother John. It seems probable that the connection with Lord Strange to which Marlowe referred when he was arrested in Flushing in 1592 dates from around this time.

Waldegrave and Penry leave Fawsley and travel to Coventry, where they are given shelter by a relative of Sir Richard Knightley's.

Thomas Cooper, Bishop of Winchester, publishes the anti-Martinist *Admonition to the People of England.*

5 (Sun.)   Lord Strange's Men probably play again at Knowsley (see George, 230–1).

7 (Tues.)   Richard Ede, lodge-keeper at the Marshalsea Prison, lodges a deposition against Robert Poley for alienating the affections of Joan Yeomans, wife of William Yeomans, cutler, of London, while Poley was a prisoner at the Marshalsea in 1583. The case was heard by William Fleetwood, Recorder of London, a figure who will recur in events connected with Marlowe.

14 (Tues.)   Francis Kett, formerly fellow of Corpus Christi College, Cambridge, burned for heresy at Norwich.

31 (Fri.)   The Comitia letter concerning Paul Fairfax is sent and no more is heard of him (see Jones, 33).

February

John Lyly, author of *Euphues*, is elected MP for Hindon, in Wiltshire. Lyly seems to have known Nashe well and was blamed by Gabriel Harvey for stirring up Nashe and Greene to attack him (see Nicholl, *Cup*, 55).

9 (Sun.)   Richard Bancroft preaches an anti-Martinist sermon at Paul's Cross.

13 (Thurs.) A proclamation declares the Martin Marprelate tracts to be seditious and orders the destruction of much of the associated writing (see Rutter, 44).

20 (Thurs.) Probable date of publication of the third Martinist tract, *Mineralls.*

28 (Fri.)   *A Ballad of the Life and Deathe of Doctor Faustus the Great Congurer* is entered in the Stationers' Register by Richard Jones (see Zimansky, 186). The relation of this to Marlowe's play is unclear and it is no longer extant.

March

It is at some stage during this month that the fourth Martinist tract, *Hay any Worke for Cooper*, appears.

7 (Mon.)   To raise money, Ralegh assigns part of his Virginia patent to a group of London merchants (see Stevens, 70–1).

11 (Tues. Julian, Sat. Gregorian) John Dee and his family set out home for Trebon in South Bohemia.

25 (Tues.) Lady Day. Start of the Elizabethan new year.

April
3 (Thurs.)   The Earl of Essex slips away from the Court to make an unauthorised expedition to Portugal. Nicholas Skeres accompanies him. The astrologer and physician Simon Forman, who may conceivably have functioned as a model for Doctor Faustus, seems also to have gone on the Portugal voyage, though this is not entirely clear (see Traister, *Notorious Astrological Physician*, 9).
9 (Wed. Julian, Sun. Gregorian) The Dee party arrives in Bremen.

April/May
Robert Waldegrave, tired of the strain of being on the run, announces that he is no longer prepared to print the Martinist tracts and leaves the country. It was also probably in May that the first anti-Martinist show, *The Maygame of Martinisme*, was played at The Theatre, and two anti-Martinist pamphlets, *A Whip for an Ape* and *Mar-Martine*, appear sometime before July, which were possibly written by John Lyly or Anthony Munday (see Nicholl, *Cup*, 68–9).

May
There is 'a great bruit' in London that the Prince of Parma is dead (Doran, 26).
12 (Mon.)   A note on this date records that by then Thomas Hariot is living in one of Ralegh's properties in Ireland (see Rukeyser, 92).
15 (Thurs. Julian, Mon. Gregorian) John Fixer is sent from Rheims to Valladolid.

June
Francis Aldrich, brother of Simon Aldrich, matriculates as a pensioner of Clare Hall, Cambridge, aged twelve. It will later be Simon Aldrich who supplies information about Marlowe's relationship with 'Mr Fineux'.
6 (Fri.)   Essex, recalled by the Queen, sails for home. The troops straggle back during this month and July and riot in London, including staging a 'mutiny' in the Strand at which Richard Cholmeley is present (see Nicholl, *Reckoning*, 268). The 'remembrances against Ric. Cholmeley' are later to be important in the story of Marlowe's death (see Kendall, *Christopher Marlowe*, 255–60), since in them Cholmeley is

quoted as saying 'that one Marlowe is able to showe more sounde reasons for Atheisme then any devine in Englande is able to geve to prove devinitie & that Marloe tolde him that hee hath read the Atheist lecture to Sir Walter Raliegh & others' (quoted in Wraight and Stern, 354).

25 (Wed.)   James Tipping is returned from the Gatehouse to the Tower.

July

8 (Tues.)   Sir Francis Walsingham signs a warrant to pay Poley for couriering letters to and from Holland.

21 (Mon.)   A warrant is issued to pay Nicholas Skeres £6 13s 4d for acting as a courier between the Earl of Essex and Sir Francis Walsingham.

22 (Tues.)   Publication of *Theses Martiniae*, a Martinist tract by 'Martin Junior'. This is followed a week later by *The Iust Censure and Reproofe of Martin Iunior*, published after Penry finds a new printer (see Nicholl, *Cup*, 69–70).

August

James VI of Scotland is married by proxy to Princess Anne of Denmark.

2 (Wed., Gregorian) Death of Henri III of France and accession of Henri IV. These events will later form the last scene of *The Massacre at Paris*.

4–6 (Mon.–Wed.) Canterbury fair held.

mid-August Publication of the anti-Martinist *A Countercuffe given to Martin Iunior*. This and its sequels, *The Returne of Pasquill* and *Pasquils Apologie*, may be wholly or partly by Thomas Nashe (see Nicholl, *Cup*, 71–2).

14 (Thurs.)   The Earl of Derby's officers find three Martinist printers in the act of printing *More Work for the Cooper* at a house on the outskirts of Manchester, and arrest them.

23 (Sat.)   Greene's *Menaphon*, containing a preface by Nashe which may glance at Marlowe (see Zimansky, 186; Rutter, 46–7; and Nicholl, *Cup*, 51–3), entered in the Stationers' Register.

24 (Sun.)   St Bartholomew's Day, marking the start of Bartholomew Fair, which ran for ten days.

Archbishop Whitgift writes to Lord Burghley about the fate of the Martinist printers.

September

Lord Strange's Men play at Knowsley.

Arrest of Henry Sharpe, a bookbinder of Northampton, who gives information to the authorities which allows them to reconstruct the movements of the Martinist pamphleteers.

11 (Thurs. Julian, Mon. Gregorian) Henri IV of France achieves a surprise victory over his Catholic adversaries, led by the Duc de Mayenne, at Arques. From this period on his affairs are eagerly followed in England (Voss, 21), and are described in, among other places, a number of news pamphlets and tracts printed by John Wolfe, perhaps at the instigation of Burghley (Voss, 29–30 and 52).

18 (Thurs.) Marlowe and his friend Thomas Watson are involved in a fight in Hog Lane in London with one William Bradley, apparently an old enemy of Watson's, and Bradley is killed. Marlowe is described as a yeoman and lately resident at Norton Folgate. Watson and Marlowe are sent to Newgate.

At some time in the same legal term, a Richard Baines is accused of uttering death threats against one Walter Spencer of London (Kendall, *Christopher Marlowe*, 169).

19 (Fri.) The agent of Bess of Hardwick, Countess of Shrewsbury opens her account ledger in London, showing that the Hardwick household were there at the time. Gristwood (458) cites this in order to show that there is in fact no evidence which conclusively disproves the idea that Marlowe was the Morley who 'read to' Arbella Stuart. Though there is equally no conclusive evidence that he *was*, therefore, nor any apparent likelihood that any such evidence will be forthcoming, the question must remain open, and the possibility cannot currently be ruled out.

28 (Sun.) The main body of 4,000 English troops, commanded by Lord Willoughby, arrives at Dieppe to assist Henri IV in his quest to secure the French throne.

October

1 (Wed.) Marlowe raises bail of £40 with Richard Kitchen, attorney of Clifford's Inn, and Humphrey Rowland, horner, as his sureties.

4 (Sat.) The remainder of Willoughby's 4,000 men arrive at Dieppe.

9 (Thurs.)   Ingram Frizer, later to be famous as Marlowe's killer, buys the Angel Inn, Basingstoke, for £20, shortly afterwards selling it on again to James Deane. An anonymous enquirer in *Notes and Queries* (20 July 1935) later referred to Ben Jonson supposedly visiting the Angel Inn, Basingstoke, and writing in its praise (B. H. N., 'Ben Jonson Queries', *Notes and Queries* 169 [1935], 47).

mid-month   Publication of the last Martinist tract, *The Protestatyon of Martin Marprelate*. This is followed within a week or two by publication of three anti-Martinist tracts, *Martins Months Minde*, *The Returne of Pasquill* and *Pappe with a Hatchet*, the last of which is by Lyly. Shortly after this the Martinist author John Penry escapes to Scotland, where he is sheltered by James VI.

November

It was probably during this month that Nashe, calling himself 'Cuthbert Curryknave', wrote his anti-Martinist pamphlet *Almond for a Parrat*, the first of the anti-Martinist writings to name Penry and Udall as responsible for the tracts (see Nicholl, *Cup*, 75).

5 (Wed.)   Date given by Gabriel Harvey for his *An Advertisement for the Papp-hatchet*, which mentions 'another Doctor Faustus' (see Zimansky, 187). This presumably indicates that there is already an existing one (though his work was not published until 1593), and so would therefore be evidence for the early date theory.

6 (Thurs.)   The Earl of Nottingham's Men, said on the title-page of the 1604 text of *Doctor Faustus* to have acted the play, are ordered by the Lord Mayor to suspend all further London performances, though they continued to perform at court until 16 February 1591. If this decree was carried out, and if *Doctor Faustus* was indeed performed by them, this too is support for the 'early date' theory.

11 (Sat. Gregorian)   Tomaso Contarini, Venetian Ambassador to Spain, writes to the Doge and Senate from Madrid mentioning David Passi.

12 (Wed.)   Letters from the Privy Council to the Archbishop of Canterbury and the Master of the Revels complain that plays have recently been dealing with 'certen matters of divinytie and State unfitt to be suffred' (see Rutter, 44–5).

Richard Dutton suggests that this precipitated the end of John Lyly's career (Dutton, 87–9).

16 (Sun.) Death of Edmund Walsingham, elder brother of Marlowe's later protector Thomas Walsingham. Thomas Walsingham inherits the Scadbury estate, and there are no further known indications of him undertaking any work for the government.

17 (Mon.) Accession Day.

Date on the preface of Thomas Hariot's *Brief and True Report of Virginia*.

20 (Thurs.) Burial of Edmund Walsingham.

23 (Sun.) James VI of Scotland and Anne of Denmark are married in Oslo.

26 (Wed. Julian, Sun. Gregorian) The Dee party leaves Bremen.

27 (Thurs.) Probable date when an inventory was taken of the possessions of Matthew Parkin, a student at Christ Church, Oxford, listing among his possessions a book called 'Doctor faustus'. If this, as seems likely, is the English Faust Book, then there must have been an early edition of it (see Fehrenbach).

December

The anti-Martinist pamphlet *A Myrrour for Martinists* is entered in the Stationers' Register.

1 (Mon.) The first three books of Spenser's *The Faerie Queene* are entered in the Stationers' Register. Patrick Cheney has recently argued that Marlowe constructed his career as a deliberate counter to Spenser's (see Cheney, *Counterfeit Profession*).

3 (Wed.) The Bradley case is heard at the Old Bailey before William Fleetwood, Recorder of London, and Sir Roger Manwood, Chief Baron of the Exchequer, on whom Marlowe later wrote an epitaph, and who is known to have owned a copy of either the 1590 or the 1592 *Tamburlaine* (see Bakeless, 160–1). Marlowe is discharged.

The Admiral's Men, who had performed *Tamburlaine the Great*, are inhibited from playing. This may contribute to the decision to publish *Tamburlaine* the following year (the title-page affirms their right in it).

10 (Wed.) Thomas Nashe's mother is buried at Lowestoft.

15 (Mon.) The Dee party arrives home to Mortlake.

1590

It was probably during this year that John Poole was released from Newgate.

A Richard Umberfield, who may conceivably have been John Marlowe's former apprentice, is recorded as one of the Puritans detained in Bridewell, along with a John Cranford, who could perhaps be the future husband of Marlowe's sister Ann (see Urry, 23).

Publication of Thomas Nashe's *Anatomie for Absurditie* and *Almond for a Parrat*. Also in this year Richard Harvey writes disparagingly of Nashe in the preface to his *The Lamb of God* (see Nicholl, *Cup*, 80).

Ralegh's 'Fifth Expedition' sails in search of the lost colony of Roanoke.

Publication of *Greenes Mourning Garment*, in which Robert Greene announces his farewell to romances and light works (see Nicholl, *Cup*, 49).

John Udall is arrested for his part in the Martin Marprelate pamphlets.

By this date the first group of players patronised by the Lord Chamberlain has disbanded (see Rutter, 21).

Publication at London of Thomas Watson's *Meliboeus*, an elegy for Sir Francis Walsingham, and of a book of madrigals on which Watson had collaborated with William Byrd, dedicated to the Earl of Essex.

Publication of Sir Philip Sidney, *The Countess of Pembroke's Arcadia*.

Special prayers for Henri IV of France, to be said in all parish churches during morning and evening prayer, are commissioned and ultimately printed by the Queen's printer Christopher Barker (Voss, 43).

John Dee returns to England.

Death of Gilbert Gifford.

Publication of William Perkins's *Armilla Aurea* ... ('The Golden Chain ...'), asserting the doctrine of absolute predestination, and of his *Foundation of Christian Religion Gathered into Six Principles*.

Publication of Henry Holland, *A Treatise Against Witchcraft*, printed by the Cambridge University printer John Legatt, which refers to a pamphlet about *Doctor Faustus* (see Zimansky, 186).

Publication of the first three books of Edmund Spenser, *The Faerie Queene*, printed by John Wolfe for William Ponsonby. On links between the iconography of *The Faerie Queene* and that of Wolfe's French news pamphlets, see Voss, 91 and 98–9; he argues that Wolfe associates Navarre with Saint George to boost support for his cause.

Tamburlaine is published in octavo, printed by Richard Jones.

Lodge and Greene, *A Looking-Glass for London and England* (argued by Peter Berek to be an imitation of *Tamburlaine*), seems to date from this year.

January

21 (Wed.) James VI of Scotland and his new wife, Anne of Denmark, cross over to Elsinore from Norway.

February

10 (Tues.) Thomas Watson is pardoned on grounds of self-defence.

12 (Thurs.) Thomas Watson is released.

23 (Mon.) Sir Thomas Heneage signs a warrant to pay Poley for couriering letters to and from Berwick.

March

Henri IV defeats the Duc de Mayenne at Ivry.

20 (Fri.) James VI of Scotland visits the astronomer Tycho Brahe at his laboratory in Denmark.

John White sets sail from Plymouth on another attempt to take supplies to the colonists at Roanoke.

24 (Tues.) Date on which Ralegh's patent for Virginia would have expired if he had not succeeded in establishing a colony by then.

25 (Wed.) Lady Day. Start of the Elizabethan new year.

April

Henri IV lays siege to Paris.

1 (Sun. Gregorian) Date on the dedication of Theodore de Bry's reprinting of Hariot's *Brief and True Report* to Sir Walter Ralegh (see Rukeyser, 107–8).

6 (Mon.) Death of Sir Francis Walsingham.

9 (Thurs.) Richard Bull, husband of Eleanor Bull in whose house Marlowe will later die, is buried at St Nicholas, Deptford.

19 (Sun.) Easter Sunday.

21 (Tues.) Canterbury Burghmoot admits John Jordan, shortly to become the husband of Marlowe's sister Margaret, as a freeman in right of his future wife's status as daughter of a freeman, on payment of 10 shillings. The experiences of both John Jordan and John Moore confirm that the Marlowe daughters were desirable matches in this respect.

22 (Sun. Gregorian) Gregorian Easter Sunday.

24 (Fri.) Henri IV is elected a Knight of the Garter.

May

Death of Charles de Bourbon. Philip II suggests his daughter, the Infanta Isabella Clara Eugenia, as an alternative Catholic candidate for the French throne.

27 (Wed.)   A pardon issued to Thomas Walsingham reveals that he has recently been imprisoned for debt in the Fleet Prison, after failing to repay 200 marks which he had borrowed from Thomas Lund. After coming into his estate, he has settled his debt and purchased his pardon.

June

There is an unsuccessful assassination attempt against Henri IV, which Voss (115) sees as closely mirrored in *The Massacre at Paris*.

15 (Mon.)   Marlowe's sister Margaret marries John Jordan, tailor, at St Mary Bredman, Canterbury.

July

Publication of the last anti-Martinist pamphlet, *Pasquils Apologie*.

8 (Wed.)   The incoming Lieutenant of the Tower is told to release James Tipping if he is willing to go to church, or if not, to indict him as a recusant (see Seaton, 'Marlowe, Poley, and the Tippings', 278).

23 (Thurs.) Sir Thomas Heneage signs a warrant to pay Poley for couriering letters to and from the Low Countries.

August

3 (Mon.)   The Earl of Essex lands at Dieppe to assist Henri IV in capturing Rouen.

4–6 (Tues.–Thurs.) Canterbury fair held.

17 (Mon.)   White lands on Roanoke and finds no trace of the colonists except the word 'Croatoan', the name of a neighbouring island. The weather makes it impossible to land on Croatoan to see if the colonists were there. Their fate remains a mystery (see Lacey, 154–5).

24 (Mon.)   St Bartholomew's Day, marking the start of Bartholomew Fair, which ran for ten days.

27 (Thurs.) Death of Pope Sixtus V (who is referred to as dead in *The Massacre at Paris*, indicating that it postdates this). Among his other claims to fame, this Pope had forbidden the Knights of Malta to molest Jews (see Roth, 216).

end-month Henri IV lifts the siege of Paris.

September

25 (Fri.)   'The true news from ffraunce broughte by the [l]aste post the 23th of September 1590' is entered in the Stationers' Register, confirming the thirst for news from France.

October

9 (Fri.)   Date on the 'certificate of allowance' for the government agent John Edge, which provides a useful comparator with the Privy Council's intervention over Marlowe's MA (see the *DNB* entry on Marlowe).

14 (Wed.) The coiner John Poole is examined in Newgate about alleged 'traitorous speeches'.

November

7 (Sat. Julian, Wed. Gregorian) Date on the letter carried by John Cecil from Father Persons at Valladolid addressed to Dr Barret, president of Rheims (which never arrived).

13 (Fri. Julian, Tues. Gregorian) John Fixer and John Cecil set out for England, apparently as part of the Catholic mission.

17 (Tues.) Accession Day. George Peele noted that Lord Strange particularly distinguished himself in the Tilts for this year (see Nicholl, *Cup*, 88).

22 (Sun.) William Ballard of Southwell in Nottinghamshire complains that the Richard Baines who is rector of Waltham has failed to repay Ballard £20 which the latter had lent him towards securing the benefice (Kendall, *Christopher Marlowe*, 312). Given the earlier suggestion of a Southwell connection for the Cambridge Richard Baines, this may make it more likely that this was indeed Marlowe's betrayer. One might also speculate on a possible connection with the John Ballard who studied at Rheims and was involved in the Babington plot.

late in the year
Michael Moody is released from the Tower.

December

8 (Tues.) Thomas Nelson enters in the Stationers' Register a pamphlet entitled 'the thinges which happened upon the Prince of Parmas retire since the 20. of Novembre, till the 27. of the same Moneth' (Voss, 69). It is the Prince of Parma whom Faustus proposes to chase 'from our land'.

17 (Thurs.) John Wolfe enters in the Stationers' Register a pamphlet entitled 'that which happened since the 27. of Novembre last' (Voss, 69).

22 (Tues.) Sir Thomas Heneage signs a warrant to pay Poley for couriering letters to and from the Low Countries.

1591

John Marlowe, now living in the parish of St Mary Breadman in Canterbury, is made churchwarden. At the Canterbury muster of this year, he is noted not now to have any of the military equipment he had possessed at the time of the Armada.

Publication of the astrologer and physician Simon Forman's only book, *The Groundes of the Longitude: With an Admonition to all those that are Incredulous and believe not of the Truth of the same* (see Traister, *Notorious Astrological Physician*, 123). Forman is seen by some as a possible model for Doctor Faustus.

Publication of *Wonderfull, Strange and Miraculous Astrologicall Prognostication*, a satire on the type of astrological writing favoured by the Harvey brothers which may be by Thomas Nashe (see Nicholl, *Cup*, 81–2).

Publication of the first of Robert Greene's tracts on 'cony-catching', *A Notable Discovery of Coosnage* and *The Second Part of Conny-catching*.

Publication of Spenser's *Complaints*, containing 'The Teares of the Muses', dedicated to Lady Strange, who was born a Spencer and with whom Edmund Spenser therefore claimed kinship.

Publication of the first edition of *Astrophel and Stella*, with a preface by Thomas Nashe, though Nashe's preface did not survive in the new and revised edition published a few months later. This seems to be an indication of displeasure on the part of Sidney's sister, the Countess of Pembroke (see Nicholl, *Cup*, 82–3).

It was during this year, Kyd later said, that he and Marlowe shared lodgings.

It was also around this time that Thomas Watson was 'reading to' William Cornwallis as a way of supplementing his income (see Nicholl, *Reckoning*, 188–90).

During the course of the year, Strange's Men and the Admiral's Men fall out with James Burbage over money, and move from The Theatre to the Rose.

Early in the year, Sir William Stanley suggests to the Jesuit Father Persons, who is much interested in the question of the succession to the English Crown, that the ideal candidate would be Stanley's cousin Lord Strange (Kuriyama, *Christopher Marlowe*, 97).

Publication at London of Edmund Spenser, *The Ruins of Time*, which Patrick Cheney sees as an important influence on Marlowe (see Cheney, *Counterfeit Profession*).

John Wolfe prints *A Discourse Uppon a Question of the Estate of this Time* and *An Answeare to the Supplication Against him, who seeming to give the*

King counsel to become a Catholike, indevoureth to stirre up his good Subjectes unto rebellion. Both deal with the affairs of Henri IV and show the extensive degree of interest felt in England in the doings and fortunes of the King. (It is notable that the title of the second tract does not even need to specify which king is meant.)

The mathematician Walter Warner starts to receive an annual pension of £20 from the Earl of Northumberland. This may be the 'Warner' who was later identified as Marlowe's friend, though that may possibly refer to the poet William Warner, author of *Albion's England*,

Publication at London of Sir John Harington, *Orlando Furioso in English Heroical Verse*, which Marlowe seems to have consulted (see Thomas and Tydeman, 159), and first performance of Robert Greene, *Orlando Furioso* (argued by Peter Berek to be an imitation of *Tamburlaine*).

Publication of Antony Colynet, *The True History of the Civil Wars of France ...*, which Marlowe may have consulted for *Massacre at Paris* (see Thomas and Tydeman, 287).

A proposal is made to marry Arbella Stuart to Rainutio Farnese, son of the Duke of Parma. 'The Prince of Parma' is mentioned in *Doctor Faustus* and it is just possible that Marlowe had 'read to' Arbella.

Winchester Cathedral is robbed by Sir Edward Bushell, Richard Williams, and others (see Nicholl, *Reckoning*, 244). Some members of the Marlowe-was-Shakespeare fraternity link Marlowe with this and occasionally assert that he funded the rest of his career from the proceeds.

Publication of William Perkins, *A Golden Chaine: or, The Description of Theologie, Containing the order of the causes of Salvation and Damnation*, another salvo in the controversy over Calvinism (see Waswo).

January

Giordano Bruno leaves Frankfurt.

5 (Sat. Gregorian.) Hieronimo Lippomano, Venetian Ambassador to the Porte, writes to the Doge and Senate mentioning David Passi in connection with Elizabeth I's attempt to ally with the Sultan against Philip of Spain.

19 (Sat. Gregorian) Lippomano writes to the Doge and Senate mentioning Passi in connection with anti-Spanish manoeuvring.

30 (Sat.)   There is a reference in the *Calendar of State Papers* for this date to 'Injunctions to Tho. Maris and others, and Richard Baynes and others [Docquets]', but this is usually taken to refer to the Oxford Baines (see Kendall, *Christopher Marlowe*, 133).

February

2 (Sat. Gregorian) Lippomano writes to the Doge and Senate mention-
     ing the possibility of a Turkish attack on Malta if the one
     on Spain is abandoned. This fear makes the premise of *The
     Jew of Malta* topical.

16 (Tues.) The Earl of Nottingham's Men are recorded as performing
     at court.
     Lippomano writes to the Doge and Senate mentioning Passi
     as agent for Don Antonio of Portugal.

March

16 (Sat. Gregorian) Lippomano writes to the Doge and Senate saying
     that Passi is in disgrace after dealings with the Grand
     Chancellor of Poland.

25 (Thurs.) Lady Day. Start of the Elizabethan new year.

April

The Jesuit Father Robert Persons, later to be the author of a controver-
sial tract on the succession to the throne, is recorded as being in
Madrid with Sir William Stanley, betrayer of Deventer.

3 April (Sat. Julian, Wed. Gregorian) Date on the document purporting to
     be Father Persons' written instructions for the Catholic priests
     John Cecil and John Fixer about approaching Lord Strange.

4 (Sun.)   Easter Sunday.

13 (Tues. Julian, Sat. Gregorian) Date on letter sent by Father Persons
     to John Cecil in Lisbon. This allegedly concerns a plot to
     approach Lord Strange to invite him to bid for the English
     throne with Catholic support, though it is possible that this
     was an attempt to frame Strange.

14 (Sun. Gregorian) Gregorian Easter Sunday.

15 (Thurs.) Richard Kitchen, Marlowe's guarantor, says in a deposition
     that he is of Great St Bartholomew's near Smithfield.

May

Michael Moody, a double agent, goes to Brussels to spy on the Welsh
Catholic Hugh Owen and his associates. Owen is in the confidence of
both Philip II and the Duke of Parma, and had travelled to Spain with
Sir William Stanley, betrayer of Deventer, the year before. (This had
been Owen's third visit to Spain.)

Lord Burghley thanks Edward Kelly for a letter which has arrived from
Prague via Marlowe's friend Matthew Roydon (Woolley, 298). Kelly is
staying there as an honoured guest of the Emperor Rudolf.

John Alleyn, brother of Edward, witnesses a dispute at The Theatre between James Burbage and members of the Admiral's Men (see Rutter, 49; and Chambers, *Elizabethan Stage*, 138).

2 (Sun.) John Cecil and John Fixer are captured (or give themselves up because at least one of them is really a double agent: see Anstruther, 64 and 118). Lord Burghley intercepts (or possibly plants) Persons' directions about approaching Lord Strange (see Nicholl, *Reckoning*, 228–9). John Cecil returns to Spain.

5 (Wed.) Sir Henry Norris, with 3,000 soldiers, arrives at St Malo to assist Henri IV.

13 (Thurs.) A warrant is issued for the arrests of Thomas Drury and Richard Cholmeley, both of whom will figure in the events surrounding Marlowe's death.

20 (Thurs.) Sir Thomas Heneage signs a warrant to pay Poley for couriering letters to and from Berwick.

July

Sir Henry Unton is sent as the Queen's ambassador to France.

15 (Tues.) Thomas Drury is sent to the Marshalsea.
Lorenzo Bernardo, back as Venetian Ambassador to the Porte, writes to the Doge and Senate confirming the fall of David Passi (see Thomas and Tydeman, 312).

23 (Fri.) Edward White enters in the Stationers' Register a now lost ballad, *The Noble departinge of the right honourable the E[a]rle of Essex lieutenant generall of her majesties forces in Ffraunce and his gallant companie*.

29 (Thurs.) Richard Cholmeley is paid £6, along with Jasper Borage, for apprehending Thomas Drury (see Nicholl, *Reckoning*, 269). Since warrants for both Drury and Cholmeley were issued on the same day, the inference seems to be that both were wanted for the same thing, and that Cholmeley has grassed.

August

The Earl of Essex, with Nicholas Skeres and Richard Williams in his train, lands at Dieppe and meets Henri of Navarre at Compiègne. Williams deserts and joins the traitor Sir William Stanley.

Michael Moody is reported to be arranging to take a Hilliard miniature of Arbella Stuart to the Duke of Parma.

Giordano Bruno returns from Germany to Venice.

4–6 (Wed.–Fri.) Canterbury fair held.

24 (Tues.) St Bartholomew's Day, marking the start of Bartholomew Fair, which ran for ten days.

September
Michael Moody travels from Antwerp to Flushing using the alias Robert Cranston and pretending to be a Scots merchant. He makes an offer to Sir Robert Sidney to turn the British Catholic Hugh Owen, who is in exile in Brussels. Sidney writes to Lord Burghley for advice (see Nicholl, *Reckoning*, 253). Sidney's dealings with Moody in this year might perhaps have left him with less patience in the matter of Marlowe and Baines the next.
John Cecil, John Fixer and three others are captured (or turned in by John Cecil, who is freed after examination).

18 (Sat.)   The first edition of Sir Philip Sidney's *Astrophel and Stella*, with the preface by Nashe, is impounded.

21 (Sat. Gregorian) Lorenzo Bernardo, Venetian Ambassador to the Porte, writes to the Doge and Senate saying that Passi has been allowed to return but predicting that he will now steer clear of politics.

October
Michael Moody writes from Flushing to Sir Thomas Heneage asking if the portrait of Arbella Stuart is ready.
Charles Paget writes to Thomas Barnes, who is employed in 'matters touching Lady Arabella [*sic*]', that he has met Thomas Morley, organist at St Paul's Cathedral (Nicholl, *Reckoning*, 342). If the implication is that he thinks Lady Arbella might be interested in this, it could mean that the Mr Morley who read to her was a relative of this Morley, rather than Marlowe.

2 (Sat. Julian, Wed. Gregorian) Michael Moody writes from Flushing to Robert Poley and to James Tipping, asking him to tell Lady Jane Percy that her mother, the Countess of Northumberland, is dead. It is Lady Jane's brother the 9th Earl whom, he will say next year, Marlowe knows well.

12 (Tues.)   Lord Burghley writes to Sir Thomas Heneage complaining that Michael Moody has extracted money from Sir Robert Sidney by promising him information about the Duke of Parma (see Nicholl, *Reckoning*, 253).

November
Michael Moody returns to Flushing with a letter from Hugh Owen to Sir Robert Sidney.
John Marlowe is selected to attend the audit of his ward, Westgate. He is also a constable of the ward in 1591–2.

8 (Mon. Julian, Fri. Gregorian) Sir Robert Sidney replies to Hugh Owen.
26 (Fri.)   Lord Burghley tells Sir Robert Sidney to cease contact with Michael Moody.
29 (Fri. Gregorian, Mon. Julian; it is unclear which is meant) A letter from the Jesuit Henry Walpole mentions that Gilbert Gifford has died in prison in Paris (see Kendall, *Christopher Marlowe*, 149).

December
James VI of Scotland writes to Arbella Stuart, his first cousin (their fathers were brothers). This is the first sign of his showing any interest in her (he claims in the letter not previously to have known where she was living) and is a mark of her new political importance. No subsequent letters are known to survive (see Gristwood, 115–16).
6 (Mon.)   The records of the court of the Stationers' Company at London record the following:

Cambridge/ Alsoe at this Courte it was motioned/ that
for quietnes to be established betwene the
Uniu'sitie of Cambridge and theire Printers
and this Companie for matters of prynting, and for
the avoidinge of divers disorders and troubles alredie
arisen and hereafter like to arise betwene the
said Partyes aboute printinge /
Yt mighte be Lawfull for the saide Uniu'sitye and
printers of Cambridge for the space of one monnethe
after the Retorne of everie ffrankford mart, to haue the
choise of anie torayne Bookes cominge from the said
marte, The same to be allowed to the saide Printers of
Cambridge and by them to be printed/

On the basis of the reference to Frankfurt here, Paul H. Kocher argued that a Cambridge printer might have obtained a copy of the German *Faustbuch* and produced an early edition of it at Cambridge, and that the translator, 'P. F.', was a Cambridge man, and suggested Peter Frenche as a possible candidate. If there was such an early edition, the only real objection to the 'early date' theory for *Doctor Faustus* is entirely removed.
20 (Mon.)   Sir Thomas Heneage signs a warrant to pay Poley for couriering letters to and from Berwick.
Christmas Lord Strange's Men give four performances at court in the course of the Christmas period.

1592

John Cranford, future husband of Marlowe's sister Ann, arrives in Canterbury. After leaving Cambridge, he has been living first in Rye in Sussex and then in Ashford in Kent.

John Udall dies in prison.

Publication of Greene's *Quip for an Upstart Courtier* and his *Repentance*.

The first mention of Sir Walter Ralegh's supposed School of Atheism can be traced to this year, with the publication of Fr Robert Persons' *Responsio ad Elizabethae edictum* ('Response to the Edict of Elizabeth'), referring to Harriot as 'Astronomo quodam necromantico' ('a certain astronomer and necromancer'), and as 'schola frequens de Atheismo' ('one who frequents a school of atheism'), summarised in English as 'Of Sir Walter Rawleys school of Atheisme by the waye, & of the Conjurer that is M[aster] thereof, and of the diligence vsed to get yong gentlemen of this schoole, where in both Moyses, & our Sauior, the ole, and the new Testatemente are iested at, and the schollers taughte, amonge other thinges, to spell God backwarde' (see Boas, *Christopher Marlowe*, 113).

Reprinting of Greene's *A Notable Discovery of Coosnage* and *The Second Part of Conny-catching* and publication of his *The Thirde and Last Part of Conny-catching*, *A Disputation betweene a Hee Conny-catcher and a Shee Conny-catcher*, and *The Black Bookes Messenger*.

Marlowe's maternal uncle Thomas Arthur is recorded as being the gaoler of Westgate prison, Canterbury.

John Marlowe quarrels with William Swaine over a gelding (Urry, 28).

John Cecil is sent by Cardinal Allen to Scotland.

Ingram Frizer, Marlowe's future killer, sues Thomas Bostock, one of the vendors of the Angel Inn, for failing to repay him £250. The case drags on until 1595.

Sir Edward Stanley, uncle of Lord Strange, is listed as a recusant.

Nicholas Breton complains that Richard Jones, the printer of *Tamburlaine*, had printed his *Bower of Delighte* 'altogether without my consent and knowledge, and many thinges of other mens mingled with a few of mine'. This might cast doubt on whether the publication of *Tamburlaine* was authorised. Also in this year a second edition of the play appears.

Publication at London of De Bellay, *Instructions for the Warre*, translated by Paul Ive, whose work Marlowe had quoted in *Tamburlaine*.

Composition of Thomas Nashe, *Summer's Last Will and Testament*.

Robert Greene, *Selimus* (argued by Peter Berek to be an imitation of *Tamburlaine*).

January

Michael Moody requests a passport from Sir Robert Sidney to return to England. He is still in Flushing in early February.

Richard Cholmeley apparently submits a report on London Catholics (see Nicholl, *Reckoning*, 269–70).

Sir Walter Ralegh receives as his new year's gift from the Queen a 99-year lease for Sherborne Castle in Dorset.

8 (Sat.)   The Earl of Essex relinquishes his command in France to Sir Roger Williams (sometimes supposed to be the original of Shakespeare's Fluellen).

26 (Wed.)   Sir Robert Sidney writes to Lord Burghley to tell him that Christopher Marlowe has been arrested in Flushing for counterfeiting money. He and Richard Baines have apparently produced one forged Dutch shilling (see Wernham). Each blames the other, and Marlowe, vouching for his own good faith and innocence, says that he is a scholar and 'says himself to be very well known both to the Earl of Northumberland and my Lord Strange'. The letter also says that Marlowe and Baines have been sharing a chamber. Marlowe, along with the goldsmith Gifford Gilbert and Evan Flud, is arrested and sent to Lord Burghley in London, escorted by Sir Robert Sidney's ensign David Lloyd. Richard Baines goes too, but only as a witness, implying that his story has been believed over Marlowe's.

February

Date given by Nicholas Skeres for his return to England from France.

3 (Fri.)   The Lord Admiral's Men, possibly in conjunction with Lord Strange's Men, are recorded as playing in Shrewsbury (see George, 233).

6 (Sun.)   First dated entry in Philip Henslowe's account book for enlarging the Rose and reconfiguring the stage area, which cost him £105 in all and continued into March (see Rutter, 47–8).

10 (Fri.)   Passports to tour abroad are issued to the Lord Admiral's Men (Wilson, 'Tragedy', 226).

19 (Sat.)   Henslowe's diary begins to record details of theatrical transactions and performances. Some plays are marked 'ne' (traditionally thought to signify a 'new' play). The first recorded is Greene's *Friar Bacon and Friar Bungay*, put on as an old play by Strange's Men and grossing 17s 3d.

20 (Sun.)   Lord Strange's Men are paid the large sum of £60 for their Christmas performances (see Rutter, 50) and put on 'Muly Mollocco' (*The Battle of Alcazar*), which grosses 29 shillings.

21 (Mon.)   Lord Strange's Men play Greene's *Orlando Furioso* at the Rose, grossing 17s 6d.

23 (Wed.)   Lord Strange's Men play the anonymous *The Spanish Comedy of Don Horatio* (presumably a spin-off of *The Spanish Tragedy*) at the Rose, grossing 13s 6d.

24 (Thurs.) Lord Strange's Men play the anonymous *Sir John Mandeville* at the Rose, grossing 12s 6d.

25 (Fri.)   Lord Strange's Men play the anonymous *Harry of Cornwall* at the Rose, grossing 32s.

26 (Sat.)   *The Jew of Malta* played at the Rose. Henslowe does not mark it 'ne', and that often indicates that it had been acted before. The takings are nevertheless 50 shillings, making it the highest-grossing performance of the week. On the same day 'mr tyllnes man' calls at the theatre for the weekly payment of 5 shillings due to Tilney for licensing the play-house. Edmund Tilney was Master of the Revels from 1581 until 1603 (nominally until 1610, but Sir George Buc was discharging the function from 1603 onwards). Though there is no reason to suppose that the visits of Mr Tilney's man were of any particular interest to Marlowe, I am noting them because they are one of the few concrete indications of a specific individual's presence in a place where Marlowe might also have been.

28 (Mon.)   Lord Strange's Men play the anonymous *Clorys and Orgasto* at the Rose, grossing 18 shillings.
            Sir Walter Ralegh's wife, Bess Throckmorton, one of the Queen's maids of honour, goes to her brother's house at Mile End to be delivered of her child in secret, since the marriage is not yet publicly known because of the Queen's dislike of her favourites marrying.

29 (Tues.) Lord Strange's Men play *The Battle of Alcazar* at the Rose, grossing 34 shillings.

March

1 (Wed.)   Robert Poley goes to Brussels. Sir Thomas Heneage signs a warrant to pay him for couriering letters.
            Lord Strange's Men play *Pope Joan* at the Rose, grossing 15 shillings.

2 (Thurs.)   Lord Strange's Men play the anonymous *Matchavell* at the Rose, grossing 14 shillings.

3 (Fri.)   Earliest recorded performance of 'harey the vi' by Strange's Men at the Rose (marked 'ne' in Henslowe's diary). This is usually identified as Shakespeare's *Henry VI*, Part One. The takings are £3 16s. 8d. Some scholars think that Marlowe may well have had a hand in the *Henry VI* plays, and it may be worth noting that Marlowe's friend Nashe had clearly seen *Henry VI*, Part One, since he writes in *Pierce Penniless*, 'How would it have joyed brave Talbot, the terror of the French, to think that after he had lain two hundred years in his tomb, he should triumph again on the stage and have his bones new embalmed with the tears of ten thousand spectators at least (at several times), who, in the tragedian that represents his person, imagine they behold him fresh bleeding!' (Nashe, 113). In the same work, Nashe also commended Edward Alleyn, who acted Tamburlaine, Barabas and Faustus (Nashe, 116).

        Burghley signs a warrant for £13 6s 8d to pay Sir Robert Sidney's ensign David Lloyd for bringing Marlowe, Gifford Gilbert and Evan Flud from Flushing.

4 (Sat.)   Lord Strange's Men play *Bindo and Richardo* at the Rose, grossing 16 shillings.

        Henslowe pays 5 shillings to 'Mr Tilney's man' in order to license plays for performance.

5 (Sun.)   Robert Poley returns from Brussels.

6 (Mon.)   Lord Strange's Men play *Four Plays in One* at the Rose, grossing 35s 6d.

7 (Tues.)   Lord Strange's Men play *Harey the VI* at the Rose, grossing £3.

8 (Wed.)   Lord Strange's Men play *The Looking Glass* at the Rose, grossing 7 shillings.

9 (Thurs.)   Lord Strange's Men play *Zenobia* at the Rose, grossing 22s 6d.

10 (Fri.)   Lord Strange's Men play *The Jew of Malta* at the Rose, grossing 56 shillings.

        Henslowe pays 5 shillings to Mr Tilney's man.

11 (Sat.)   Lord Strange's Men play *Harey the vi* at the Rose, grossing 47s 6d.

13 (Mon.)   Lord Strange's Men play *The Spanish Comedy of Don Horatio*, grossing 29 shillings.

14 (Tues.) Lord Strange's Men play *Jeronymo* (*The Spanish Tragedy*), grossing £3 15s.

16 (Thurs.) Lord Strange's Men play *Harey the vi*, grossing 31s 6d.

17 (Fri. Gregorian, Tues. Julian) Sir Henry Unton, the English ambassador in France, sends Lord Burghley a letter labelled 'To my Lord Treasurer: by Mr Marlin'. This has sometimes been identified as Marlowe, but the entry for 23 March of this year proves that it was not.

Lord Strange's Men play *The Battle of Alcazar* at the Rose, grossing 28s 6d.

Henslowe pays 5 shillings to Mr Tilney's man.

18 (Sat.) Lord Strange's Men play *The Jew of Malta* at the Rose, grossing 39 shillings.

19 (Sun.) The Privy Council issues a warrant for the arrest of Richard Cholmeley (Bakeless, 126).

20 (Mon.) Lord Strange's Men play *The Spanish Tragedy* at the Rose, grossing 38 shillings.

21 (Tues.) Lord Strange's Men play the anonymous *Constantine* at the Rose, grossing 12 shillings.

22 (Wed.) Lord Strange's Men play 'Q Jerusallem' at the Rose, grossing 18 shillings.

23 (Thurs.) Lord Burghley signs a warrant to pay William Marlin 100 shillings for bringing letters from France. The first name definitively establishes that Unton's 'Mr Marlin' was not Christopher Marlowe.

Lord Strange's Men play *Harry of Cornwall* at the Rose, grossing 13s 6d.

24 (Fri.) Good Friday. Henslowe pays 5 shillings to Mr Tilney's man.

25 (Sat.) Lady Day. Start of the Elizabethan new year.

Lord Strange's Men play *Friar Bacon and Friar Bungay* at the Rose, grossing 15s 6d.

26 (Sun.) Easter Sunday.

27 (Mon.) Lord Strange's Men play *The Looking Glass* at the Rose, grossing 55 shillings.

28 (Tues.) Lord Strange's Men play *Harey the vi* at the Rose, grossing £3 8s. Henslowe's diary records several more payments for repairs to the Rose (see Rutter, 49). He also pays 5 shillings to Mr Tilney's man.

29 (Wed. Julian) Lord Strange's Men play *The Battle of Alcazar* at the Rose, grossing £3 2s.

Sir Walter Ralegh's wife Bess gives birth to a son, Damerei, a name which hints at royal blood in Ralegh's family tree since it was the name of an ancestor, Damerei Clare, who was of Plantagent descent (see Lacey, 167).

29 (Sun. Gregorian) Gregorian Easter Sunday.

30 (Thurs. Julian) Lord Strange's Men play *The Spanish Comedy of Don Horatio* at the Rose, grossing 39 shillings.

31 (Fri.) Lord Strange's Men play *The Spanish Tragedy* at the Rose, grossing £3.

April

By this month the second edition on Sir Philip Sidney's *Astrophel and Stella*, minus the preface by Nashe, has been brought out.

Also in this month Elizabeth I hears privately of reverses in Henri IV's Breton campaigns, though the news is suppressed, and of the Duke of Parma forces the lifting of the siege of Rouen (Doran, 41).

1 (Sat.) Lord Strange's Men play *Sir John Mandeville* at the Globe, grossing 30 shillings.

3 (Mon.) *Arden of Faversham* entered in the Stationers' Register by Edward White. The play, which was published later in the year, shows a clear debt to *Edward II* (see Tucker Brooke, 376), and has occasionally been attributed to Marlowe, not least because it was set in his home county of Kent. However, its bourgeois setting makes it very different from the rest of his work.

Lord Strange's Men play *Matchevell* at the Rose, grossing 22 shillings.

4 (Tues.) Lord Strange's Men play *The Jew of Malta* at the Rose, grossing 43 shillings.

5 (Wed.) Lord Strange's Men play *Harey the vi* at the Rose, grossing 41 shillings.

6 (Thurs.) Lord Strange's Men play 'brandymer' at the Rose, grossing 22 shillings.

7 (Fri.) Lord Strange's Men play *The Spanish Tragedy* at the Rose, grossing 26 shillings.

Henslowe pays 5 shillings to Mr Tilney's man.

8 (Sat.) Lord Strange's Men play *The Battle of Alcazar* at the Rose, grossing 23 shillings.

10 (Mon.) Lord Strange's Men play *The Spanish Tragedy* at the Rose, grossing 28 shillings.

Sir Walter Ralegh's son Damerei is secretly baptised, with the Earl of Essex as godfather. This is presumably attributable to Ralegh's wish to have powerful friends on his side, but serves as a reminder that Ralegh and Essex were not always at odds.

11 (Tues.)   Lord Strange's Men play a new play, *Titus and Vespasian*, at the Rose, grossing £3 4s.

12 (Wed.)   Lord Strange's Men play *Bindo and Richardo* at the Rose, grossing 23 shillings.

13 (Thurs.) Lord Strange's Men play *Harey the vi* at the Rose, grossing 26 shillings.

14 (Fri.)   Lord Strange's Men play *The Spanish Tragedy* at the Rose, grossing 33 shillings.
            Henslowe pays 5 shillings to Mr Tilney's man.

15 (Sat.)   Lord Strange's Men play *Sir John Mandeville* at the Rose, grossing 26 shillings.

21 (Fri.)   Lord Strange's Men play *Harey the vi* at the Rose, grossing 33 shillings.
            Henslowe pays 5 shillings to Mr Tilney's man.
            Defence of Conny-Catching entered in the Stationers' Register. This purports to be a confutation of Greene but Nicholl argues that it is the result of a collaboration between him and Nashe (Nicholl, *Cup*, 126–7).

22 (Sat.)   Lord Strange's Men play 'the comodye Jeronymo' (presumably *The Spanish Comedy of Don Horatio*) at the Rose, grossing 17 shillings.

24 (Mon.)   Lord Strange's Men play 'Jeronymo' (presumably *The Spanish Tragedy*) at the Rose, grossing 28 shillings.

25 (Tues.) Lord Strange's Men play *Jerusalem* at the Rose, grossing 46 shillings.

26 (Wed.)   Lord Strange's Men play *Friar Bacon and Friar Bungay* at the Rose, grossing 24 shillings.

27 (Thurs.) Lord Strange's Men play *The Battle of Alcazar* at the Rose, grossing 26 shillings.
            Sir Walter Ralegh's wife, Bess, returns to court, having left her baby with a wet nurse and thus far successfully concealed his existence.

28 (Fri.)   Lord Strange's Men play a new play, *The Second Part of Tamar Cham* (a derivative of *Tamburlaine*) at the Rose, grossing £3 4s.
            Henslowe pays 5 shillings to Mr Tilney's man.

29 (Sat.)   Lord Strange's Men play *Harry of Cornwall* at the Rose, grossing 26 shillings.
30 (Sun.)   Lord Strange's Men play *The Battle of Alcazar* at the Rose, grossing 58 shillings.

May

The *English Faust Book, The Historie of the damnable life, and deserved death of Doctor John Faustus*, translated from the German by 'P. F., Gent.', is entered in the Stationers' Register by Abel Jeffes and is printed later that year by Thomas Orwin. If this is indeed the first actual printing of it rather than merely the first *known* printing, the 'late date' theory for *Doctor Faustus* would have to be accepted. However, Orwin's title-page refers to the text being 'newly imprinted, and in convenient places imperfect matter amended', which seems to suggest that there had been an earlier edition.

Imprisonment of Giordano Bruno in Venice.

Date at the end of the epistle dedicatory of John Stow's *The Annals of England* (a new edition of his *Chronicles*), which Marlowe consulted for *Edward II* (see Thomas and Tydeman, 343).

2 (Tues.)   Lord Strange's Men play *The Spanish Tragedy* at the Rose, grossing 34 shillings.
3 (Wed.)   Lord Strange's Men play *Titus and Vespasian* at the Rose, grossing 57s 6d.
4 (Thurs.)   John Wolfe enters in the Stationers' Register *Twooe discourses to be joyned in one booke, The one a true relacon of the Frenche kinges good successe against the Duke of Parma, the other of a certen mountaine borninge in the Isle of Palme five or sixe weeks.*
Lord Strange's Men play *Harey the vi* at the Rose, grossing 56 shillings.
5 (Fri.)   Lord Strange's Men play *The Jew of Malta* at the Rose, grossing 41 shillings.
Henslowe pays 5 shillings to Mr Tilney's man.
6 (Sat.)   Lord Strange's Men play *Friar Bacon and Friar Bungay* at the Rose, grossing 14 shillings.
Sir Walter Ralegh sets sail from Falmouth but is almost immediately recalled, perhaps because his marriage has been discovered. The secret is certainly out before the end of the month though the Queen seems to have been playing a double game of feigning ignorance of the marriage in the hope that Ralegh would tell her himself.

7 (Sun.)   (or Tues. 9 May – there appears to be a confusion in Henslowe's diary) Lord Strange's Men play *Harey the vi* at the Rose, grossing 22 shillings.

8 (Mon.)   Lord Strange's Men play either 'brandimer' at the Rose, grossing 24 shillings, or *Titus and Vespasian*, grossing 30 shillings (again there is a confusion in Henslowe's diary).

9 (Tues.)   Marlowe bound over in the sum of £20 to keep the peace towards Allen Nicholls, Constable of Holywell Street, Shoreditch, and Nicholas Helliott, beadle, and to appear at the General Sessions in October. It is not known what moved Nicholls and Helliot to this suit.

Lord Strange's Men play *The Spanish Tragedy* at the Rose, grossing 26 shillings.

10 (Wed.)   Lord Strange's Men play *The Second Part of Tamar Cham* at the Rose, grossing 37 shillings.

Henslowe pays 5 shillings to Mr Tilney's man.

11 (Thurs.) Lord Strange's Men play *The Jew of Malta* at the Rose, grossing 34 shillings.

13 (Sat.)   Lord Strange's Men play *The Spanish Tragedy* at the Rose, grossing £3 4s.

Henslowe pays 5 shillings to Mr Tilney's man.

14 (Sun.)   Whitsunday. Lord Strange's Men play *Harey the vi* at the Rose, grossing 50 shillings.

15 (Mon.)   Lord Strange's Men play *Titus and Vespasian* at the Rose, grossing £3.

16 (Tues.)   Lord Strange's Men play *Sir John Mandeville* at the Rose, grossing 40 shillings.

17 (Wed.)   Lord Strange's Men play *The Battle of Alcazar* at the Rose, grossing 36s 6d.

18 (Thurs.) Lord Strange's Men play *Harry of Cornwall* at the Rose, grossing 26 shillings.

19 (Fri.)   Lord Strange's Men play *Harey the vi* at the Rose, grossing 30 shillings.

20 (Sat.)   Lord Strange's Men play *The Jew of Malta* at the Rose, grossing 54 shillings.

Henslowe pays 5 shillings to Mr Tilney's man.

21 (Sun.)   Lord Strange's Men play *The Spanish Comedy of Don Horatio* at the Rose, grossing 28 shillings.

22 (Mon.)   Lord Strange's Men play *The Spanish Tragedy* at the Rose, grossing 27 shillings.

23 (Tues.)   Sir Robert Cecil writes to Sir Thomas Heneage asking him if he knows where Robert Poley is.

Lord Strange's Men play a new play, *The Tanner of Denmark*,
at the Rose, grossing £3 13s 6d.

24 (Wed.) Lord Strange's Men play *Titus and Vespasian* at the Rose,
grossing 30 shillings.

25 (Thurs.) Lord Strange's Men play *Harey the vi* at the Rose, grossing
24 shillings.

26 (Fri.) Sir Robert Cecil writes to Sir Thomas Heneage telling him
that he has now spoken to Robert Poley.
Lord Strange's Men play *Tamar Cham* at the Rose, grossing
36s 6d.

27 (Sat.) Lord Strange's Men play *The Spanish Tragedy* at the Rose,
grossing 23 shillings.

29 (Mon.) Lord Strange's Men play *Matchevell* at the Rose, grossing
26 shillings.

30 (Tues.) Lord Strange's Men play *The Jew of Malta* at the Rose, grossing 33 shillings.

31 (Wed.) Lord Strange's Men play *The Battle of Alcazar* at the Rose,
grossing 23 shillings.
Sir Walter Ralegh is arrested by Sir Robert Cecil as a result of
his clandestine marriage, but is allowed to return to
Durham House, and enters a period of limbo.

May–July
Nashe is composing *Pierce Penniless* (see Nicholl, *Cup*, 89).

June
1 (Thurs.) Robert Poley leaves the court at Greenwich for Berwick-
upon-Tweed.

3 (Sat.) Lady Ralegh is arrested.

5 (Mon.) Lord Strange's Men play *Bindo and Richardo* at the Rose,
grossing 32 shillings.

6 (Tues.) Lord Strange's Men play *Titus and Vespasian* at the Rose,
grossing 42 shillings.

7 (Wed.) Lord Strange's Men play *The Looking Glass* at the Rose,
grossing 29 shillings.

8 (Thurs.) Lord Strange's Men play *Tamar Cham* at the Rose, grossing
40 shillings.

9 (Fri.) Lord Strange's Men play *The Spanish Tragedy* at the Rose,
grossing 28 shillings.
Henslowe pays 5 shillings to Mr Tilney's man.

10 (Sat.) According to Henslowe, this date saw the first performance
of *A Knack to Know a Knave*, which, Curt Zimansky argued,

is influenced by *Doctor Faustus*. Zimansky argued that Marlowe *must* therefore have had access to an edition of the *English Faust Book* published earlier than the one licensed in May of this year. *A Knack to Know a Knave* grossed £3 12s. Since Henslowe unusually does not give the precise date, there is a slim possibility that the performance could in fact have taken place on Sunday, 11 June, but it would be very unusual for Lord Strange's Men to give a Sunday performance and not a Saturday one, whereas performances on Sunday (though by no means unknown) were illegal. However, see the following entry for possible evidence for a Sunday date.

11 (Sun.)   There is a riot at a playhouse, according to a letter written the following day by Sir William Webbe, Lord Mayor of London, to Lord Burghley (see Rutter, 61–2).

12 (Mon.)   Lord Strange's Men play *Harey the vi* at the Rose, grossing 32 shillings.

13 (Tues.)   Lord Strange's Men play *The Battle of Alcazar* at the Rose, grossing 20 shillings.

14 (Wed.)   Lord Strange's Men play *The Jew of Malta* at the Rose, grossing 38 shillings.
Henslowe pays 5 shillings to Mr Tilney's man.
By this date Richard Harvey has seen much of the manuscript of Nashe's *Pierce Penniless* (see Nicholl, *Cup*, 89).

15 (Thurs.) Lord Strange's Men play *A Knack to Know a Knave* at the Rose, grossing 52 shillings.

16 (Fri.)   Lord Strange's Men play *Sir John Mandeville* at the Rose, grossing 20 shillings.

18 (Sun.)   Lord Strange's Men play *The Spanish Tragedy* at the Rose, grossing 24 shillings.

19 (Mon.)   Lord Strange's Men play *Harey the vi* at the Rose, grossing 31 shillings.
A Catholic called Charles Chester, who lives near Chester, is arrested. Nashe refers to this event (see Nashe, 87–9) and Ben Jonson may glance at Chester in his character Carlo Buffone in *Every Man out of his Humour*. Charles Nicholl suggests that Chester was arrested at the behest of his erstwhile friend Sir Walter Ralegh, about whom he had been gossiping, and whose affairs were currently at a crisis because of the discovery of his secret marriage to Bess Throckmorton (see Nicholl, *Cup*, 104–5).

20 (Tues.) Lord Strange's Men play *The Spanish Comedy of Don Horatio* at the Rose, grossing 15 shillings.
21 (Wed.) Lord Strange's Men play *Tamar Cham* at the Rose, grossing 32 shillings.
22 (Thurs.) Lord Strange's Men play *A Knack to Know a Knave* at the Rose, grossing 27 shillings.
23 (Fri.) Sir Thomas Heneage signs a warrant to pay Poley for couriering letters to and from Berwick.
Because of plague and concern about public order (particularly rumours that apprentices plan trouble at midsummer), London theatres are ordered to close until 28 September, although in fact the restraint was to last well beyond that. Playwrights and actors will have to look for alternative livelihoods, or go on tour (see Rutter, 62).
27 (Tues.) The Queen formally confirms her gift of Sherborne Castle to Ralegh. It looks as though he is being given an opportunity to mollify her during this period, but he does not take it.
29 (Thurs.) A plea roll in Canterbury civil court mentions John Benchkin as still a student at Cambridge at this date. By November he is back in Canterbury as an admitted freeman (Kuriyama, *Christopher Marlowe*, xvii).

July
Gabriel Harvey's brother John dies in London, presumably because of the plague which is now raging.
John Marlowe is rebuked for failing to maintain the butts in his ward of Westgate and failing to inspect the small arms kept in the ward.
13 (Thurs.) A warrant for paying Lord Strange's Men for performing issued by the Canterbury Chamberlain shows that they were touring Kent at this period (see Rutter, 63).
26 (Wed.) Arthur Gorges writes to Sir Robert Cecil that 'Sir W. Ralegh will shortly grow to be Orlando Furioso if the bright Angelica [i.e. the Queen] persevere against him a little longer' (see Lacey, 170).
31 (Mon.) Bess of Hardwick, Countess of Shrewsbury, sets off for London from Derbyshire and her granddaughter, Arbella Stuart, follows shortly after (see Gristwood, 118). Arbella may have expected to return to court shortly, but in fact she is to become a virtual prisoner at her grandmother's house, Hardwick Hall, principally because Sir William

Stanley, betrayer of Deventer, is rumoured to have been plotting to put her on the throne (Gristwood, 124).

August

Gabriel Harvey arrives in London to sort out the affairs of his late brother, John. He stays apparently at the house of John Wolfe in St Paul's Churchyard. This is where booksellers have their stalls and Marlowe is likely to frequent it. John Wolfe will later enter Marlowe's *Hero and Leander* in the Stationers' Register and has recently been printing news from France.

John Dee and Thomas Hariot have a meeting.

The Queen 'discovers' Sir Walter Ralegh's secret marriage. Ralegh falls from favour.

4–6 (Fri.–Sun.) Canterbury fair held.

7 (Mon.)   Sir Walter Ralegh and his wife are sent to the Tower.

8 (Tues.)   *Pierce Penniless* is entered in the Stationers' Register. It carries a dedication to Lord Strange, whom Nashe calls 'Amyntas'. Nashe's extremely bawdy poem *The Choice of Valentines*, also known as 'Nashe's Dildo', which was also dedicated to Lord Strange, may well belong to this year too (see Nicholl, *Cup*, 90).

24 (Thurs.) St Bartholomew's Day, marking the start of Bartholomew Fair, which ran for ten days.

September

There are fears of a Spanish landing in Scotland.

Thomas Nashe is now in the service of the Archbishop of Canterbury at Croydon, where he composes *Summers Last Will and Testament*.

1 (Fri.)   Gabriel Harvey arrives in London (see Nicholl, *Cup*, 130).

3 (Sun.)   Death of Robert Greene. Later in the month publication of his *Groats-worth of Witte*, which includes the words 'Wonder not ... thou famous gracer of Tragedians, that *Greene*, who hath said with thee (like the foole in his heart) There is no God', can only be a reference to Marlowe, and publicly identifies him as an atheist.
            Sir Thomas Heneage signs a warrant to pay Robert Poley for a trip to Antwerp.

4 (Mon.)   Burial of Robert Greene.

6 (Wed.)   The Thames dries up.

7 (Thurs.) Probable date of publication of Harvey's pamphlet inveighing against Greene.

8 (Fri.)   Publication of Thomas Nashe, *Pierce Pennilesse*. Along with
Gabriel Harvey's *Foure Letters* and Nashe's own *Strange
Newes*, both also published this year, this established the
alias of 'Pierce' for Nashe, on the basis of which Paul
Kocher argued that the phrase 'A per se a' suggested that
Nashe was responsible for the prose scenes in the 'A' text of
Doctor Faustus (see Kocher, 'Nashe's Authorship', 23). *Pierce
Pennilesse* contains the lines 'I heare say that there be
Mathematicians abroad, that will prove men before Adam'
(Nashe, 68); this comes close to one of the opinions later
attributed in the Baines Note to Marlowe (see Nicholl, *Cup*,
106–7), and 'Mathematicians' presumably glances at Hariot
and Walter Warner. Nashe also criticises Spenser for not
including Lord Strange in his catalogue of English heroes in
The Faerie Queene (Nashe, 143). In this Nashe may show
knowledge of Chapman's *Shadow of Night* in manuscript
(Nicholl, *Cup*, 108–9), and satirises the Earl of Leicester,
perhaps because he, as a protector of Puritans, can be seen
as similar to Sir Walter Ralegh (Nicholl, *Cup*, 112–15). This
might cast an interesting light on the notably favourable
treatment which Marlowe's *Edward II* gives to its Earl of
Leicester. Nicholl suggests that, on the whole, *Pierce Penniless* in particular, and Nashe's political writing in general,
could well be read as suggesting that he had Catholic sym-
pathies (Nicholl, *Cup*, 118).
A Spanish carrock, the *Madre de Dios*, is brought into Dart-
mouth. Fear that her rich cargo will be totally looted by the
locals prompts the Queen to release Sir Walter Ralegh from
the Tower and dispatch him to deal with it. Although he is
afterwards imprisoned again, he and his wife are perman-
ently released by Christmas.

12 (Tues.) Gabriel Harvey completes the fourth of his *Fowre Letters*.
On or around this date, Robert Poley leaves to carry letters
to Dover. Constance Kuriyama suggests that Marlowe may
have travelled with him or also been en route to Dover.

15 (Fri.)   Marlowe is involved in a street fight with the Canterbury
tailor William Corkine near the corner of High Street and
Mercery Lane in Canterbury. Marlowe is arrested and 12d
'mainprise' is paid by his father to redeem him from jail.

16 (Sat.)   Date on the preface of Gabriel Harvey's *Fowre Letters and
Certain Sonnets*, which was published around the end of the

month. This denounces Nashe as well as Greene, and compares Marlowe to the notoriously licentious Italian poet Aretino.

21 (Thurs.) Bess of Hardwick, Countess of Shrewsbury, writes to Lord Burghley about her granddaughter Arbella Stuart, referring to 'One Morley, who hath attended on Arabella [*sic*] and read to her for the space of three year and a half, showed to be much discontented since my return into the country, in saying he had lived in hope of having some annuity granted him by Arabella out of her land, or some lease of grounds to the value of £40 a year, alleging that he was so much damnified by leaving of the University ... I understanding by divers that Morley was so much discontented, and withal of late having some cause to be doubtful of his forwardness in religion (though I cannot charge him with papistry), took occasion to part with him. After he was gone from my house, and his stuff carried from hence, the next day he returned again, very importunate to serve' (Nicholl, *Reckoning*, 341).

As the first cousin of James VI of Scotland and a descendant of Margaret Tudor, Arbella had a claim to the thrones of both England and Scotland, and was thus a personage of the highest importance politically. It is unlikely that this Morley was Marlowe, but it does not currently appear to be impossible: Nicholl ruled it out primarily on the grounds that a lengthy stay in Derbyshire would be incompatible with Marlowe's known presence in London for some of the relevant period, but at least one of Arbella's two surviving letters from this period comes from London. It may also be noteworthy that in a letter that she was subsequently to write on 4 March 1592, Arbella quoted a tag from Lucan's *Pharsalia*, which Marlowe had translated (Gristwood, 224).

24 (Sun.)   On or around this date, Poley returns from Dover.

25 (Mon.)   Corkine sues Marlowe.

Sir Thomas Heneage signs a warrant at Oxford to pay Poley for couriering letters between Dover and Oxford while the Queen was staying at Christ Church.

26 (Tues.) Marlowe's counter-suit against Corkine is heard at the Quarter Sessions.

Marlowe's friend Thomas Watson is buried at St Bartholomew the Less.

29 (Fri., week beginning) Marlowe is due to appear at the General Sessions of the Peace for Middlesex, but does not do so.

October

Robert Poley returns to Scotland with letters for the Court.

1 (Sun.) The Privy Council decides to postpone the Michaelmas law term because of the plague. It does not commence until November.

2 (Mon.) The civil case of *Corkine v Marlowe* is heard. The case is adjourned.

9 (Mon.) The case of *Corkine v Marlowe* is dropped. This is the last known mention of Marlowe's presence in Canterbury.

11 (Wed.) Gabriel Harvey is granted administration of the estate of his late brother John. Nashe will later refer scathingly to the harsh way in which Harvey treated his brother's widow.

22 (Sun.) Edward Alleyn marries Joan Woodward, stepdaughter of Philip Henslowe, who owned the Rose playhouse.

29 (Sun.) The Catholic propagandist Richard Verstegan reports that Sir Robert Sidney has burned almost all his books and fears damnation (see Nicholl, *Reckoning*, 381).

Autumn

Publication at London of Thomas Watson, *Amintae Gaudia*, with a posthumous dedication to the Countess of Pembroke signed 'C. M.'. Mary Sidney, Countess of Pembroke, was a famous patron of literature and the sister of Sir Philip Sidney (and also of Sir Robert Sidney who had arrested Marlowe in Flushing). The friendship between Watson and Marlowe makes it very probable that 'C. M.' was Christopher Marlowe, especially since, having fallen out with Lord Strange at some stage after the staging of *Massacre at Paris*, Marlowe will have his last play, *Edward II*, put on by the Earl of Pembroke's Men. However, Constance Kuriyama suggests that 'C. M.' stands for Christopher Morley, who she thinks may have been the brother of William Byrd's protégé Thomas Morley and thus known to Watson through the Byrd connection, and whom she also suggests as the tutor of Arbella Stuart (*Christopher Marlowe*, 88–9).

The campaign against Rouen, led by Essex on behalf of Henri IV, fails, with the loss of Essex's younger brother Walter Devereux.

Also during this year the travelling diary of a Würtemberg merchant, now no longer extant, is claimed to have recorded the performance of several plays by 'the famous Herr Christopher Marlowe' at the Frankfort autumn fair (see Brooke, 'Reputation', 381). This seems rather too good to be true, and is certainly no longer verifiable.

November
The Richard Baines who is rector of Waltham performs two christenings and four burials there (see Kendall, *Christopher Marlowe*, 317).

3 (Fri.)   The postponed Michaelmas Term begins at Hertford.

8 (Wed.)   Lord Buckhurst writes to Sir John Puckering about Thomas Drury (see Kendall, 'Richard Baines', 540).

10 (Fri.)   Thomas Watson's *Amintae Gaudia* is entered in the Stationers' Register.

12 (Sun.)   Another letter from Buckhurst mentions Drury again, this time in conjunction with Lord North, almost certainly Roger North. North was the stepbrother of Alice Arden, whose murder of her husband is dramatised in the anonymous *Arden of Faversham*, sometimes wholly or party attributed to Marlowe. (See Kendall, *Christopher Marlowe*, 248–9.)

17 (Fri.)   Accession Day.

19 (Sun.)   Arthur Throckmorton, brother of Sir Walter Ralegh's wife Bess, records in his diary that this was the day he first learned of his sister's secret marriage to Ralegh.

20 (Mon.) *Soliman and Perseda* licensed. This tells the story referred to in the subplot of Kyd's *The Spanish Tragedy*, which cannot be securely dated, but may well belong to the period of Kyd's friendship with Marlowe. It is unclear whether *Soliman and Perseda* is itself by Kyd.

December
Death of the Prince of Parma.

8 (Fri.)   Henry Chettle, *Kind Heart's Dream*, entered in the Stationers' Register and published shortly afterwards. Noting that Marlowe and Shakespeare have both been offended by Greene's references to them in Greene's *Groatsworth of Wit*, in whose publication he had been involved, Chettle remarks, 'With neither of them that take offence was I acquainted, and with one of them I care not if I neuer be ... For the first [i.e. Marlowe], whose learning I reuerence, and, at the perusing of Greene's book, stroke out what then in conscience I thought he in some displeasure writ, or, had it beene true, yet to publish it was intollerable, him I would

wish to vse me no worse than I deserue'. Chettle also has the ghost of Greene exhorting Nashe to retaliate more energetically against Gabriel Harvey.

14 (Thurs.) Anne Burnell, whom Thomas Watson had encouraged in her delusion that she was the King of Spain's daughter, is whipped through the City of London (see Nicholl, *Reckoning*, 185–6).

Robert Poley returns to Hampton Court.

Death of Sir Roger Manwood, on whom Marlowe seems to have written a Latin epitaph.

16 (Sat.) Robert Poley is paid £43. Shortly afterwards he leaves for Scotland again.

18 (Mon.) A ballad on the whipping of Anne Burnell is entered in the Stationers' Register.

The following entry appears in the Court of the Stationers' Company:

Abell Ieffes	Yt is ordered: that if the book of Dcor ffaustus shall not
Tho. Orwin	be found in the [bch] hall book entred to Richard Oliff before Abell Ieffes claymed the same wch was about May last. That then the seid copie shall Remayne to the said Abell as his prop. copie from the tyme of his first clayme wch was about May last as aforesaid.

This seems to imply that one Richard Oliff had a prior claim on the *English Faust Book* before Jeffes entered it in the Stationers' Register in the previous May, and presumably, therefore, that it was already extant.

Arrest of Giordano Bruno. He is imprisoned in the Castel' Sant Angelo in Rome.

26 (Tues.) Lord Burghley's agent Ralph Birkenshaw has his ears cut off in Flushing (see Nicholl, *Reckoning*, 247). This indicates the very real danger in which Marlowe had probably been when he was arrested there, and perhaps also the diminishing tolerance for English spies in Flushing.

27 (Wed.) The Earl of Pembroke's Men, who would next year stage *Edward II*, are paid for performing at court.

Lord Strange's Men perform at Hampton Court.

29 (Fri.) Lord Strange's Men return to the Rose, playing *The Battle of Alcazar* and grossing £3 10s.

30 (Sat.)   Lord Strange's Men play *The Spanish Tragedy* at the Rose, grossing £3 8s.

31 (Sun.)   Lord Strange's Men play *A Knack to Know a Knave* at the Rose, grossing 30 shillings.

1593

This was the year during which, William Vaughan later claimed, Marlowe wrote a book against the Trinity.

Publication of the 'Wagner book', a sequel to the German *Faustbuch* (see Jones, 10).

Lord Burghley's agent Thomas Webbe is charged with coining, as Marlowe and Baines had been.

Death of Sir Thomas Perrot, husband of Lady Dorothy Devereux.

Fortunatus Greene, bastard son of Robert Greene, buried at Shoreditch.

The Earl of Northumberland gives Thomas Hariot £24, a substantial sum for the time and an indication of considerable favour.

Robert Poley acts as the executor of the will of Rose Crayford, widow of Shoreditch.

January

Death of the father of Drew Woodleff, who will later complain of having been subsequently swindled by Nicholas Skeres at some time after the death of his father.

The Richard Baines who is rector of Waltham performs two christenings and a marriage there (see Kendall, *Christopher Marlowe*, 317).

1 (Mon.)   Lord Strange's Men perform *The Jew of Malta* at the Rose, grossing 56 shillings. They also perform at Hampton Court the same evening.

3 (Wed.)   Lord Strange's Men perform *A Knack to Know a Knave* at the Rose, grossing 29 shillings.

4 (Thurs.) Lord Strange's Men play *Sir John Mandeville* at the Rose, grossing 12 shillings.

5 (Fri.)   Lord Strange's men perform a new play, 'the gelyous comodey', at the Rose, grossing 44 shillings.

6 (Sat.)   Pembroke's Men perform at court.
           Robert Poley returns to Hampton Court. Sir Thomas Heneage signs a warrant to pay for him for going to Scotland.
           Lord Strange's Men play *Titus and Vespasian* at the Rose, grossing 52 shillings.

8 (Mon.)   Lord Strange's Men play *The Spanish Tragedy* at the Rose, grossing 22 shillings.

9 (Tues.) Lord Strange's Men play *The Battle of Alcazar* at the Rose, grossing 20 shillings.

10 (Wed.) Lord Strange's Men play *Friar Bacon and Friar Bungay* at the Rose, grossing 24 shillings.

12 (Fri.) Lord Strange's Men play 'the comodey of cosmo' at the Rose, grossing 44 shillings.
           Nashe's *Strange Newes* is entered in the Stationers' Register.

13 (Sat.) Lord Strange's Men play *Sir John Mandeville* at the Rose, grossing 9 shillings.

14 (Sun.) Lord Strange's Men play *A Knack to Know a Knave* at the Rose, grossing 24 shillings.

15 (Mon.) Lord Strange's Men play *Titus and Vespasian* at the Rose, grossing 30 shillings.

16 (Tues.) Lord Strange's Men play *Harey the vi* at the Rose, grossing 46 shillings.

17 (Wed.) Lord Strange's Men play *Friar Bacon and Friar Bungay* at the Rose, grossing 20 shillings.

18 (Thurs.) Lord Strange's Men play *The Jew of Malta* at the Rose, grossing £3.

19 (Fri.) Lord Strange's Men play *Tamar Cham* at the Rose, grossing 36 shillings.

20 (Sat.) Lord Strange's Men play *The Battle of Alcazar* at the Rose, grossing 20 shillings.

22 (Mon.) Lord Strange's Men play *The Spanish Tragedy* at the Rose, grossing 20 shillings.

23 (Tues.) Lord Strange's Men play *Cosmo* at the Rose, grossing 30 shillings.

24 (Wed.) Lord Strange's Men play *A Knack to Know a Knave* at the Rose, grossing 24 shillings.

25 (Thurs.) Lord Strange's Men play *Titus and Vespasian* at the Rose, grossing 30 shillings.

? 26 (Fri.) 'the tragedye of the gvyes' – i.e. *The Massacre at Paris* – is played by Lord Strange's Men at the Rose and noted by Henslowe as 'ne'. The takings were £3 14s. Henslowe's diary actually gives the date as 30 January, but there seems to be a misnumbering here and the actual performance was almost certainly earlier (see Rutter, 68–9). In the few remaining days before plague shut the playhouses, Lord Strange's Men played *Sir John Mandeville*, grossing 12 shillings, *Friar Bacon* and *Friar Bungay*, grossing 12 shillings, *Harey the vi*, grossing 26 shillings, and *The Jew of Malta*, grossing 35 shillings. Misnumbering in Henslowe's diary makes it difficult to establish the exact sequence, but it seems clear that *The Jew of Malta* was the last play performed, and thus almost certainly the last performance of a Marlowe play during his lifetime.

28 (Sun.)   The Privy Council recommends the closing of the playhouses on account of plague.

February

The Earl of Essex is appointed to the Privy Council. Essex had worked hard to engineer this as it would give him greater power and prestige. Scholars who see Essex as responsible for Marlowe's death often see this as the starting point of the 'conspiracy' against Marlowe, and generally consider Marlowe to have been a pawn in Essex's struggle against his enemy, Ralegh.

During this month, Thomas Nashe is at Conington in Huntingdonshire, as the guest of Sir Robert Cotton, and is composing *The Terrors of the Night* there (see Nicholl, *Cup*, 146).

The Richard Baines who is rector of Waltham performs a burial there (see Kendall, *Christopher Marlowe*, 317). This is the last burial he performs until July, which might seem to indicate an absence, though in a small parish it could simply mean that there were no deaths during the period.

1 (Thurs.)   Henslowe's diary entries cease, presumably because of the closing of the playhouses due to plague.

4 (Sun.)   John White writes a letter to a friend from Sir Walter Ralegh's estates in Ireland. Nothing further is heard of him (see Stevens, 71).

12 (Mon.)   Sir Thomas Heneage signs a warrant to pay Poley for couriering letters to and from the Low Countries.

17 (Sat.)   A coffin with the remains of a Separatist, Roger Rippon, is carried by protesters from Newgate to Cheapside, to the house of Justice Richard Young. Riggs (315) dates to this the subsequent religious crackdown which he thinks brought Marlowe to his death.

March

Robert Poley is in Scotland again.

John Mathews, later to be known as Christopher Marler, takes his BA at Trinity College, Cambridge.

John Penry is arrested in London for his part in the Martin Marprelate pamphlets.

The Richard Baines who is rector of Waltham performs three christenings there (see Kendall, *Christopher Marlowe*, 317).

Parliament debates the extent of the economic privileges to be allowed to immigrants.

4 (Sun.) Twenty-six sectarians are arrested by Archbishop Whitgift's Court of High Commission for Ecclesiastical Causes, seen by Riggs as evidence that the search for religious nonconformity of whatever sort is intensifying and that the net is therefore tightening around Marlowe.

7 (Wed.) Lord Strange's Men are paid £30 for several unidentified performances given at court over the Christmas period, a valuable financial lifeline during the closure of the theatres.

19 (Mon.) The Privy Council issues a warrant for the arrest of Richard Cholmeley and Richard Strange.

21 (Wed.) The House of Commons votes to extend the privileges of resident aliens, overruling the objections of Sir Walter Ralegh. According to some theories, the resulting unrest will be an important factor in Marlowe's death.

Archbishop Whitgift indicts two Puritans, Henry Barrow and John Greenwood. In 1581 Marlowe had allowed John Greenwood, a former Corpus man, to eat in Hall in his place.

22 (Thurs.) Arrest of the Puritan pamphleteer John Penry, an associate of Greenwood, whom Archbishop Whitgift believed to be responsible for the Marprelate tracts.

23 (Fri.) Lady Day. Start of the Elizabethan new year.

Robert Poley returns from Scotland. Sir Thomas Heneage signs a warrant to pay him for having gone there 'for her heighnes speciall and secret affayres of great importaunce' (Boas, *Christopher Marlowe*, 266).

Arrest of two Separatist leaders, Henry Barrow and John Greenwood, and of the printers who had published their work.

24 (Sat.) Last of the 'Stranger' debates in Parliament.

26 (Mon.) The Queen creates a new Royal Commission to seek out religious deviants, counterfeiters, and vagrants.

April

The Richard Baines who is rector of Waltham performs two christenings there (see Kendall, *Christopher Marlowe*, 317). These are the last he performs there until July.

6 (Fri.)   Greenwood and Barrow are hanged.

15 (Sun.)   Easter Sunday.

16 (Mon)   Easter Monday. In the wake of the extension of the privileges of resident alients, the Privy Council write a letter to the Lord Mayor of London worrying that one anti-stranger 'placard' had already appeared and that others would follow.

18 (Sun., Gregorian) Gregorian Easter Sunday.

18 (Wed.)   Shakespeare's *Venus and Adonis* is entered in the Stationers' Register by Richard Field. *Venus and Adonis*, like Marlowe's *Hero and Leander*, is an epyllion – a comic short epic poem on love – but it is not clear which came first. The publication of *Venus and Adonis* may suggest that *Hero and Leander* was already being read in manuscript and that Shakespeare was anxious to emulate it; alternatively, Marlowe may have started work on *Hero and Leander* in the last weeks of his life as a response to *Venus and Adonis*, and his death shortly after would explain why it appears unfinished (though some critics argue that Marlowe meant to end where he did).

22 (Sun.)   The Privy Council appoints Dr Julius Caesar, Master of the Court of Requests, to lead a five-man commission to investigate the authorship of the writings against the 'strangers' – i.e. foreign residents – 'by secret means'. The committee included William Waad and Thomas Phelippes, both Walsingham men.

26 (Thurs.) Nicholas Skeres, charged with extortion before the Star Chamber, testifies that Matthew Roydon shares a debt of £150 to John Wolfall, and says Roydon is lodging in the Blackfriars.

27 (Fri.)   Date which appears at the end of Gabriel Harvey's *Pierce's Supererogation*, a satire on Marlowe's friend Nashe.

29 (Sun.)   The Privy Council issues a licence permitting Lord Sussex's Men, who have clearly abandoned hope of the London playhouses being reopened, to go on tour.

May

Fears of a Spanish landing in Lancashire lead the Earl of Derby, father of Lord Strange, to be empowered to raise more forces there.

Henri IV decides to convert to Catholicism, though the news does not reach England until June (Doran, 41).

2 (Wed.)   A letter received by Edward Alleyn by this date shows that Lord Strange's Men are by now touring the provinces (see Rutter, 70). It may have been at or around this time that the Earl of Derby perhaps encouraged the building of a playhouse at Prescot in Lancashire to reduce the dependence of his and his family's players on London performances (see George, 234–5; and Keenan, 153).

4 (Fri.)   Completion of a census of immigrants in London shows their number to stand at 4,300.

5 (Sat.)   A threat against the 'strangers' appears on the wall of the Dutch Churchyard in Broad Street. It is signed 'Tamburlaine' and contains allusions to *The Jew of Malta* and *The Massacre at Paris*. Though the style means this cannot possibly have been by Marlowe, he is thus drawn into the controversy over the presence of 'strangers' in London. Charles Nicholl has recently suggested Richard Cholmeley as the most likely author of what has come to be known as 'the Dutch Church libel'.

6 (Sun.)   The Privy Council issues a licence for Lord Strange's Men to go on tour, though they have in fact been away since at least the beginning of May (see Rutter, 70).

8 (Tues.)   Date later given by Heneage for Robert Poley's departure from Croydon for The Hague on the Queen's service.

Henslowe notes in his diary that he has lent his nephew Francis, a player, £15 to go on tour with the Queen's Men, another company who have clearly despaired of the London season restarting (see Rutter, 70).

10 (Thurs.) The Lord Mayor of London offers a reward for information about recent libels concerning 'strangers'.

The plague is now so bad that the Court of Aldermen make plans for building 'a house for receiving of infected persons' (see Rukeyser, 132).

11 (Fri.)   The Privy Council orders that anyone suspected in connection with the Dutch Church Libel be arrested and their premises searched. Authorisation for torture is given.

12 (Sat.)   This is the date heading the document beginning:

> Vile hereticall Conceiptes
> denyinge the deity of Jhesus
> Christe our Saviour fownd
> emongest the papers of Thos
> Kydd prisoner

Below this, in a different ink, appear the words:
> which he affirmethe That he
> had ffrom Marlowe.

The document in question is a copy of a fragment of John Proctor's *The Fal of the Late Arrian*, which was old by now and not really heretical. It was apparently found among Kyd's papers when he was arrested, presumably in connection with the Dutch Church Libel. Kyd said it belonged to Marlowe and that Marlowe had left it there when the two had been roommates a year or two before. Kyd was tortured, and his death the following year may well have been due to the effects of this. It is not clear when Kyd implicated Marlowe; if it was not done immediately, he might already have known that Marlowe was dead and therefore could not come to any further harm by being named. On the other hand, the fact that a warrant was issued for Marlowe's arrest might well be attributable to Kyd's incrimination of him.

18 (Fri.)   Warrant issued by the Privy Council to Henry Maunder, 'one of the messengers of Her Majesty's Chamber, to repair to the house of Mr. T. Walsingham, in Kent or to anie other place where he shall understand Christopher Marlowe to be remayning and by virtue hereof to bring him to the Court in his companie, and in case of need to requyre ayd'. 'Mr. T. Walsingham' was Thomas Walsingham of Scadbury in Kent, a young relative of the late Sir Francis Walsingham and an erstwhile messenger for him. Some scholars, apparently actuated mainly by the principle of *'cherchez la femme'*, have tried to implicate Thomas Walsingham's wife Audrey in the death of Marlowe, but it is unclear whether Thomas and Audrey Walsingham were married by this date. It has often been asserted that they were not, and that their only son Thomas was not born until 1600; however, Constance Kuriyama has recently argued that he is more likely to have been born in or before 1595, and that the Walsinghams must therefore have married in the early 1590s (Kuriyama, *Christopher Marlowe*, 100).

20 (Sun.)   Marlowe is arrested at Scadbury. Since it was a Sunday and the law courts were closed, he returned with the warrant officer to Nonsuch to be interviewed by members of the Privy Council, and was given bail on condition that he reported back to them every day until given leave to do otherwise.

21 (Mon.)   John Penry, probable author of the Martin Marprelate tracts, is tried and convicted.

26 (Sat.)   This is the earlier of the two possible dates for the receipt of the Baines Note by the Privy Council. The Note was headed 'A note containing the opinion of one Christopher Marly concerning his damnable judgment of religion, and scorn of God's word', and made the following allegations about Marlowe's supposed beliefs and statements:

> That the Indians, and many authors of antiquity, have assuredly written of above 16 thousand years agone, whereas Adam is proved to have lived within six thousand years.He affirmeth that Moses was but a juggler, and that one Herlots [i.e. Thomas Harlot] being Sir Walter Raleigh's man can do more than he.

> That Moses made the Jews to travel 40 years in the wilderness (which journey might have been done in less than one year) ere they came to the promised land, to the intent that those who were privy to many of his subtleties might perish, and so an everlasting superstition reign in the hearts of the people.

> That the beginning of religion was only to keep men in awe.

> That it was an easy matter for Moses being brought up in all the arts of the Egyptians to abuse the Jews, being a rude and gross people.

> That Christ was a bastard and his mother dishonest.

> That he was the son of a carpenter, and that if the Jews among whom he was born did crucify him, they best knew him and whence he came.

> That Christ deserved better to die than Barabas, and that the Jews made a good choice, though Barabas were both a thief and a murderer.

> That if there be any God or any good religion, then it is in the Papists, because the service of God is performed with more ceremonies, as elevation of the mass, organs, singing men, shaven crowns, etc. That all Protestants are hypocritical asses.

> That if he were put to write a new religion, he would undertake both a more excellent and admirable method, and that all the New Testament is filthily written.

> That the woman of Samaria and her sister were whores and that Christ knew them dishonestly.

That Saint John the Evangelist was bedfellow to Christ and leaned always in his bosom; that he used him as the sinners of Sodoma.

That all they that love not tobacco and boys are fools.

That all the apostles were fishermen and base fellows, neither of wit nor worth; that Paul only had wit, but he was a timorous fellow in bidding men to be subject to magistrates against his conscience.

That he had as good a right to coin as the Queen of England, and that he was acquainted with one Poole, a prisoner in Newgate, who hath great skill in mixture of metals, and having learned some things of him, he meant through help of a cunning stamp-maker to coin French crowns, pistolets, and English shillings.

That if Christ would have instituted the sacrament with more ceremonial reverence, it would have been in more admiration; that it would have been much better being administered in a tobacco pipe.

That the angel Gabriel was bawd to the Holy Ghost, because he brought the salutation to Mary.

That one Richard Cholmley hath confessed that he was persuaded by Marlowe's reasons to become an atheist.

29 (Tues.) Execution of John Penry, probable author and certainly principal instigator of the Martin Marprelate tracts. Some 'Marlowe-was-Shakespeare' conspiracy theorists suggest that Penry's body was recovered afterwards and 'stood in' for Marlowe's at the inquest.

30 (Wed.) Death of Marlowe at the house of Eleanor Bull, in Deptford. The circumstances of his death remain mysterious; all that is known for sure is that he had spent the day in the company of Nicholas Skeres, Ingram Frizer and Robert Poley, that there had been a quarrel, and that during the course of it Marlowe was fatally stabbed. The account given to the coroner was that:

after supper the said Ingram & Christopher Morley were in speech & uttered one to the other divers malicious words for the reason that they could not be at one nor agree about the payment of the sum of pence, that is, le Reckoninge, there; & the said Christopher Morley then lying upon a bed in the room where they supped, & moved with anger against the said Ingram ffrysar upon the words aforesaid spoken between them, and the said Ingram then & there sitting in the room aforesaid with his back towards the bed where the said Christopher Morley was then lying, sitting near the bed, that is, *nere the Bedd*, & with the front part of his body towards the towards the table & the aforesaid Nicholas Skeres & Robert Poley sitting on either side of the said Ingram in such a manner that the same Ingram frrysar in no wise could take flight; it so befell that the said Christopher Morley on a sudden & of his malice towards the said Ingram aforethought, then & there maliciously drew the dagger of the said Ingram which was at his back, and with the same dagger the said Christopher Morley then & there maliciously gave the aforesaid Ingram two wounds on his head of the length of two inches & of the depth of a quarter of an inch; whereuopon the said Ingram, in fear of being slain, & sitting in the manner aforesaid between the said Nicholas Skeres & Robert Poley so that he could not in any wise get away, in his own defence & for the saving of his life, then & there struggled with the said Christopher Morley to get back from him his dagger aforesaid; in which affray the same Ingram could not get away from the said Christopher Morley; and so it befell in that affray that the said Ingram, in defence of his life, with the dagger aforesaid to the value of twelve pence, gave the said Christopher then & there a mortal wound over his right eye of the depth of two inches & of the width of one inch.

There has been much debate about whether such a wound would indeed have caused death (see particularly Tannenbaum, 41–2; and Urry, 91–2).

June

'Unkindness' is reported between Sir Robert Cecil and the Earl of Essex (see Nicholl, *Reckoning*, 391). This has sometimes been interpreted as a result of Marlowe's death.

1 (Fri.)   Inquest on Marlowe's body. Marlowe is buried at St Nicholas' Church, Deptford. The phrasing of the dedication of *Hero and Leander* perhaps implies that Sir Thomas Walsingham, the dedicatee, and the stationer Edward Blount, who wrote the dedication, were both present.

2 (Sat.)   The second possible date for the receipt of the Baines Note by the Privy Council. As with Kyd's confession, the document would read very differently if the man it implicated were already dead.

3 (Sun.)   Whitsunday. This is an important date because the revised copy of the Baines Note is headed: 'A note delivered on Whitsun eve last of the most horrible blasphemes and damnable opinions uttered by Xpofer Marly who <since Whitsunday dyed> within iii dayes after came to a soden & <vyolent deathe.> fearfull end of his life'. Also on this date a Mrs Tipping of Grub Street, probably a relation of James and Thomas Tipping, helps 'four poor scholars for Douai' to leave England around Whitsun.

8 (Fri.)   Date later given by Heneage for Robert Poley's return to Nonsuch from his trip to The Hague on the Queen's service.

10 (Sun.)   Marlowe's sister Ann marries John Cranford, shoemaker, at St Mary Bredman, Canterbury. Even if news of Marlowe's death had already reached Canterbury by then, it would probably have been impracticable to delay the wedding because Ann Marlowe appears to have been pregnant. Ann and John Cranford subsequently keep a local inn, the Windmill.

12 (Tues.)   Richard Stonley, teller of the Exchequer, buys *Venus and Adonis* for 6d, proving that it was certainly on sale by then. Sir Thomas Heneage, Treasurer of the Chamber, signs a warrant to pay Robert Poley £30 'for carrying of letters in post for Her Majesty's special and secret affairs of great importance, from the Court at Croydon the viijth of May 1593 into the Low Countries to the town of the Hague in Holland, and for returning back again with letters of answer to the Court at Nonsuch the viijth of June 1593, being in Her Majesty's service all the aforesaid time' (see Nicholl, *Reckoning*, 32). This formula seems unusually insistent, and one of its implications is that Poley was on official business at the time of Marlowe's death.

15 (Fri.)   One of the Queen's clerks writes to the coroner, William Danby, asking to see the writ of *certiorari* 'concerning the death of Christopher Morley'.

23 (Sat.)   George Peele paid £3 by the Earl of Northumberland for *The Honour of the Garter*, praising Watson and Marlowe. Plague closure of all playhouses in London.

27 (Wed.) Date which appears at the end of Nashe's *The Unfortunate Traveller* (published 1594), which draws a parallel between Marlowe and Aretino.
28 (Thurs.) Ingram Frizer, Marlowe's killer, is pardoned by the Queen on grounds of self-defence.
Richard Cholmeley arrested.
29 (Fri.) Drew Woodleff signs a 'statute staple' in favour of Thomas Walsingham to cover his debt to Ingram Frizer (see Nicholl, *Reckoning*, 23), pledging himself to pay £200 by 25 July 1593. This seems to indicate that Marlowe's killer and the man with whom Marlowe had been staying just before his death remained on good terms.

Summer
At some point in the summer Lord Strange's Men, who were touring in the provinces while plague closed the London theatres, appear to have disbanded (Rutter, 20).

July
Henri IV of France converts to Catholicism.
6 (Fri.) *Edward II* is licensed for publication by William Jones.
14 (Sat.) Robert Poley is paid for couriering letters to and from France.

August
1 (Wed.) Thomas Drury writes to Anthony Bacon that 'There was a command layed on me latly to stay on|e| Mr Bayns, which did use to resort unto me, which I did pursue ... and got the desired secrett at his hand' (see the *DNB* entry on Marlowe). This appears to indicate a connection between Thomas Drury and Richard Baines. Anthony Bacon was closely associated with the Earl of Essex.
17 (Fri.) Thomas Drury writes to thank Sir Robert Cecil for giving him money and arranging his release from prison.
Marlowe's maternal uncle Thomas Arthur dies, almost certainly of plague.
29 (Wed.) John Arthur, son of Thomas, is buried.

September
Composition of Gabriel Harvey's 'Newe Letter of Notable Contents', which calls Marlowe a 'Lucian' and also speaks of the death of 'Tamburlaine', but seems to imply that he had died of the plague.

Charles Nicholl argues convincingly that this refers in fact to the death of Peter Shakerley (see Nicholl, *Reckoning*, 64).
Robert Poley is arrested in the Netherlands and examined by the States General after accusations made by the English agent Roger Walton. Poley is released soon after.

2 (Sun.)   William Bayons and John Bayons baptised at All Saints, Waltham. These are the twin sons of the Richard Baines who was rector of Waltham (Kendall, *Christopher Marlowe*, 319). For other Bayons baptisms and burials during this period which may possibly be connected with this family, see Kendall, *Christopher Marlowe*, 317–18.

6 (Thurs.)   Death of Marlowe's cousin Elizabeth, daughter of Thomas and Ursula Arthur.

7 (Fri.)   Death of William, son of Thomas and Ursula Arthur.

8 (Sat.)   Entry in the Stationers' Register of Thomas Nashe's *Christ's tears over Jerusalem*, which castigates atheism. Nashe had been friendly with Marlowe and might be attempting here to dissociate himself from his dangerous acquaintance.

13 (Thurs.) Ursula Arthur buried.

14 (Fri.)   Burial of Daniel, son of Thomas and Ursula Arthur. Dorothy, the only surviving member of the family, enters the Marlowe household.

15 (Sat.)   John and Katherine Marlowe, together with their friends Thomas Plessington, baker, and Laurence Applegate, tailor, are bound in the sum of 200 marks to administer the estate of Thomas Arthur, and instructed to produce an inventory of the estate by Christmas.

16 (Sun.)   Richard Hesketh is handed a letter to give to Lord Strange by the Cecil agent 'Mr Hickman' at the White Lion Inn in Islington (see Nicholl, *Reckoning*, 248). It is possible that 'Mr Hickman' was John Dee's scryer Bartholomew Hickman (Woolley, 317).

18 (Tues.)   Burial of Peter Shakerley.

25 (Tues.)   Henry, 4th Earl of Derby, dies. His eldest son Lord Strange succeeds him in the title.

27 (Thurs.) Richard Hesketh visits Lord Strange, now 5th Earl of Derby, suggesting a *coup d'état* in his favour. Strange informs the Queen.

28 (Fri.)   *Hero and Leander* is entered in the Stationers' Register by John Wolfe.

A letter from Philip Henslowe mentions the serious financial distress of Pembroke's Men, who he says have been forced to pawn their apparel while on tour. This is the first of three apparently separate acting companies of that name (see Rutter, 21).

October

Publication of Gabriel Harvey's *Pierce's Supererogations*, an attack on Marlowe's friend Thomas Nashe, together with his 'New Letter of Notable Contents'.

6 (Sat.) William Dudley and William Shaw are charged with unlawful assembly and assault and battery against one Richard Cholmeley after he, Thomas Allen of Stafford and a tailor called Samuel were attacked on the road at Forebridge (see Hammer, 233–4). It is uncertain whether this is the same Richard Cholmeley as figures in the intrigues surrounding Marlowe's death.

22 (Mon.) Thomas Edwards' *Narcissus*, praising Watson and Marlowe and showing clear signs of knowledge of *Hero and Leander*, is entered in the Stationers' Register by John Wolfe. This would seem to suggest that *Hero and Leander* had been circulating in manuscript.

November

Essex writes to Sir Edward Littleton, Sir Edward Aston and Richard Bagot to thank them for their help in the matter of his servant Cholmeley (see Hammer, 232–5).

29 (Thurs.) Richard Hesketh is hanged and quartered at St Albans.

December

Henslowe's diary resumes.

John Marlowe enrolls Thomas Mychell as an apprentice.

14 (Fri.) Lord Strange protests to the Earl of Essex about followers who have defected from him to the Earl.

27 (Thurs.) Henslowe's diary records Lord Sussex's Men beginning to play at the Rose.

31 (Mon.) George Chapman's *The Shadow of Night* is entered in the Stationers' Register. This is sometimes thought to supply evidence for the existence of a 'School of Night' of which Lord Strange is alleged to have been the head, and Marlowe a member.

1594

Marriage of Lady Dorothy Devereux, sister of the Earl of Essex, to the Earl of Northumberland.

Lord Chamberlain's Men resurface, apparently composed principally of the residue of Lord Strange's Men (see Rutter, 21).

John Marlowe's former apprentice William Hewes is fined for an assault on him.

John Bedle sues John Marlowe for detention of goods.

Publication of *The Second Report of Doctor John Faustus*, allegedly written by 'an English gentleman, student in Wittenberg ... University', which Jones sees as 'written much in the style of Nashe' (Jones, 11).

John Cecil leaves Scotland for Rome and is captured by (or gives himself up to) Sir Francis Drake.

Publication, probably in Antwerp, of *A conference about the next succession to the crowne of Ingland*, dedicated to Essex. The author's name was said to be 'R. Doleman', probably a pseudonym for the Jesuit Robert Persons. This suggested that the Spanish Infanta should be the heir to the Crown, and the dedication seems intended to suggest that the Earl agreed, something which would have seriously compromised him.

Publication of the first known quarto of *Edward II*. It is possible that there was an earlier one, now lost.

Publication of *Dido, Queen of Carthage*, printed by Thomas Woodcock, and saying on the title-page that it was written by Marlowe and Nashe. This is the only surviving early printing of the work, though there may have been a second edition, containing an elegy on Marlowe by Nashe, of which no copies now survive (see Bakeless, *Christopher Marlowe*, 326–7). This first edition was also thought lost, and *Dido* supposed not to survive, until the late eighteenth century.

Publication of Thomas Nashe, *The Unfortunate Traveller*, which refers to Agrippa and his entertainment for the Emperor Charles V, episodes which seem to be echoed in *Doctor Faustus* (Nashe, 297–9). It also includes a satirical account of an entertainment at 'Wittenberg University', which seems to be based on Cambridge (see Nicholl, *Cup*, 26), praises Aretine (Nashe, 310–11), with whom Marlowe was sometimes compared, and refers to the death of Lucan (Nashe, 352).

Publication of *A Looking Glasse for London and England*, by Greene and Lodge (composed *c.* 1589–91), and of Lodge's *The Wounds of Ciuill War* (composed *c.* 1588), both of which Paul Kocher adduced as evidence that Nashe wrote the prose scenes of the A text *Faustus* (see Kocher, 'Nashe's Authorship', 35–7).

Publication of Robert Ashley's *Of the Interchangeable Course, or Variety of Things in the Whole World*, a translation of Loys LeRoy, which seems to take the idea of Tamburlaine's footstool from Marlowe's play rather than the original text (see Brown, 'Marlowe's Debasement', 45).

Publication at London of George Chapman's *The Shadow of Night*, with a dedication to Matthew Roydon. In the preface Chapman says:

> I remember, my good Mat, how joyfully oftentimes you reported unto me that most ingenious Derby, deep-searching Northumberland and skill-embracing heir of Hunsdon had most profitably entertained learning in themselves, to the vital warmth of freezing science, & to the admirable lustre of their true nobility.

'Derby' here is Lord Strange, and the 'heir of Hunsdon' is Sir George Carey. Since Roydon was known to be a friend of Marlowe's, this might give an indication of the kind of company which Marlowe had been keeping.

January

6 (Sun.) Baptism of Ann Cranford, first child of Marlowe's sister Ann and her husband John Cranford, some seven months after their marriage. Since she is not mentioned in Katherine Marlowe's will, Ann probably died young.

17 (Thurs.) Essex replies to Lord Strange disallowing his complaint about followers who have defected.

26 (Sat.) Thomas Kyd's *Cornelia*, translated from the French of Robert Garnier, is licensed for publication. Kyd's dedication to the Countess of Sussex speaks of 'those so bitter times and priuie broken passions that I endured in the writing it'. He dies soon after. *Cornelia* is another Lucanian work, since Cornelia was the wife of Pompey and figures in the *Pharsalia*.

27 (Sun.) Nicholas Colbrand, landlord of the Lion in Canterbury, alleges that Thomas Gradwell, future husband of Marlowe's sister Dorothy, has accused him of stealing five pots.

February

4 (Mon.) Sussex's Men, who may have included former members of Lord Strange's Men and of Pembroke's Men, play *The Jew of Malta* at the Rose, grossing 50 shillings. It is their only performance of any Marlowe play during a seven-week run which included thirty performances.

5 (Tues.)   Arrest of the Queen's Jewish physician, Dr Rodrigo Lopez, on charges of treason and attempted poisoning. His trial is referred to in the House-courser scene of *Doctor Faustus*, which is therefore evidence of posthumous additions to the play. The Lopez affair brings a new lease of life to *The Jew of Malta*, which becomes newly topical.

Thomas Drury writes to Lord Burghley asking for an appointment as a herald.

6 (Wed.)   According to Henslowe's diary, last performance of Lord Sussex's Men at the Rose.

14 (Thurs.) John Cecil writes to Sir Robert Cecil explaining that he had been captured by Drake. He is allowed to leave and departs for Madrid.

28 (Thurs.) Trial of Dr Lopez.

March

12 (Tues.)   *The First Part of the Contention between the two famous houses of York and Lancaster* entered in the Stationers' Register by Thomas Millington. This may be either a source for or a garbled version of *Henry the Sixth,* Part One, in which some critics see Marlowe as having had a hand.

21–28 (Thurs.–Thurs.) An inquiry into Ralegh's alleged atheism is held at Cerne Abbas in Dorset. Some scholars argue that the death of Marlowe was connected with an attempt by Essex to entrap Ralegh, which did not bear fruit until this point but was well under way in the previous year.

April

1 (Mon.)   Henslowe's diary records that Sussex's Men and the Queen's Men play at the Rose for a week (ending Monday, 8 April).

3 (Wed.)   Sussex's Men and the Queen's Men play *The Jew of Malta* at the Rose, grossing £3.

7 (Sun.)   Sussex's Men and the Queen's Men play *The Jew of Malta* at the Rose, grossing 26 shillings.

11 (Thurs.) Richard Kitchen is indicted at the Guildhall for an assault on John Finch.

16 (Tues.)   Death of Ferdinando Stanley, Earl of Derby (formerly Lord Strange). Because this was sudden and the Earl was a young man, this was attributed at the time to poison, and generally blamed on Catholics displeased at his reluctance to ally himself with an attempt at a *coup d'état*. His family connec-

tion with the Tudors might in fact have meant that he suffered from the hereditary disease porphyria, now thought to have been responsible for the premature death of Mary, Queen of Scots' father, James V of Scotland, as well as, famously, for 'the madness of King George'. (Arbella Stuart seems also to have been a sufferer.)

22 (Mon.) Death of Thomas Woodcock, printer of *Dido, Queen of Carthage*, which must therefore have appeared before this.

John Marlowe belatedly submits an inventory of the estate of Thomas Arthur, which was worth £56 7s 6d.

26 (Thurs.) William Hewes, formerly apprenticed to Marlowe's father John, is admitted as freeman of the city of Canterbury.

May

2 (Thurs.) *Taming of a Shrew*, the so-called 'bad quarto' of Shakespeare's *The Taming of the Shrew*, is entered in the Stationers' Register. This contains five apparent borrowings from *Doctor Faustus* (see Bowers, 3).

14–16 (Tues.–Thurs.) The re-formed Admiral's Men play at the Rose. On 14 May they put on *The Jew of Malta*, grossing 48 shillings.

17 (Fri.) *The Massacre at Paris* is entered in the Stationers' Register by Nicholas Linge and Thomas Millington. No ensuing edition is known to have been published.

20 (Mon. Julian, Fri. Gregorian) Camillo Caetani, papal nuncio in Madrid, writes to Cardinal Aldobrandino mentioning that John Cecil had been there some months previously on his way from the Scottish Catholics to the King of Spain, and that the nuncio had helped him on his way.

John Cecil writes to Camillo Caetani from Prague discussing plans for a Spanish landing in Scotland.

29 (Wed.) John Benchkin applies for a licence to marry Katherine Grawnte of Kingston near Canterbury. Constance Kuriyama suggests that he had observed a year's mourning for Marlowe (Kuriyama, 'Second Selves', 93), but without further evidence this remains purely speculative.

June

4 (Tues.) The Lord Admiral's Men and the Lord Chamberlain's Men put on *The Jew of Malta* at the Rose, grossing 10 shillings.

7 (Fri.) Execution of Dr Lopez.

14 (Fri.) The Lord Admiral's Men and the Lord Chamberlain's Men put on *The Jew of Malta* at the Rose, grossing 4 shillings.

17 (Mon.)   The Admiral's Men begin to play at the Rose.

19 (Wed.)   Marlowe's sister Dorothy marries Thomas Cradwell or Gradwell, vintner, at St Mary Bredman, Canterbury.
            The Massacre at Paris is performed by the Admiral's Men at the Rose, grossing 54 shillings.

23 (Sun.)   The Admiral's Men perform *The Jew of Malta* at the Rose, grossing 23 shillings.

25 (Tues.) The Admiral's Men perform *The Massacre at Paris* at the Rose, grossing 36 shillings.

28 (Fri.)   Ingram Frizer, Marlowe's killer, takes out a three-year lease on a house in St Saviour's, Southwark, from Thomas Smyth.

30 (Sun.)   The Admiral's Men perform *The Jew of Malta* at the Rose, grossing 41 shillings.

July

3 (Wed.)   The Admiral's Men perform *The Massacre at Paris* at the Rose, grossing 31 shillings.

8 (Mon.)   The Admiral's Men perform *The Massacre at Paris* at the Rose, grossing 27 shillings.

10 (Wed.)   The Admiral's Men perform *The Jew of Malta* at the Rose, grossing 27 shillings.

August

Richard Williams, who had deserted from the Earl of Essex's forces in France, is hanged for treason and for other crimes, including the robbery of Winchester Cathedral (see under 1591).

19 (Mon.)   Robert Poley is paid for couriering letters to and from Brussels.

28 (Wed.)   First recorded performance of *Tamburlaine the Great*, Part One at the Rose Playhouse.

October

3 (Thurs.) A Richard Baines is imprisoned in the Marshalsea on suspicion of felony and murder and will be hanged at Tyburn later in the year (see Kendall, *Christopher Marlowe*, 322–3). The presiding judge was Sir John Popham, whose great-nephew, the Caroline playwright John Ford, was later to show considerable signs of having been influenced by Marlowe (see Hoy). Kendall suggests an allusion to this Baines's crime in the 1602 additions to *Doctor Faustus* and wonders whether this might mean that the authors of the

additions were aware of a connection between this Baines and Marlowe (see Kendall, *Christopher Marlowe*, 327), but I find this very tenuous.

16 (Wed.)   Death at Rome of Cardinal Allen.

17 (Thurs.) Ingram Frizer takes out a suit against Edmund Ballard for recovery of possession of his house in Southwark. He wins the case and is granted £5 damages and 6d costs.

December

6 (Fri.)   The Richard Baines who had earlier been imprisoned in the Marshalsea is hanged at Tyburn. A ballad entitled 'The Woful Lamentacon of Richard Baynes, executed at Tyborne' is entered in the Stationers' Register the same day (see Nicholl, *Reckoning*, 335; and Kendall, *Christopher Marlowe*, 323–4). It is unlikely but not impossible that this was the Baines of the Baines Note.

8 (Sun.)   The Admiral's Men play *Doctor Faustus* at the Rose, grossing 15 shillings.

9 (Mon.)   The Admiral's Men play *The Jew of Malta* at the Rose, grossing 3 shillings.

17 (Tues.) The Admiral's Men play *Tamburlaine the Great*, Part One, at the Rose, grossing 31 shillings.

19 (Thurs.) The Admiral's Men play *Tamburlaine the Great*, Part Two, at the Rose, grossing 46 shillings.

20 (Fri.)   The Admiral's Men play *Doctor Faustus* at the Rose, grossing 18 shillings.

23 (Mon.) Thomas Mychell apprenticed to Marlowe's father John.

27 (Fri.)   The Admiral's Men play *Doctor Faustus* at the Rose, grossing 52 shillings.

30 (Mon.) Thomas Kyd's parents renounce the administration of his goods, presumably indicating that they feel he has disgraced them.

           The Admiral's Men play *Tamburlaine the Great*, Part One, at the Rose, grossing 22 shillings.

1595

Thomas Gradwell is accused of maltreatment of a gelding which has been lodged in the stables of the George Inn, Canterbury, of which he is by now landlord, and he and his wife Dorothy are accused of not taking communion.

Publication at London by Thomas Millington of *The True Tragedy of Richard, Duke of York, and the death of good King Henry the Sixth ... as it was sundry times acted by the Right Honourable the Earl of Pembroke his servants* (no Stationers' Register entry). This is either a source text or a garbled version of *Henry the Sixth,* Part Two.

Publication at London of William Covell, *Polimanteia,* describing Shakespeare as Watson's heir, and thus indicating the continued esteem in which Watson is held.

Publication at London of Thomas Edwards, *Narcissus.*

1 (Wed.)   The Admiral's Men play *Tamburlaine the Great,* Part Two at the Rose, grossing £3 2s.

9 (Thurs.) The Admiral's Men play *Doctor Faustus* at the Rose, grossing 22 shillings.

February–April

During these months – it was later alleged in an action brought in summer 1596 by John Browne – Thomas Gradwell, husband of Marlowe's sister Dorothy, accused Browne of having committed adultery with Dorothy 'seven times in one nyght'.

March

13 (Thurs.) Nicholas Skeres and fourteen others are arrested for doing business in the house of Edmund Williamson in Philip Lane, near Cripplegate, suspected to be a centre of sedition because Williamson's brother Nicholas, a Catholic, was under interrogation.

14 (Fri.)   Skeres and all but Williamson and another of his brothers released.

April

John Marlowe is recorded as no longer serving as churchwarden of St Mary Breadman.

1 (Tues.)   Robert Poley is paid for couriering letters to and from Antwerp.

7 (Mon.)   Nicholas Skeres deposes that Robert Poley was 'threatened to be apprehended' in the Low Countries, indicating the continuing danger of service in the Netherlands even for so experienced a hand as Poley.

30 (Wed./Thurs., 1 May) Presumably on one of these dates (Henslowe wrote '31 April', which does not exist), the Admiral's Men play *Doctor Faustus* at the Rose, grossing 22 shillings.

May

21 (Wed.) The Admiral's Men play *Tamburlaine the Great*, Part One, at the Rose, grossing 22 shillings.

22 (Thurs.) The Admiral's Men play *Tamburlaine the Great*, Part Two, at the Rose, grossing 25 shillings.

June

14 (Sat.) Lord Burghley signs a warrant to pay Thomas Drury £16, suggesting that he is now in good favour

26 (Thurs.) Last day of the Admiral's Men's season at the Rose. They presumably tour the provinces between now and their return.

July

27 (Sun.) Anthony Cranford, son of Marlowe's sister Ann and her husband John Cranford, baptised at St Margaret's, Canterbury. The use of the name Anthony might conceivably suggest a link with Anthony Marlowe; alternatively, it might be a name associated with Cranford's family, but the International Genealogical Index shows no baptisms for any Anthony Cranfords.

August

1 (Fri.) Robert Poley is paid for couriering letters to and from Brussels.

25 (Mon.) The Admiral's Men return to the Rose.

September

11 (Thurs.) The Admiral's Men play *Doctor Faustus* at the Rose, grossing 30s 2d.

15 (Mon.) The Admiral's Men play *Tamburlaine the Great*, Part One, at the Rose, grossing 21 shillings.

November

11 (Tues. Julian, Sat. Gregorian) John Cecil reaches Rome.

12 (Wed.) The churchwardens of St Mary Breadman complain that John Marlowe 'denieth to paye the clarkes wages as he himself hath always payd ... and is nowe behind for three quarters of a yere at midsomer last past' (Urry, 28).

1596

John Cecil is reported to be in Salamanca. John Fixer is also in Spain, sending despatches to Sir Robert Cecil (see Anstruther, 118).

Another accusation is made that the Gradwells are not taking communion. Thomas Gradwell wins money in a wager over the rumoured death of Sir Francis Drake.

George Byng sues the Marlowes for £500 which he claims is owed him from Thomas Arthur's estate. There is no record of the outcome of the case.

John Marlowe appears to have helped himself to a 'legacy' from the estate of Thomasina Moore, mother of Ursula Arthur, without waiting for probate (see Urry, 19).

Edward Alleyn is involved in selling the lease of the parsonage at Firle, in Sussex, to a member of the local Langworth family.

Publication of Thomas Nashe's *Have with You to Saffron-Walden*, an attack on Gabriel Harvey which castigates him for, amongst other things, his references to Greene and Marlowe after their deaths.

January
9 (Fri.)   The Admiral's Men play *The Jew of Malta* at the Rose, grossing 52 shillings.

February
27 (Fri.)   Last performance by the Admiral's Men at the Rose until April.

March
John Mathews, later to be known as Christopher Marler, takes his MA at Trinity College, Cambridge.

10 (Wed.)   Thomas Gradwell, husband of Marlowe's sister Dorothy, is found guilty of slanderously alleging that John Browne had slept with her. Gradwell was ordered to do penance and, when he refused, was excommunicated.

19 (Fri.)   Eleanor Bull, in whose house Marlowe had died, is buried at St Nicholas's, Deptford.

April
12 (Mon.)   The Admiral's Men resume playing at the Rose.

30 (Fri.)   Ingram Frizer purchases land at Great Missenden, in Buckinghamshire, from Drew Woodleff and his mother. In

the same year they are also in trouble for selling other lands
without a licence to do so.

May

1 (Sat.) Probable date of death of John Alleyn, elder brother of
Edward (Cerasano, in Reid and Maniura, 13).

5 (Fri.) The Admiral's Men play *Doctor Faustus* at the Rose, grossing
20 shillings.

14 (Sun.) The Admiral's Men play *The Jew of Malta* at the Rose, grossing 24 shillings.

June

12 (Sat.) The Admiral's Men play *Doctor Faustus* at the Rose, grossing
17 shillings.

21 (Mon.) The Admiral's Men play *The Jew of Malta* at the Rose, grossing 13 shillings.

July

3 (Sat.) The Admiral's Men play *Doctor Faustus* at the Rose, grossing
14 shillings.

28 (Wed.) The Admiral's Men give their last performance of the
summer at the Rose.

August

Thomas Gradwell finally agrees to perform his penance.

6 (Fri.) Philip Henslowe consults Simon Forman, a famous Elizabethan astrologer and supposed magician. Although this is
the first extant record of contact between Henslowe and
Forman, S. P. Cerasano suggests that Marlowe may have
known, or known of, Forman and that he may have been an
influence on the conception of Doctor Faustus (Cerasano,
'Philip Henslowe', 148–50).

September

16 (Thurs.) Thomas Gradwell is certified to have performed his
penance. However, failure to pay his legal fees soon leads to
further trouble and results in imprisonment and renewed
excommunication.

28 (Sat., Gregorian) A letter from Dr Richard Barret, rector of the
English college in Douai, to Robert Persons, who is in
Rome, mentions Cardinal Allen's secretary Roger Baines,

who Kendall suggests may be a relative of Marlowe's betrayer (see Kendall, *Christopher Marlowe*, 147).

October
27 (Wed.)   The Admiral's Men return to the Rose.
28 (Thurs.) The Admiral's Men play *Doctor Faustus* at the Rose, grossing 27 shillings.

November
Parnella Watson of Canterbury accuses Dorothy Gradwell of stealing cloth from her.
4 (Thurs.) The Admiral's Men play *Doctor Faustus* at the Rose, grossing 17 shillings.

December
3 (Fri.)   Robert Poley paid £20.
17 (Fri.)   The Admiral's Men play *Doctor Faustus* at the Rose, grossing 9 shillings.
29 (Wed.)   Michael Moody is reported as being dead.

1597

Simon Aldrich receives his BA from Trinity College, Cambridge.
John Cranford, husband of Marlowe's sister Ann, is appointed sealer and examiner of leather.
Publication of *Devoreux*, containing the fragment 'I walkt along a stream', which was republished in *England's Parnassus* (1600) and later erroneously attributed to Marlowe.
Publication at Edinburgh of King James's *Daemonologie*. This indicated that the likely successor to the English throne had an interest in witchcraft, and so will have made *Doctor Faustus* newly topical again.
Tamburlaine the Great is reprinted.
Probable composition of *The Merry Wives of Windsor*, which when eventually published in 1623 included an apparent reference to a scene found in the B text of *Doctor Faustus* but absent from the A text (see Bowers, 1 and 16).
Publication of Thomas Beard, *Theatre of God's Judgements*, containing the following inaccurate account of Marlowe's death:

> It so fell out that in London streets, as he purposed to stab one whom he ought a grudge unto with his dagger, the other party perceiving, so avoided the stroke that withal catching hold of his wrist, he stabbed his own dagger into his own head, in

such sort that notwithstanding all the means of surgery that could be wrought, he shortly after died thereof.

Apart from curiosity value, the only real point of interest here is the reference to 'London streets', which may represent a genuine mistranscription of a possible address for Eleanor Bull's house – Deptford did have a London Street.

February

5 (Sat.) Philip Henslowe consults Simon Forman again (see Cerasano, 'Phillp Henslowe', 150).

12 (Sat.) The Admiral's Men cease playing at the Rose.

16 (Wed.) Thomas Gradwell agrees to pay his legal fees and applies for the excommunication to be lifted.

March

3 (Thurs.) The Admiral's Men resume performances at the Rose.

5 (Sat.) Date on a letter from Robert Poley dated from Hogesden.

7 (Mon.) Robert Poley paid for couriering letters to and from The Hague.

25 (Fri.) Note of a further payment to Robert Poley.

April

6 (Wed.) A case brought by Dorothy Gradwell against John Browne, alleging that he has defamed her, is dismissed, and results in further legal fees.

23 (Sat.) Garter Feast for which *The Merry Wives At Windsor* may have been commissioned.

July

Queen Elizabeth visits Scadbury and knights Thomas Walsingham.

16 (Sat.) The Admiral's Men give their last performance of the summer at the Rose.

23 (Sat.) Note of a further payment to Robert Poley.

August

Ben Jonson, imprisoned for his part in writing *The Isle of Dogs*, is committed to the Marshalsea, where he may have encountered Robert Poley (see Nicholl, *Reckoning*, 336-7).

21 (Mon.) Marlowe's cousin Dorothy Arthur, who had been taken in by the Marlowes after being orphaned by plague in the summer of 1593, speaks her will, which leaves everything to the Marlowes.

26 (Fri.)   Dorothy Arthur is buried at St Dunstan's, Canterbury.
27 (Sat.)   John and Katherine Marlowe are granted probate of
               Dorothy Arthur's estate.

October
8 (Sat.)   Ben Jonson is released from the Marshalsea.
11 (Wed.)   The Admiral's Men return to the Rose, along with
               Pembroke's Men, to give the last recorded performance of
               the rôle of Dr Faustus by Edward Alleyn before his retire-
               ment from the stage.
21 (Fri.)   From now on Henslowe begins to keep detailed records of
               income he receives from the Admiral's Men and Pembroke's
               Men.
22 (Sat.)   The Lord Admiral, Charles Howard, is created Earl of
               Nottingham, though Henslowe continues to refer to him
               simply as the Lord Admiral until 1599.

November
5 (Sat.)   Last performance by the Admiral's Men at the Rose
               recorded in Henslowe's diary.

December
20 (Tues.)   Date chosen by J. P. Collier for his forged addition to
               Henslowe's diary referring to 'Marloes Tamberlan'.
29 (Thurs.) By this date Edward Alleyn has retired from the stage, appar-
               ently because he hoped, with the help of his wife's step-
               father Henslowe, to obtain the court appointment of Master
               of the Bears, Bulls, and Mastiff Dogs (Cerasano, 98–112).

1598

Publication of *Hero and Leander* by Edward Blount, with Marlowe's
name on the title-page and a dedication to Thomas Walsingham. There
appear to have been two separate printings of it in this year (see
Bakeless, 323).
Edward II is reprinted.
Humphrey Rowland's goods are assessed at the small sum of £3.
Publication at London of George Chapman, *De Guiana*, and *Achilles'
Shield*, dedicated to Thomas Hariot. The Earl of Northumberland starts
paying a pension to Thomas Hariot, which continues until the latter's
death.

William Vaughan, soon to give the most accurate account of Marlowe's death, dedicates a volume of poems to the Earl of Essex.

The Woodleffs finally complain about Ingram Frizer's behaviour.

Publication of *Mucedorus*, which, Paul Kocher argued, imitated the goblet scene of *Doctor Faustus* ('Nashe's Authorship', 37). The date of the play's composition is unknown, but it was in or before 1596.

Publication of *The Second Part of Hero and Leander. Conteyning their further Fortunes*, by Henry Petowe.

Publication of Francis Meres, *Palladis Tamia*, containing the following mentions of Marlowe's death:

> As Jodelle, a French tragical poet, being an epicure and an atheist, made a pitiful end, so our tragical poet Marlowe for his epicurism and atheism had a tragical death.
>
> As the poet Lycophron was shot to death by a certain rival of his, so Christopher Marlowe was stabbed to death by a bawdy serving-man, a rival of his in his lewd love.

As in the case of Beard's account, this is remarkable principally for its complete inaccuracy in all ascertainable respects.

January

8 (Sun.)   Alice Cranford, daughter of Marlowe's sister Ann and her husband John Cranford, is baptised at St Margaret's, Canterbury. Since she is not mentioned in Katherine Marlowe's will, Alice probably died young.

Henslowe's diary records 'lent vnto the company when they fyrst played dido at nyght the some of thirtishillynges which wasse the 8 of Jenewary 1597 I saye'. As usual, Henslowe is dating the new year here from 25 March, so he means 1598. It is not clear if 'dido' refers to *Dido, Queen of Carthage*, but it seems a reasonable supposition.

20 (Mon.)   A Richard Baynes is robbed of a cloak worth 11d at Southwark. Constance Kuriyama argues that this is so cheap that the Baines in question is very unlikely to be Marlowe's betrayer and that this is therefore testimony to the relative commonness of the name (Kuriyama, 'Marlowe's Nemesis', 354).

March

2 (Thurs.) The copyright of *Hero and Leander* is assigned by Edward Blount to Paul Linley, who in the same year published a version concluding with Chapman's continuation.

4 (Sat.)   Henslowe's list of money received from the Admiral's Men
             and Pembroke's Men comes to an end. However, Henslowe
             does begin to list expenditure.
10 (Fri.)   An inventory of the Lord Admiral's Men's stock, thought to
             have been written in this year, mentions, among other
             things, 'j tombe of Dido', 'Tamberlyne bridell', 'j dragon in
             fostes', and 'j cauderm for the Jewe'.

June
4 (Sun.)   Edward Alleyn is staying at the house of Mr Arthur
             Langworth at the Brille in Sussex.

August
9 (Wed.)   Henslowe lends Richard Alleyn 8s 6d to despatch a debt to
             a Mr Kitchen. The Richard Kitchen who acted as a surety
             may well be meant here.

November
19 (Sun.)   The actor William Birde (alias Borne) borrows 12 shillings
             from Henslowe 'to embroider his hat for the Guise', indic-
             ating that he is about to star in a revival of *The Massacre at
             Paris* and needs to refurbish his costume.
27 (Mon.)   Birde/Borne borrows a further 20 shillings 'to bye a payer of
             sylke stockens to playe the gwisse'.

December
19 (Tues.)   Robert Poley is paid for couriering letters to and from the
             Governor of Bayonne.

1599

Publication of Thomas Nashe, *Lenten Stuff*, containing a parody of
Hero and Leander (see Holmes, 155–6) and the more serious question,
'Let me see, hath anybody in Yarmouth heard of Leander and Hero, of
whom divine Musaeus sung, and a diviner muse than him, Kit
Marlowe?' (Nashe, 424).
Probable date of *As You Like It*. This contains references to Marlowe's
death and to the burning of his *All Ovids Elegies* as well as allusions to
'The Passionate Shepherd to his Love' and *Hero and Leander*.
Publication at London of *The Passionate Pilgrim*, containing the first
three stanzas of Marlowe's poem 'The Passionate Shepherd to his Love'
and an abbreviated version of Sir Walter Ralegh's 'The Nymph's Reply
to the Shepherd'.

John Cecil is living in Paris and publishes there his *A discovery of the errors committed and injuries done to his majesty of Scotland ... by a malicious mythology titled an apology, and compiled by William Criton, priest and professed Jesuit.* This interestingly brings together the prevailing themes of the Scottish succession, Catholicism, and double agents.

Francis Aldrich, brother of Simon Aldrich, becomes a fellow of Sidney Sussex College, Cambridge.

January
13 (Sat.) Death of Edmund Spenser.

May
19 (Sat., or just conceivably Wed., 19 May Gregorian) John Poole, presumably the same man as the one of that name who taught Marlowe to coin, was said by Robert Persons to have written him a letter on this date (see Kendall, *Christopher Marlowe*, 174).

26 (Sat.) First reference in Henslowe's diary to the Admiral's Men as the Earl of Nottingham's Men. On the title-page of the 1604 quarto, the Earl of Nottingham's Men are said to have acted *Doctor Faustus*.

30 (Thurs.) John Matthew or Matthews, alias Christopher Marler, MA of Trinity College, Cambridge, is admitted to the English Seminary at Valladolid.

June
1 (Sat.) 'Davies' Epigrams, with Marlowe's Elegies' is called in by the bishops. This refers to Marlowe's translation of Ovid's *Amores*, which had been printed along with Sir John Davies' *Epigrams*. The reason for the bishops' objection was the rather racy subject matter.

4 (Tues.) Marlowe's *Ovid's Elegies* is burnt at Stationers' Hall by order of the Archbishop of Canterbury.

26 (Tues.) Christening at St Helen's, Bishopsgate of Christopher Morley, son of Thomas Morley, friend of Thomas Watson, and possibly brother of the 'other' Christopher Morley (see Kuriyama, 'Second Selves', 98).

July
30 (Mon.) William Vaughan's brother John is knighted by the Earl of Essex in Ireland.

October

3 (Wed.)   William Warner, author of *Albions England* and possible friend of Marlowe, marries Anne Dale, a widow, at Great Amwell in Hertfordshire.

1600

Paul Ive dedicates a treatise on fortification to the Earl of Northumberland.

Publication at London of *England's Helicon*, containing the six-stanza version of 'The Passionate Shepherd to his Love', and Sir Walter Ralegh's 'The Nymph's Reply to the Shepherd'.

Publication at London of 'England's Parnassus', containing the fragment 'Description of Seas, Waters, Rivers, &c.', erroneously attributed to 'Ch. Marlowe'.

Hero and Leander is reprinted.

Publication of Marlowe's translation of the First Book of Lucan's *Pharsalia*, printed by P. Short for Thomas Thorpe, who, dedicating it to Edward Blount, writes of Marlowe that his 'ghoast or Genius is to be seene' in St Paul's 'Churchyard in (at the least) three or foure sheets' (i.e. of paper, referring to his works). This is the only known early printing.

Simon Aldrich commences MA at Trinity College, Cambridge.

Publication of William Vaughan's *Golden Groue*, with the following reference to Marlowe:

> Not inferior to these was one Christopher Marlow, by profession a playmaker, who, as it is reported, about 7 years ago wrote a book against the Trinity. But see the effects of God's justice: so it happened, that at Deptford, a little village about three miles distant from London, as he meant to stab with his poignard one named Ingram, that had invited him thither to a feast, and was then playing at tables, he quickly perceiving it, so avoided the thrust, that withall drawing out his own dagger for his defence, he stabbed this Marlowe into the eye, in such sort that his brains coming out at the dagger's point, he shortly after died. Thus did God, the true executioner of divine justice, work the end of impious atheists.

February

7 (Mon., Gregorian) Giordano Bruno burned at the stake.

March

30 (Sun.) Elizabeth Cranford, daughter of Marlowe's sister Ann and her husband John Cranford, is baptised at St Margaret's, Canterbury.

June

1 (Sun.) Richard Kitchen gives evidence for William Williamson, landlord of the Mermaid Tavern in Bread Street. The Mermaid was a tavern much frequented by theatre people, so Kitchen's familiarity with its landlord may explain his willingness to act as a surety for Marlowe in the Hog Lane affair.

July

10 (Thurs.) Robert Poley is paid for couriering letters to and from the Queen's agent at The Hague.

August

4 (Mon.) *As You Like It* is entered in the Stationers' Register.

Winter

(between Tues., 11 November and Sun., 14 December) Edward Alleyn returns to the stage (see Cerasano, 98).

December

17 (Wed.) Robert Poley writes to Sir Robert Cecil complaining that 'it pleasde your Honor to sequester mee from your seruice and bountye' (see Boas, *Christopher Marlowe*, 290).

21 (Sun.) Robert Poley is paid for couriering letters to and from Sir John de Laye in France.

1601

Publication at London of John Deacon and John Walker, *A Dialogicall Discourse of Spirits and Diuels.*

A Mabel Jordan baptised at St Margaret's, Canterbury in this year may have been the daughter of Marlowe's sister Margaret and her husband John Jordan, but if so she may have died shortly after birth as she is not mentioned in the will of Katherine Marlowe. No baptisms can be traced for Margaret Jordan's three known children, John, Elizabeth and William, who are mentioned in Katherine Marlowe's will.

Marlowe's sister Dorothy Gradwell accuses Thomas Peeling, a local
blacksmith, of assaulting her.
John Fixer is imprisoned at the instigation of Father Persons.
Death of Thomas Nashe.
John Cecil goes to Rome.

January
Death of Humphrey Rowland.
7 (Wed.)   'A booke called the plaie of Dcor ffaustus' is entered into
            the Stationers' Register by Thomas Bushell. Subsequently
            printed in 1604 by Valentine Simmes. This will be what
            becomes known as the A text of *Doctor Faustus*.

February
7 (Sat.)   The Lord Chamberlain's Men put on a play about Richard
            II (probably but not certainly Shakespeare's) at the Earl of
            Essex's behest, apparently in a bid to get the audience into
            a suitable frame of mind for the following day's rebellion.
            This tactic of using literary works for political purposes
            might perhaps be thought reminiscent of the presence of
            the signature 'Tamburlaine' in the Dutch Church Libel.

March
18 (Wed.)   Execution of the Earl of Essex.

May
19 (Tues.) Henslowe's diary records the purchase of 'divers thinges for
            the Jewe of Malta'.

July
Robert Poley is detained at Dover by the Warden of the Cinque Ports
trying to smuggle in his cousin George Cotton, who had been studying
at St Omer for two years. This seems further to muddy the waters on
the question of Poley's true allegiances.
3 (Fri.)   *The True History of George Scanderbeg* is entered in the
            Stationers' Register by Edward Alde. It is often said that
            Marlowe wrote a lost play on the history of the Albanian
            patriot Scanderbeg, but the only evidence for this is Gabriel
            Harvey's reference to 'a Scanderbegging wight' in 'Gorgon',
            which Charles Nicholl has convincingly suggested actually
            refers to Peter Shakerley.

31 (Fri.)   The Council issues a warrant for Nicholas Skeres to be taken
             from Newgate to Bridewell.

August
4 (Tues.)   Sir Robert Cecil issues a warrant to pay Robert Poley.

September
5 (Sat.)   Sir Robert Cecil issues a warrant to pay Robert Poley. This is
             the last recorded government payment to him.

November
26 (Thurs.) A tailor named Radford receives final settlement from
             Henslowe of £7 14s 6d for cloth for costumes for *The
             Massacre at Paris*.

1602

John Mathews, alias Christopher Marler or Marlowe, is consecrated
priest.
Dorothy Gradwell sues Anthony Howe, landlord of the Saracen's Head,
for defamation.
The Earl of Worcester's Men take up residence at the Rose.

January
18 (Mon.)   *The Merry Wives of Windsor* is entered in the Stationers'
             Register. The text which appeared later in the year does not
             contain the allusion to *Doctor Faustus* but is not generally
             reliable (see Bowers, 16).
             Edward Alleyn is paid £6 by Henslowe 'for three books
             which were played' including 'The Massacre of France'.

June
Ingram Frizer is described in a deed of sale as living at Eltham.

July
4 (Sun. Julian, Thurs. Gregorian) William Vaughan, author of *Golden
             Grove*, writes from Pisa mentioning John Matthew/
             Christopher Marlor (see Nicholl, *Reckoning*, 359).
7 (Wed.)   Sir Ralph Winwood, English ambassador to Paris, writes to
             Lord Burghley complaining that Italian actors have repres-
             ented the Queen on stage in Paris, and that the French

authorities are refusing to act on the grounds that 'the Death of the Duke of Guise hath ben plaied at London ... and ... that the Massacre of St. Bartholomews hath ben publickly acted' (quoted in Bakeless, *Christopher Marlowe*, 251). Presumably this refers to *The Massacre at Paris*, of which news had clearly reached Paris. Bakeless comments that 'One sees why nothing further is heard of Marlowe's play, upon the boards' (251).

18 (Sun.)   Robert Poley writes to Cecil giving him information about a priest.

November

22 (Mon.)   William Birde and Samuel Rowley are paid £4 by Philip Henslowe on behalf of the Admiral's Men for revisions to *Doctor Faustus*.

December

27 (Mon.)   Margery, daughter of Peter Frizer of Kingsclere in Hampshire, is christened. Peter Frizer may perhaps have been Ingram Frizer's brother (see Hopkins, 'New Light on Marlowe's Murderer').

29 (Wed.)   John Manningham, later to be famous for the diary he kept while a student at the Middle Temple in London, journeys to Canterbury for legal dealings with the Aldriches.

1603

Trial of Sir Walter Ralegh.

Publication of Richard Knolles, *The Generall Historie of the Turks*, containing an engraving of Tamburlaine which has been claimed as a portrait of Edward Alleyn in the role (see Martin Holmes).

Publication of Thomas Dekker, *The Wonderful Year*, in which he refers to 'Death (like a Spanish Leagar, or rather like stalking *Tamberlaine*)'.

Marlowe's sister Anne Cranford is accused by the Churchwardens of St Mary Breadman, Canterbury, of being 'a malicious contentious uncharitable person, seeking the unjust vexation of her neighbors as the fame goeth in our said parish', and 'a scold, a common swearer, a blasphemer of the name of god'.

February

18 (Fri.)   Wolstan Randall, who sat on the jury at the inquest into Marlowe's death, makes his will.

March
24 (Thurs.) Death of Elizabeth I.

Spring
John Mathews, alias Christopher Marlowe, is sent back to England.

June
John Cecil is captured off Gravesend and imprisoned.

November
19 (Sat.)   Christening at Faversham of John, son of Thomas Marloe, whom Michael Frohnsdorff suggests is Marlowe's younger brother (Frohnsdorff, vi).

December
Ingram Frizer is granted the lease in reversion of some lands of the Duchy of Lancaster for the benefit of Audrey, Lady Walsingham.

1604

Publication of the A text of *Doctor Faustus*.
Matthew Roydon is recorded as living with James I's favourite William Hamilton, Earl of Haddington.
John Marlowe is licensed 'to keep comon victualling in his now dwelling house'. He may also have been parish clerk of St Mary Breadman.
Some time between 1604 and 1606, Queen Anne's Men play *Edward II* at the Red Bull (see Bakeless, *Christopher Marlowe*, 194).

March
15 (Thurs.) Edward Alleyn makes a temporary return to the stage to play the Genius of the City in the 'Magnificent Entertainment' presented by the City of London to King James I.

June
Death of Paul Ive.
'Christopher Marlowe *alias* Mathews, a seminary preist' is committed to the Gatehouse Prison, Westminser, by the Lord Chief Justice (see Boas, *Christopher Marlowe*, 24).

July
22 (Sun.)   A Margaret Jordan is christened in St Margaret's, Canterbury. This might be a daughter of Marlowe's sister Margaret, but she is not mentioned in Katherine Marlowe's will.

August

11 (Sat.)   Marlowe's father John acts as a professional bondsman for a couple seeking a marriage licence.

September

23 (Sun.)   'Christopher Marlowe *alias* Mathews, a seminary preist' is recorded as indebted for his food and lodging for seven weeks in the Gatehouse Prison, Westminster.

November

Death of Richard Kitchen.

6 (Tues.)   John Cranford, husband of Marlowe's sister Ann, sues Thomas Gradwell, husband of Marlowe's sister Dorothy, in one suit, and Thomas and Dorothy jointly in another.

29 (Thurs.) Edward Alleyn is finally successful in his quest to obtain the Mastership of the Bears, Bulls, and Mastiff Dogs, jointly with Henslowe.

1605

Publication of Samuel Rowley's *When You See Me You Know Me*.

Tamburlaine the Great is reprinted.

Death of Sir Thomas Isham of Lamport Hall, where previously unknown editions of *Hero and Leander* and *All Ovids Elegies* would be discovered in 1867. It seems likely that this Sir Thomas was the purchaser.

Ingram Frizer is made churchwarden.

In this year all three of Marlowe's quarrelsome brothers-in-law are charged with offences – Thomas Gradwell with assault on John Reynoldes, labourer, John Jordan with unlicensed victualling, and John Cranford with selling unknown beer in pots not 'sysed'.

January

23 (Wed.)   Marlowe's father John makes his will.

26 (Sat.)   Marlowe's father John buried at St George's, Canterbury. He is termed 'clerk of St Maries'.

February

21 (Thurs.) The inventory of John Marlowe's goods is taken. The contents of the house are valued at £21 14s 2d.

March

17 (Sun.)   Marlowe's mother Katherine makes her will, leaving lega-
cies to her three surviving daughters. However, disagree-
ments over the will led to John Cranford, husband of Ann,
and Thomas Gradwell, husband of Dorothy, suing each
other, while the third daughter, Margaret, and her husband
John Jordan fell out with the Cranfords.

28 (Thurs.) Katherine Marlowe is buried at All Saints', Canterbury, not
at St George's as she had requested.

July

22 (Mon.)   Probate of Katherine Marlowe's will is granted.

1606

Tamburlaine the Great is reprinted.
Hero and Leander is reprinted.

June

24 (Tues.) Collimore Cranford, son of Marlowe's sister Ann and her
husband John Cranford, is baptised at St Mary Breadman,
Canterbury. He died in 1608.

December

30 (Tues.) Simon Aldrich is licensed to marry Elizabeth Hamon in
Canterbury.

1607

Publication of *D. Johann Fausten Gauckeltasche* (Dr Faustus' Conjuring
Bag) (see Jones, 10).
Simon Aldrich graduates as Bachelor of Divinity in Trinity College,
Cambridge.

June

21 (Sun.)   Agnes, daughter of Peter Frizer of Kingsclere in Hampshire,
is christened.

1608

Francis Aldrich, brother of Simon Aldrich, is appointed master of Sidney Sussex College by the Earl of Kent.
English actors on tour abroad perform *Doctor Faustus* and *The Jew of Malta* at Gratz (see Bakeless, 148).

February
28 (Sun.)   Date when Thomas Harriot said he gave the *Ars Naupegica* ('Art of Navigation') to Captain Edmund Marlowe, possibly a relation of Christopher Marlowe, for 'Mr. Baker the ship-write' (see Boas, *Christopher Marlowe*, 114).

April
4 (Mon.)   John Barber, who sat on the jury at the inquest into Marlowe's death, makes his will.

June
2 (Thurs.)   Ingram Frizer attends the funeral of Sir James Deane, who had purchased the Angel Inn from him. The connection between Frizer and Deane may afford one of the few slender clues to Frizer's background and connections.

December
13 (Sun.)   James Jordan, son of Marlowe's sister Margaret and her husband John Jordan, baptised at All Saints', Canterbury.

1609

The A text of *Doctor Faustus* is reprinted.
Hero and Leander is reprinted.
Death of Sir Edward Stanley.
Francis Aldrich becomes a Doctor of Divinity.

January
18 (Wed.)   Henry Oxinden, to whom Simon Aldrich later spoke about Marlowe, born in Canterbury.

March
9 (Thurs.)   William Warner is buried at Great Amwell in Hertfordshire.

June

26 (Mon.) John Cranford, husband of Marlowe's sister Ann, is appointed as one of Canterbury's four serjeants-at-mace, empowering him to make arrests and serve writs.

November

1 (Wed.) Francis Aldrich makes his will.

December

27 (Wed.) Death of Francis Aldrich.

1610

Dorothy Gradwell sues Margery White for defamation. Some time in the previous two years Dorothy has also been temporarily excommunicated over unpaid legal fees.

April

5 (Thurs.) Burial of the Richard Baines who is rector of Waltham (see Kendall, *Christopher Marlowe*, 114). For details of his will and of the inventory of his possessions, see Kendall.

June

17 (Sun.) 'Richearde Baynes sonne of Richearde Baynes clarke late deceased' baptised at Waltham (see Kendall, *Christopher Marlowe*, 318), indicating that the Waltham Baines' wife was pregnant when he died.

1611

Birth of Owen Cranford, son of Marlowe's sister Ann Cranford and her husband John. Baptised at St Mary Breadman, Canterbury, he died in 1638. This is the last Cranford child whose baptism can be traced, but there were also Margaret, Katherine, John, Rebecca, a second daughter called Elizabeth, and possibly one called Sarah (Urry, 34–5).

The A text of *Doctor Faustus* is reprinted.

Ingram Frizer is made parish tax-assessor at Eltham and is recorded as holding land valued at 20 shillings.

January

19 (Sat.)   Christening of Faversham of John, son of Thomas Marlowe. Michael Frohnsdorff suggests that this is another son of the man whom he identifies as Marlowe's brother, though the register does not record the death of the previous John (Frohnsdroff, vi).

May

27 (Mon.)   Barbara Baines, widow of the Richard Baines who was rector of Waltham, marries his successor Christopher Markham. She had been born Barbara Wentworth and was the daughter of Francis Wentworth of Waltham (see Kendall, *Christopher Marlowe*, 318).

July

16 (Tues.)   Ingram Frizer gives evidence about charities at East Greenwich.

October

2 (Wed.)   Burial at All Saints, Waltham of Francis Wentworth, father of Barbara Baines.

1612

A musical setting of 'The Passionate Shepherd to his Love' is published by William Corkine, probably the son of the tailor with whom Marlowe had his 1592 fight, in his *Second Book of Ayres*.
Edward II reprinted.

January

1 (Wed.)   Philemon Jordan, son of Marlowe's sister Margaret and her husband John Jordan, is baptised at St Mary Breadman, Canterbury.

April

6 (Mon.)   William Curry, who sat on the jury at the inquest into Marlowe's death, makes his will.

19 (Sun.)   Elizabeth, daughter of Peter Frizer of Kingsclere in Hampshire, is christened.

October
15 (Thurs.) Burial at Faversham of John, son of Thomas Marlowe.

1613

John Cranford, husband of Marlowe's sister Ann, becomes parish clerk of St Mary Breadman.
Hero and Leander is reprinted.
Publication at Cambridge of William Perkins, *A Discourse of Witchcraft*.

January
4 (Mon.) Laurence Applegate the tailor, who had been a friend of John Marlowe since at least 1564, is buried at St George's, Canterbury.

May
17 (Mon.) Edward Alleyn begins construction of the College of God's Gift at Dulwich.

December
Last mention of John Fixer, still under restraint.

1614

Publication of Sir Walter Ralegh, *History of the World*, in which the description of Tamburlaine's footstool has been seen as influenced by Marlowe (see Brown, 'Marlowe's Debasement', 46).
Jonson's *Bartholomew Fair*, which contains a parody of *Hero and Leander*.

April
14 (Thurs.) Christening at Faversham of Bennet, daughter of Thomas and Elizabeth Marlowe (see Frohnsdorff, vi).
17 (Sun.) Christening at Faversham of Nicholas, son of Thomas and Elizabeth Marlowe (see Frohnsdorff, vi).

September
7 (Wed.) Alice, daughter of Peter Frizer of Kingsclere in Hampshire, is christened.

24 (Sat.)   Christening at Faversham of Marie, daughter of Thomas and Elizabeth Marlowe (see Frohnsdorff, vi). It is hard to imagine what could explain three christenings in one year, so these may perhaps refer to different couples.

1615

John Stow in *The Life and Death of Sir Francis Drake* sums up his importance with 'In briefe, he was as famous in Europe and America as Tamberlaine in Asia and Africa' (Bawlf, epigraph).

December
Death of John Cranford, husband of Marlowe's sister Ann.

1616

Publication of the B text of *Doctor Faustus*.
Hero and Leander is perhaps reprinted (see Bakeless, 323).
The Pope commends John Cecil to Marie de' Medici.

January
6 (Sat.)   Death of Philip Henslowe.

March
10 (Sun.)   Bennet, daughter of Thomas Marlowe, buried at Faversham.

April
23 (Tues.) Death of Shakespeare.

September
The chapel at Dulwich College, Edward Alleyn's foundation, is consecrated by George Abbot, Archbishop of Canterbury.

1617

Hero and Leander is reprinted.

March
30 (Sun.)   Christening at Faversham of Sara, daughter of Thomas and Elizabeth Marlowe. This Sara Marlowe may have married in 1642 (Frohnsdorff, vi).

April

9 (Wed.)   Philip Henslowe's widow Agnes, Edward Alleyn's mother-in-law, is buried in Dulwich Chapel.

May

9 (Fri.)   Elizabeth Marlowe, wife of Thomas, buried at Faversham. Thomas Marlowe shortly afterwards marries Maria Wigges and then disappears from the Faversham registers (Frohnsdorff, vii).

December

2 (Tues.)   John Benchkin deposes that he wrote out the will of Sir Thomas Harflete, knight, on 18 September at the latter's request.

1618

A Robert Poley, gentleman, is licensed to travel abroad (though not to Rome) with three other men. One of these was named John Shelton; William Urry speculates that this may be the same Poley and that there may be some significance to the fact that Shelton was the maiden name of Audrey Walsingham (Urry, 96).

Thomas Coryat refers to the popularity of Tamburlaine in a letter written from Agra (see Bowers, 362).

April

17 (Fri.)   Edward Alleyn is shown over the Earl of Arundel's collection of pictures and statues by the earl's servant.

May

(Mon.)   Joan, daughter of Peter Frizer of Kingsclere in Hampshire, is christened.

1619

The B text of *Doctor Faustus* is reprinted.

September

13 (Mon.)   Edward Alleyn reads the Deed of Foundation of Dulwich College. The event is attended by, among others, Francis Bacon, Inigo Jones, Sir John Bodley and Thomas Howard, 2nd Earl of Arundel.

1620

The B text of *Doctor Faustus* is reprinted.
An anonymous account describes how 'men goe to the Fortune in Golding-lane to see the Tragedie of Doctor Faustus. There indeed a man may behold shagge-hayr'd Deulls runne roaring ouer the Stage with Squibs in their mouthes, while Drummers make Thunder in the Tyring-house, and the twelue-penny Hirelings make artificiall Lightning in their Heauens' (quoted in Bakeless, 146).

October
18 (Wed.)   'Tamberlane, s.[on of] William Bowdler' christened at Ludlow. The choice of name presumably testifies to an admiration for Marlowe's play, which had been acted in nearby Leominster some time in 1619–20 (see Bowers, 362).

1621

April
Sir Henry Yelverton, giving evidence to the House of Lords, compares James I's favourite, the Duke of Buckingham, to Edward II's favourite, Hugh Despenser, suggesting something of the paradigms within which Marlowe's play was likely to be read (see Perry).

June
29 (Fri.)   Thomas Hariot makes his will.

July
2 (Mon.)   Death of Thomas Hariot.

1622

Edward II is reprinted, presumably as a result of its newfound topicality in the light of James I's liaison with the Duke of Buckingham.
Hero and Leander is reprinted.
Margaret Cranford, daughter of Marlowe's sister Ann and her husband John Cranford, marries Richard Maple, bricklayer, at All Saints, Canterbury.

1623

Thomas Gradwell, husband of Marlowe's sister Dorothy, is bound over to keep the peace.

The Lord Mayor's Show for this year, written by Thomas Middleton, includes Tamburlaine among its six worthies (see Bowers, 362).

June

6 (Thurs.) Burial at All Saints Waltham of Barbara Markham, formerly Baines, widow of the Richard Baines who was rector of Waltham.

28 (Sat.) Death of Edward Alleyn's wife Joan.

December

3 (Wed.) Edward Alleyn marries Constance Donne, daughter of the poet John Donne.

1624

The B text of *Doctor Faustus* is reprinted.

Publication of Thomas Heywood, *The Captives; or, the Lost Recovered,* and *Gunaikeion or, Nine Bookes of Various History Concerning Women,* both containing parts of the narrative of the friar sub-plot in *The Jew of Malta.*

Death of Audrey, Lady Walsingham, wife of Marlowe's friend Thomas Walsingham.

Robert Pooley, Esq., is recorded as MP for Queenborough. Apart from the coincidence of name, there is no evidence to suggest this is Robert Poley, but see Urry (96) for further information on him.

1625

Death of Thomas Gradwell, husband of Marlowe's sister Dorothy. There is no burial record for a Dorothy Gradwell, so she may have remarried and been buried under a different name.

November

17 (Thurs.) Thomas Gradwell's will is proved.

25 (Fri.) Dorothy Gradwell sues her son John (or conceivably her stepson: Thomas appears to have left two sons both called John) over Thomas Gradwell's will.

1626

Year in which the portrait of Edward Alleyn now at Dulwich College was painted. On what this may tell us about Alleyn's stage appearance, particularly in the rôle of Tamburlaine, see Cerasano ('Tamburlaine', 175).

February
14 (Tues.)   Thomas Gradwell's will is pronounced genuine in court.

May
9 (Tues.)   Date on the will of one Robert Poley, 'citizen and habber-
             dasher of London', whom Bakeless (217) suggested might
             be the Poley who knew Marlowe.

November
25 (Sat.)   Death of Edward Alleyn.

December
21 (Thurs.) Death of John Cecil.
26 (Tues.)   Last known mention of Marlowe's sister Dorothy Gradwell,
             who is reported to have various suitors (Urry, 38).

1627

Drayton writes in *Of Poets and Poetry* of 'Neat Marlowe, bathed in the
Thespian Springs'.

May
Marlowe's sister Ann Cranford assaults William Prowde with sword and
knife.

August
14 (Tues.)   Ingram Frizer is buried in Eltham church.

1628

The B text of *Doctor Faustus* is reprinted.
Katherine Cranford, daughter of Marlowe's sister Ann and her husband
John Cranford, marries John Anthony of London, saddler.
First printing of Francis Hubert's poem *The Historie of Edward II*, which
had been circulating in manuscript since some time in the 1590s (see
Perry).

1629

Hero and Leander is reprinted, in an edition containing annotations
about Marlowe and 'Mr Fineux'.

Francis Hubert's poem *The Historie of Edward II* is reprinted.
Publication at London of R. M., *Micrologia*, containing the information that when Bridewell inmates are made to clean the streets, 'as they passe, the people scoffing say, / "Holla, ye pampered jades of Asia!"'

1630

May
3 (Mon.)   Sir Thomas Walsingham conveys some property to Henry Sholton, presumably a relative of his late wife, Audrey. The document is at the Folger Shakespeare Library and bears his signature. Walsingham dies later in the year.

1631

The B text of *Doctor Faustus* is reprinted. This was the last printing of *Doctor Faustus* still to use black letter type, more normally associated with the Bible (see Sachs, 633–4).
Walter Warner edits Thomas Harriot's work on algebra.

1632

November
5 (Mon.)   Death of Henry Percy, 9th Earl of Northumberland.

1633

First publication of *The Jew of Malta*, with a prologue by Thomas Heywood. This is the only known early printing of the play.
William Prynne's *Histrio-Mastix* describes how 'the visible apparition of the Devill on the Stage at the Belsavage Play-house, in Queene Elizabeth's dayes, (to the great amazement both of the Actors and Spectators) whiles they were prophanely playing the History of Faustus (the truth of which I have heard from many who now live, who well remember it,) there being some distracted with that fearfull sight' (quoted in Bakeless, 146–7).

1637

Publication of a new edition of *Hero and Leander*. Except for the 1663 *Doctor Faustus*, this was to be the last Marlowe edition until Dodsley's *Old Plays* in 1744.

1639

June

3 (Mon.)   Peter Frizer of Kingsclere makes his will.

1641

February

10 (Wed.)   Henry Oxinden notes that Simon Aldrich had told him that:

> Marlo who wrot Hero & Leander was an Atheist: & had writ a booke against the Scripture; how that it was al one man's making, & would haue printed it but could not be suffered. He was the son of a shomaker in Cant. He said hee was an excellent scoller & made excellent verses in Lattin & died aged about 30; he was stabd in the head with a dagger & dyed swearing.

Aldrich further reported that 'Sir Walter Raleigh was an Atheist in his younger days' (see Eccles, 41).

12 (Fri.)   Henry Oxinden writes down the following information received from Simon Aldrich about a Mr Fineux of Dover:

> Mr Ald. sayd that mr Fineux of Douer was an Atheist & that hee would go out at midnight into a wood, & fall down uppon his knees & pray heartily that that Deuil would come, that he might see him (for hee did not beleiue that there was a Deuil) Mr Ald: sayd that hee was a verie good scholler, but would neuer haue aboue one booke at a time, & when hee was perfect in it, hee would sell it away & buy another: he learnd all *Marlo* by heart & diuers other bookes: *Marlo* made him an *Atheist*. This Fineaux was faine to make a speech uppon *The foole hath said in his heart there is no God*, to get his degree. Fineaux would say as Galen sayd that man was of a more excellent composition then a beast, & thereby could speake; but affirmed that his soule dyed with his body, & as we remember nothing before wee were borne, so we shall remember nothing after wee are dead. (see Eccles, 40)

This used to be identified as Thomas Fineux, who matriculated at Corpus Christi in the Easter Term of 1587, but Constance Kuriyama has recently suggested that it might have been his younger brother John, who was an exact contemporary of Simon Aldrich (*Christopher Marlowe*, 160).

1642

Death of Marlowe's sister Margaret Jordan.

1652

Death of John Jordan, husband of Marlowe's sister Margaret.

December

7 (Tues.)   Marlowe's sister Ann Cranford is buried at All Saints Church Canterbury, aged 81.

1653

Izaak Walton's *The Compleat Angler* prints 'The Passionate Shepherd' and ascribes it to Marlowe.

1654

Publication of Edmund Grayton, *Festivous Notes on Don Quixote*, which claims that at festivals players were often asked to act 'sometimes *Tamburlaine*, sometimes *Jugurth*, sometimes *The Jew of Malta*, and sometimes parts of all these'.

April

8 (Sat.)   'a comedie called *The Maidens Holiday* by Christopher Marlow and John Day' is entered in the Stationers' Register. No one now accepts the attribution to Christopher Marlowe.

1655

A second edition of *The Compleat Angler* prints a slightly different version of 'The Passionate Shepherd'.

July

23 (Mon.)   Death of Simon Aldrich.

1662

May

26 (Mon.) Samuel Pepys saw a performance of *Doctor Faustus*, 'but so wretchedly & poorly done that we were sick of it' (see Bakeless, 147).

1663

Publication at London of a a version of *Doctor Faustus* rewritten as a farce.
Publication of a quarto edition of *Doctor Faustus*.

1670

Sir Sackville Crow, who is in charge of the manufacture of tapestries at Mortlake, describes the story of Hero and Leander as one of only six 'worth the making' (see Bakeless, *Christopher Marlowe*, 303).

April

10 (Sun.) 'Tamberlaine, s. of Mr. Tamb: Davies was buried' at Ludlow, another sign of the popularity of the name there. It is intriguing that Mr Tamberlaine Davies became one of Ludlow's wealthiest citizens, in the true style of his name-sake (see Bowers, 362).

1675

Milton's nephew Edward Phillips in his *Theatrum Poetarum* calls Marlowe 'a kind of a second *Shakesphear*' but assigns *Tamburlaine* to Thomas Newton, author of *A Notable Historie of the Saracens*.
The Duke of York's company play *Doctor Faustus* before Charles II.

1681

Charles Saunders' *Tamerlane the Great* is acted. When it was censured as 'only an Old Play transcrib'd', Saunders claimed never to have heard of Marlowe's play, or to have found anyone else who had either (see Boas, 300).

1686

Probable first production of William Mountford's rewriting of *Doctor Faustus* (see Brooke, 386).

1691

Anthony Wood in *Athenae Oxonienses* assigns *Tamburlaine* to Marlowe, correctly identifies him as a student at Cambridge and a contemporary of Shakespeare, and says that he used to be an actor. Gerard Langbaine, writing in the same year, cannot conceive why Phillips should have ascribed *Tamburlaine* to Newton.

1695

October
10 (Thurs.) 'Tamberlaine, s. of Thomas Davies & Elinor' baptised in Ludlow. This child died shortly after birth but in 1702 Thomas and Elinor gave the same name to another son, and the name continued to appear, presumably among members of the same family, into the nineteenth century (see the International Genealogical Index).

1697

Publication at London of William Mountford, *The Life and Death of Doctor Faustus, Made into a Farce. By Mr Mountford. With the Humours of* Harlequin *and* Scaramouche, *As they were several times Acted by Mr. Lee and Mr. Jevon, at the Queens Theatre in* Dorset *Garden. Newly Revived, at the Theatre in* Lincolns Inn Fields, *With Songs and* Dances *between the Acts.*

1724

Publication of *Harlequin Dr. Faustus*, by the dancing-master John Thurmond.

1744

Publication of Dodsley's *Old Plays*, including *Edward II*.

1752

William Rufus Chetwode's *British Theatre* declares that Marlowe was stabbed in 1592 by a man whom he disturbed in the bedchamber of a loose woman with whom he was having an affair.

1753

Colley Cibber speaks of Marlowe as blaspheming the Trinity (see Kendall, *Christopher Marlowe*, 185).

1754

Date at which Thomas Warton later said that he had seen a copy of *Dido, Queen of Carthage* in T. Osborne's shop which included a copy of Nashe's now lost elegy on the death of Marlowe (see Boas, *Christopher Marlowe*, 50).

Thomas Godfrey's *Prince of Parthia*, the first American play acted on the English stage, shows a clear debt to the Tamburlaine story, albeit in Rowe's redaction.

1759

Death of John Warburton, last person known to have seen the text of *The Maiden's Holiday*. Like many others of his playscripts, it was probably used to line pie-dishes by his cook, Betsy (see Greg). Warburton's only comment on the play was to record it as 'The Mayden Holaday by Chris. Marlowe'.

1764

David Erskine Baker in his *Companion to the Playhouse* declares that Marlowe and Day co-authored *The Maiden's Holiday*.

1774–81

Publication of Thomas Warton's *History of English Poetry*, the first serious critical engagement with Marlowe.

1777

Publication at London of John Berkenhout, *Biographia Literaria*, containing a forged letter purporting to be from George Peele to Marlowe about Shakespeare, Jonson and Alleyn (see Brooke, 391).

1780

The second edition of Dodsley's *Old Plays*, including *The Jew of Malta*.

1782

Joseph Ritson discovers the Baines Note (see Kendall, *Christopher Marlowe*, 264–5).

1785

Death of the actor John Henderson, who is said to have bought Henry Oxinden's copy of *Dido, Queen of Carthage* (see Bakeless, 325).

1795

Death of Major-General J. A. Hamilton, a Scot who became Master of the Royal Household of Sweden and probably took with him the copy of the 1628 edition of *Doctor Faustus* which eventually reached the Kungliga Biblioteket in Stockholm.

1796

Goethe plans a work on the Hero and Leander story (see Bakeless, 150).

1807

Publication at London of Percy and Steevens, *Poems in Blank Verse (not Dramatique) prior to Milton's Paradise Lost*, including Marlowe's translation of Lucan.
The great-grandson of Henry Oxinden bequeaths his library to the parish of Eltham. Many books are subsequently borrowed and not returned, and Oxinden's collection is broken up.

1808

Charles Lamb, in *Specimens of English Dramatic Poets*, praises the death scene of Edward II.

1810

Publication of Scott's *The Ancient British Drama*, which included *Edward II* and *The Jew of Malta*.

1811

February
28 (Thurs.) Edmond Malone writes in his copy of Langbaine that he believes *Tamburlaine* to have been written by Nicholas Breton. A previous MS annotation by Malone ascribes it to Nashe.

1814

Publication at London of C. W. Dilke, *Old English Plays*, including *Doctor Faustus* and *Edward II*.

1815

Publication at London of Sir Egerton Brydges, *Restituta*, including *Hero and Leander*.
Last performances of Nicholas Rowe's *Tamerlane*, which has held the stage since 1702.

1816

Publication at London of a further edition of Dodsley's *Old Plays*, including *Doctor Faustus*.

1818

James Broughton, in his privately printed edition of *Tamburlaine*, expresses disbelief in Marlowe's authorship.
Publication at London of W. Oxberry, in separate texts, of *The Jew of Malta*, *Edward II*, *Doctor Faustus*, *Lust's Dominion*, sometimes then attributed to Marlowe, and *The Massacre at Paris*.
Publication of the first German translation of *Doctor Faustus*.

April

24 (Fri.) Edmund Kean revives *The Jew of Malta*. This seems to have been the first time that a Marlowe play had been seen on the stage since the 1633 *Doctor Faustus*.

June

11 (Thurs.) Goethe records in his diary 'Dr. Faust von Marlowe' (see Bakeless, 150).

1819

J. P. Collier starts to produce a series of articles 'On the Early English Dramatists' for the *Edinburgh Magazine*, of which the first deals mainly with Marlowe.

The Monthly Review publishes the first known speculation that Marlowe was in fact a pseudonym of Shakespeare (see Kuriyama, *Christopher Marlowe*, 170).

April

29 (Thurs.) Alexander Blair discusses Marlowe in a letter to John Wilson (quoted in full in Kuriyama, *Christopher Marlowe*, 168–9).

1820

Rev. Jones of St Nicholas's church, Deptford assures James Broughton that Marlowe was killed by 'Francis Archer'. This inaugurated a confusion that would last some considerable time.

W. Oxberry publishes the two parts of *Tamburlaine*.

Publication at London of William Hazlitt, Lectures *Chiefly on the Dramatic Literature of the Age of Elizabeth*, praising Marlowe.

Publication at London of J. P. Collier, *Poetical Decameron*, discussing Marlowe.

1821

An anonymous article in *Retrospective Review, and Historical and Antiquarian Magazine*, vol. 4, dismisses the rumours of Marlowe's atheism on the grounds that his plays are highly moral.

1824

Goethe discusses *Doctor Faustus* (see Bakeless, 150).

1825

Publication at London of Hurst and Robinson's *Old English Drama*, including *Dido, Queen of Carthage*.
John Payne Collier announces the 'discovery' (?) of the *Massacre at Paris* leaf, a much longer version of a speech from the play, which he says is in the hands of the London bookseller Rodd (see Adams, 447). Collier's known habits of forgery leave a question mark over the authenticity of this, but *The Massacre at Paris* certainly does read like a garbled and truncated text, and there is nothing inherently implausible in the 'Collier leaf'.

1826

Publication of the first collected edition of Marlowe, probably by George Robinson.

1827

Oxberry's editions are all brought out together, along with *Dido, Queen of Carthage*, as *The Dramatic Works of Christopher Marlowe, with Prefatory Remarks, Notes, Critical and Explanatory*, by W. Oxberry, Comedian.

1829

Goethe praises *Doctor Faustus* in conversation with Henry Crabb Robinson, exclaiming 'How greatly is it all planned!' (see Bakeless, 150).

1831

Publication of the first German translations of *The Jew of Malta* and *Edward II*.

1834

The 1629 edition of *Hero and Leander* containing Henry Oxinden's annotations is sold to an unnamed buyer (see Bakeless, 331).

1837–39

Henry Hallam, *Introduction to the Literature of Europe*, praises Marlowe.

1844

Leigh Hunt, *Imagination and Fancy*, praises Marlowe.

1850

First of Alexander Dyce's editions of Marlowe, *Introductory Account of Marlowe and his Writings*, including for the first time the A text as well as the B text. This included information about the Marlowe family and the first mention of the fact of Marlowe's attendance at the King's School, Canterbury.

May

18 (Sat.)   A contributor to *Notes and Queries* claims to possess a sixteenth-century MS containing sixteen sonnets and an eclogue signed 'Ch. M.', which he says are by Marlowe. The sonnets are addressed to an Elizabethan painter named Seager (presumably William Segar). There was no further known sighting of them until 1988, when Sukanta Chaudhuri was able to disprove the attribution to Marlowe.

1858

Second of Alexander Dyce's editions of Marlowe.
Publication of the first French translation of *Doctor Faustus*.

1860

Sale, in New York, and last sighting of a copy of *Dido, Queen of Carthage* which may have been the one containing Nashe's elegy on Marlowe (see Bakeless, 327). It had been in the library of the English actor William E. Burton.

1865

Hippolyte Taine, *History of English Literature*, praises Marlowe.

1867

The antiquarian Sir Charles Edmonds discovers the only two known copies of Paul Linley's 1598 *Hero and Leander* at Lamport Hall in Northampton, together with a volume binding together the 1599 edition of

Venus and Adonis, a first edition of the 1599 *Passionate Pilgrim*, and the *Epigrammes of Sir John Davies and Certaine of Ovid's Elegies: translated by Christopher Marlowe*. These may have belonged to John Isham, who was a student at Cambridge in the late sixteenth century, and bought many books for himself and also to read to his blind father (Wraight and Stern, 221–3). Until this discovery, it was not known that the 1598 *Hero and Leander* had contained a dedication to Audrey, Lady Walsingham (the wife of Marlowe's friend Sir Thomas) signed by George Chapman.

1876

A copy of the previously unknown 1594 edition of *Edward II* is discovered in the Landesbibliothek in Kassel. English actors had visited the court of Kassel in 1594 (see Bakeless, 329–30).

1885

A. H. Bullen's edition of Marlowe, including only the A text of *Doctor Faustus*.

1887

Havelock Ellis makes the Baines Note available in its entirety (in an appendix to his *Sexual Inversion*) for the first time since Ritson's original 1782 publication of it (see Kendall, *Christopher Marlowe*, 265).

1889

Publication of a collected edition of Marlowe translated into French.

1891

Henry Irving unveils a memorial to Marlowe in Canterbury.

1893

Havelock Ellis's Mermaid edition.
Sidney Lee's *DNB* article on Marlowe.
Publication of the first German edition of *Tamburlaine the Great*, Part One.

1894

Sidney Lee in *The Athenaeum* identifies Marlowe as one of the participants in the Hog Lane fight.

1898

Publication of the first Italian translation of *Doctor Faustus*.

1903

August
10 (Mon.) William Poel produces *Edward II* for the Elizabethan Stage Society.

1904

Publication at London of J. H. Ingram, *Christopher Marlowe and His Associates*.

1907

February
18 (Mon.) The discovery of the 'Grafton' portrait of Shakespeare is announced in the *Manchester Guardian*. A. D. Wraight and Virginia F. Stern have argued that this is in fact of Marlowe (Wraight and Stern, 219). However, as always, the subtext of Wraight's work here is the desire to 'prove' that Shakespeare *was* Marlowe.

1909

G. C. Moore Smith identifies and publishes the Corpus Christi records of Marlowe's residences in college.

1910

C. F. Tucker Brooke's old-spelling edition, *Works of Christopher Marlowe*. At some time between 1910 and 1920, a copy of the previously unknown 1628 edition of *Doctor Faustus* is discovered in the library of Lincoln College, Oxford.

1911

Doctor Faustus is translated into Spanish.

1912

Doctor Faustus is translated into Polish.
Ivan Bloch declares that Marlowe died in a quarrel over a soldiers' camp follower (see Bakeless, 240).

1913

Publication of Alfred Noyes' *Tales of the Mermaid Tavern*, in which Marlowe is pictured drinking and swapping stories with Ben Jonson, Lyly, Peele, Lodge and Drayton, mischievously sharing his and Jonson's plan for coining with the unpleasant puritan Master Richard Bame (something which is particularly interesting in the light of the fact that Marlowe's arrest for coining in Flushing had not yet come to light), and is eventually fatally stabbed on board the *Golden Hind* by one Archer, lover of the wicked woman to whom he has inadvisedly given his heart, and dying in the arms of Thomas Nash. It also has 'Bame' habitually referring to Marlowe as 'wormal' and suggests that this is a common alias for him in literature of his time.

1914

Publication of the first Italian translation of *Edward II*.

1917

An article called 'Marlowe and the Heavy Wrath of God', written by a vicar, proposes that Marlowe and his characters were all damned (see Bakeless, 238).
The London bookseller Dobell sells the copy of the 1629 *Hero and Leander* which contained Oxinden's additions to an unknown buyer. It has not been seen since (see Bakeless, 330–1).

1919

June
3 (Tues.)   Sir Frank Benson unveils a memorial tablet to Marlowe in
              Deptford parish church.

1920

Students at Birkbeck College, London, produce *Edward II*.

1922

The Phoenix Society puts on *The Jew of Malta* in London.
A 'highly modernist' production of *Edward II* is staged in Prague (Bakeless, 194).

1923

The Phoenix Society puts on *Edward II* at the Regent Theatre, London.

1925

Publication of Leslie Hotson, *The Death of Christopher Marlowe*, identifying Marlowe's killer as Ingram Frizer and revealing the circumstances of his death.

1926

The Marlowe Society produces *Edward II* at Cambridge.

1929

F. S. Boas, *Marlowe and his Circle*.

1930–33

The six-volume critical edition of Marlowe appeared under the general editorship of R. H. Case.

1933

February
9–11 (Thurs.–Sat.) *Edward II* is performed at Christ Church, Oxford.

1934

Mark Eccles, *Christopher Marlowe in London*. This carries the first account of the papers relating to the fight with William Bradley at Hog Lane, which Eccles had discovered.

C. E. Lawrence's play *The Reckoning* is acted at the Royal Academy of Dramatic Art.

1937

February
27 (Sat.)   A letter in the *Times Literary Supplement* first proposes the identification of Marlowe with the Morley who 'read to' Arbella Stuart.

March
6 (Sat.)   A reply in the *Times Literary Supplement* contests the proposed identification.

1938

Publication of John Bakeless, *Christopher Marlowe*.

1939

James Smith's *Scrutiny* essay contests the view of Marlowe as a purely subjective artist.
Frank W. Tyler discovers Katherine Benchkin's will, with the only known signature of Marlowe, in the Canterbury archives.

1940

Publication of F. S. Boas, *Christopher Marlowe*.
The memorial tablet to Marlowe in Deptford parish church is destroyed by enemy action.

1941

Publication of Roy W. Battenhouse, *Tamburlaine: A Study in Renaissance Moral Philosophy*.
Timur the Lame exhumed.

1942

June
1 (Mon.)   57 St George's Street, Canterbury, the house identified by local tradition as Marlowe's childhood home, is destroyed

during a German air raid. On the question of whether it was really Marlowe's house, see Kuriyama, *Christopher Marlowe*, 13.

1946

Publication of Paul H. Kocher, *Christopher Marlowe, A Study of his Thought, Learning and Character*.

1950

Publication of W. W. Greg's double edition of the two texts of *Doctor Faustus, The Tragical History of the Life and Death of Doctor Faustus*.

1951

Publication of Michel Poirier, *Christopher Marlowe*.
Tamburlaine (a condensed version of Parts One and Two) is staged at the Old Vic Theatre with Donald Wolfit in the title rôle.

1952

Publication of Harry Levin, *The Overreacher: A Study of Christopher Marlowe*.
Publication of John Bakeless, *The Tragicall History of Christopher Marlowe*.

1953

Publication of a revised edition of F. S. Boas, *Christopher Marlowe*.
Discovery of the Corpus Christi portrait of a young man aged 21 in 1585.

1955

Calvin Hoffman proposes the identification of the Corpus Christi portrait as Marlowe, and although there is no real evidence for the identification, the portrait is now habitually used as a cover for books on Marlowe and has become indelibly associated with him.

1956

Edward II is put on at the Theatre Royal, Stratford East, directed by Joan Littlewood.

May

1 (Tues.)   Sir Thomas Walsingham's tomb at Scadbury is opened by Calvin Hoffman in pursuit of evidence for his theory that Marlowe survived the stabbing in Deptford and wrote the works of Shakespeare. The tomb was found to contain nothing but sand, intended to serve as a damp course. Actual burials were in the vault below, to which the Home Office refused to grant entry.

1957

The Association of Men of Kent and Kentish Men erects a replacement memorial tablet to Marlowe in Deptford parish church.

1961

In 1961–2 *Doctor Faustus*, directed by Michael Benthall, is performed at the Old Vic.

1962

Publication of J. D. Jump's Revels edition of *Doctor Faustus*.
Publication of Douglas Cole, *Suffering and Evil in the Plays of Christopher Marlowe*.
Publication of David M. Bevington, *From Mankind to Marlowe: Growth of Structure in the Popular Drama of Tudor England*.
Publication of E. M. Waith, *The Herculean Hero*.
Publication of J. P. Brockbank, *Marlowe: Dr. Faustus*.

1963

Publication of Irving Ribner's edition of *The Complete Plays of Christopher Marlowe*.

1964

Four hundredth anniversary of Marlowe's birth.
Tulane Drama Review 8 is entirely devoted to Marlowe.
Publication of J. B. Steane, *Marlowe: A Critical Study*.

Publication of Clifford Leech, ed., *Marlowe: A Collection of Critical Essays*, the first book of essays devoted to Marlowe.

1970

A Dutch-language made-for-TV film called *Christoffel Marlowe*, directed by Dré Poppe, is released in Belgium. Characters include Hariot, Shakespeare, Roydon, Ralegh and Poley.

1971

The full text of the Dutch Church Libel is discovered.

1976

Discovery by R. B. Wernham of the Flushing coining episode.

1981

Publication of Stephen Greenblatt, *Renaissance Self-Fashioning*, which contains an influential essay on 'Marlowe and the Will to Absolute Play'.

1986

Publication of Clifford Leech, *Christopher Marlowe: A Poet for the Stage*.

1991

Derek Jarman's film of *Edward II*.

1992

First edition of Charles Nicholl, *The Reckoning*.

1996

The 660th anniversary of the birth of Timur the Lame is widely celebrated in Uzbekistan. Events include a conference held by the Uzbek Women's Committee to celebrate his progressive attitude towards women (see Norton).

1999

Publication of Yuzo Yamada's *Writing under Influences: A Study of Christopher Marlowe*, the first monograph on Marlowe published in Japan.

2002

July
Publication of Constance Kuriyama, *Christopher Marlowe: A Renaissance Life*.
Second edition of Charles Nicholl, *The Reckoning*.
11 (Thurs.) Unveiling by the actor Sir Antony Sher of an engraved panel dedicated to Marlowe in the memorial window of Poets' Corner in Westminster Abbey. The inscription controversially included a question mark after the 1593 date of death, reflecting the Marlowe Society's conspiracy theory that Marlowe survived Deptford and wrote the works of Shakespeare.

2004

Publication of Patrick Cheney, ed., *The Cambridge Companion to Christopher Marlowe*.
Publication of David Riggs, *The World of Christopher Marlowe*.

Who's Who in the Marlowe Chronology

Agrippa, Heinrich Cornelius. Supposed magician and author of several books; a possible influence on *Doctor Faustus*.

Aldrich, Simon. Canterbury and Cambridge man who tells an anecdote about Marlowe and 'Mr Fineux' (see under 1641).

Allen, William, Cardinal. Responsible for the imprisonment of Richard Baines at Douai (see under 1582).

Alleyn, Edward. Actor. Took the leading rôle in *Tamburlaine*, *The Jew of Malta* and *Doctor Faustus*.

Alleyn, John. Brother of Edward.

Arthur, Dorothy. Marlowe's cousin, who came to live with his family after she was orphaned.

Arthur, Thomas. Marlowe's maternal uncle.

Babington, Anthony. Catholic conspirator entrapped by Robert Poley (see under 1586).

Baines, Richard. Studied at Douai; detained with Marlowe in Flushing for coining (see under 26 January 1592); author of the 'Note' alleging that Marlowe held heretical opinions (see under 26 May 1593).

Ballard, John. One of the Babington conspirators (see under 1586).

Benchkin, John. Canterbury and Cambridge man who may have been a friend of Marlowe's.

Blount, Christopher. Catholic and eventual stepfather of the Earl of Essex; on the fringes of a number of big political events. His mother was a Poley so he may have been connected with Robert Poley.

Bridgeman, Jacob. Marlowe's successor as Parker Scholar.

Bruno, Giordano. Author; eventually burned for heresy; probably the source of the name 'Bruno' in *Doctor Faustus*.

Bull, Eleanor. Owner of the house in which Marlowe died.

Catlin, Maliverny. Walsingham *agent provocateur*.

Cecil, John. Catholic priest and possible double agent (see under 1590).

Chapman, George. Playwright and apparent friend of Marlowe; completed *Hero and Leander*.

Cholmeley, Richard. Alleged to have been converted to atheism by Marlowe (see under 1593).

Corkine, William. Canterbury tailor with whom Marlowe had a street fight on 15 September 1592.

Cranford, John. Husband of Marlowe's sister Ann.

Dee, John. Self-styled wizard and member of the Ralegh circle.

Drury, Thomas. Associate of Richard Cholmeley who was involved in the machinations surrounding Marlowe's death.

'Fagot'. Spy in the house of the French ambassador to London; possibly the alias of Giordano Bruno.

Fairfax, Paul. Possible candidate for the 'P. F.' who translated the *English Faust Book*.

Faunt, Nicholas. Canterbury and Cambridge man and Walsingham spy.

Fineux, John. Possible candidate for the 'Mr Fineux of Dover' who is alleged to have learned all Marlowe's works by heart.

Fineux, Thomas. Brother of John and the other possible candidate.

Fixer, John. Catholic priest associated with John Cecil.

Fleetwood, William. Recorder of London before whom Marlowe appeared.

Forman, Simon. Self-styled magus; possible influence on Faustus.

Frenche, Peter. Possible candidate for the 'P. F.' who translated the *English Faust Book*.

Frizer, Ingram. Marlowe's killer.

Gifford, Gilbert. Double agent for Walsingham.

Gilbert, Gifford. Goldsmith detained for coining in Flushing with Marlowe and Baines. (NB Gilbert Gifford and Gifford Gilbert do appear to be two different people.)

Gosson, Stephen. Canterbury man who wrote anti-theatrical tracts.

Gradwell, Thomas. Husband of Marlowe's sister Dorothy.

Hariot, Thomas. Mathematician; travelled to Virginia in 1585; friend of Ralegh; mentioned in the Baines Note.

Harvey, Gabriel. Writer who traded published insults with a number of Marlowe's friends.

Harvey, Richard. Brother of Gabriel and rector of Scadbury, where Sir Thomas Walsingham lived.

Heneage, Sir Thomas. Walsingham's successor as chief of the intelligence service.

Henslowe, Philip. Theatrical entrepreneur who ran the Rose Theatre.

Hesketh, Richard. Walsingham spy and *agent provocateur*.

Howard, Charles, Admiral. Patron of the Admiral's Men, the company for which Marlowe wrote his early plays.

Ive, Paul. Walsingham agent and author of a treatise on fortification which Marlowe used in *Tamburlaine*.

Jones, Richard. Printer of Tamburlaine.

Jordan, John. Husband of Marlowe's sister Margaret.

Kett, Francis. Tutor at Corpus Christi; subsequently executed for heresy.

Kitchen, Richard. Acted as surety for Marlowe when he was arrested in 1589.

Kyd, Thomas. Dramatist; friend and at one stage roommate of Marlowe; implicated him in the possession of heretical documents (see under 1593).

Laski, Albert. Polish magnate who visited England in 1583.

Lewgar, Thomas. Marlowe's roommate at Corpus Christi.

Lyly, John. Canterbury-born dramatist.

Manwood, Sir Roger. Chief Baron of the Exchequer, on whom Marlowe wrote an epitaph.

Marlowe, Ann. Sister.

Marlowe, Dorothy. Sister.

Marlowe, Jane or Joan. Sister.

Marlowe, John. Father.

Marlowe, Katherine. Mother.

Marlowe, Margaret. Sister.

Marlowe, Mary. Sister.

Marlowe, Thomas. Brother.

Marprelate, Martin. Pseudonym of John Penry and John Udall.

Mathews, John. Catholic priest who used 'Christopher Marler' as an alias.

Micques, João. Also known as Nassi. A Jew who was created Duke of Cyprus by Sultan Selim II.

Moody, Michael. Walsingham double agent.

Moore, John. Husband of Marlowe's sister Jane or Joan.

Morgan, Thomas. Agent of Mary, Queen of Scots.

Nashe, Thomas. Pamphleteer and prose writer; friend and possible collaborator of Marlowe.

Northumberland, Henry Percy, 9th earl of. Friend of Hariot and possibly of Marlowe.

Nottingham, Earl of. See Howard, Charles, Admiral.

Ortelius, Abraham. Low Countries cartographer whose maps Marlowe used.

Oxinden, Henry. Man to whom Simon Aldrich told the 'Mr Fineux' anecdote.

Paget, Charles. Agent for Mary, Queen of Scots.

Parker, Matthew. Archbishop of Canterbury; founder of the Parker scholarships.

Parry, William. Executed for planning to assassinate Elizabeth.

Pashley, Christopher. Marlowe's predecessor as Parker scholar.

Passi, David. Suggested by Thomas and Tydeman as an analogue to Barabas.

Penry, John. Principal author of the Martin Marprelate tracts.

Perkins, William. Calvinist theologian.

Persons, Father. Jesuit who published a tract arguing that the Spanish Infanta should succeed to the English Crown.

Poley, Robert. Spy who was in the room when Marlowe died.

Poole, John. Coiner who seems to have taught Marlowe how to counterfeit money.

Puckering, Sir John. Lord Keeper; person to whom Kyd addressed his letter about Marlowe.

Rowland, Humphrey. Acted as surety for Marlowe when he was arrested in 1589.

Roydon, Matthew. Poet and friend of Marlowe.

Shelton, Audrey. See Walsingham, Audrey.

Sidney, Mary, Countess of Pembroke. Sister of Sir Philip and Sir Robert Sidney and dedicatee of Thomas Watson's posthumous *Amintae Gaudia*.

Sidney, Sir Robert. Brother of Mary and Sir Philip and Governor of Flushing, before whom Marlowe was brought when he was arrested there.

Skeres, Nicholas. One of the men in the room when Marlowe died.

Sledd, Charles. Student at the English College in Rome who may have been an associate of Richard Baines.

Spira, Francis. Died of despair at the possibility of his salvation. His story was subsequently dramatised.

Stanley, Sir Edward. Uncle of Lord Strange who fought at the Siege of Malta.

Stanley, Sir William. Relative of Lord Strange who betrayed Deventer to the Spanish.

Strange, Ferdinando Stanley, Lord. Nobleman and theatrical patron whom some Catholics hoped to see on the throne.

Stransham, George. English Catholic who studied at Rheims; also known as Potter and Popham.

Stuart, Lady Arbella. Potential claimant to the throne for whom Marlowe may conceivably have acted as tutor.

Tipping, James. Minor player in the events surrounding Marlowe's death.

Tirrell, Anthony. Associate of John Ballard.

Udall, John. One of the authors of the Martin Marprelate tracts.

Vaughan, William. Author of the most accurate of the early accounts of Marlowe's death.

Waldegrave, Robert. Printer of the Martin Marprelate tracts.

Walsingham, Audrey. Wife of Sir Thomas Walsingham.

Walsingham, Sir Francis. Head of the intelligence service.

Walsingham, Sir Thomas. Nephew of Francis Walsingham and friend of Marlowe.

Warner, Walter. Mathematician; possible candidate for the 'Warner' said to be a friend of Marlowe.

Warner, William. Poet; the other possible Warner.

Watson, Thomas. Poet and friend of Marlowe.

White, John. Travelled to Ralegh's colony, Roanoke, in Virginia, at the same time as Hariot and painted what he saw there.

Wolfe, John. Printer of *Hero and Leander*.

Woodleff, Drew. Conned by Nicholas Skeres.

Works Cited

Adams, Joseph Q. 'The *Massacre at Paris* Leaf', *The Library* 14 (1934): 447–69.

Anstruther, Godfrey. *The Seminary Priests: A Dictionary of the Secular Clergy of England and Wales 1558–1850*, Vol. 1: Elizabethan 1558–1603. Ware and Durham: St Edmund's College and Ushaw College, 1968.

Bakeless, John. *Christopher Marlowe*. London: Jonathan Cape, 1938.

Baron, Frank. *Doctor Faustus from History to Legend*. Munich: Wilhelm Fink, 1978.

Battenhouse, Roy W. 'Protestant Apologetics and the Subplot of 2 *Tamburlaine*', *English Literary Renaissance* 3 (1973): 30–43.

Bawlf, Samuel. *The Secret Voyage of Sir Francis Drake*. Harmondsworth: Penguin, 2003.

Berek, Peter. '*Tamburlaine's* Weak Sons: Imitation as Interpretation before 1593', *Renaissance Drama* 13 (1982): 55–82.

Binding, Paul. *Imagined Corners: Exploring the World's First Atlas*. London: Hodder Headline, 2003.

Bingham, Caroline. *The Life and Times of Edward II*. London: Weidenfeld and Nicolson, 1973.

Boas, F. S. 'New Light on Marlowe and Kyd', *Fortnightly Review* (February 1899): 212–25.

——. *Christopher Marlowe: A Biographical and Critical Study*. Oxford: The Clarendon Press, 1940.

——. *University Drama in the Tudor Age*. Oxford: The Clarendon Press, 1914.

Bossy, John. *Giordano Bruno and the Embassy Affair*. [1991] London: Vintage, 1992.

Bowers, Fredson. 'Marlowe's *Doctor Faustus*: The 1602 Additions', *Studies in Bibliography* 26 (1973): 1–18.

Bowers, Rick. 'Tamburlaine in Ludlow'. *Notes and Queries* 243 (1998): 361–3.

Briggs, William Dinsmore. 'On a Document Concerning Christopher Marlowe', *Studies in Philology* 20 (1923): 153–9.

Brooke, C. F. Tucker. 'The Reputation of Christopher Marlowe'. *Transactions of the Connecticut Academy of Arts and Sciences* 25 (June 1922): 347–408.

Brown, William J. 'Marlowe's Debasement of Bajazet: Foxe's *Actes and Monuments* and *Tamburlaine, Part I*', *Renaissance Quarterly* 24 (1971): 38–48.

Butcher, Andrew. '"only a boy called Christopher Mowle"'. In *Christopher Marlowe and English Renaissance Culture*. Edited by Darryll Grantley and Peter Roberts. Aldershot: Scolar, 1996. 1–16.

Campbell, Lily B. '*Doctor Faustus*: A Case of Conscience', *Publications of the Modern Language Association of America* 67 (1952): 219–39.

Carroll, D. Allen. 'Thomas Watson and the 1588 MS Commendation of *The Faerie Queene*: Reading the Rebuses', *Spenser Studies* 16 (2002): 105–23.

Cerasano, S. P. 'Edward Alleyn's "Retirement" 1597–1600'. *Medieval and Renaissance Drama in England* 10 (1998): 98–112.

200 A Christopher Marlowe Chronology

——. 'Edward Alleyn: 1566–1626'. In *Edward Alleyn: Elizabethan Actor, Jacobean Gentleman*. Edited by Aileen Reed and Robert Maniura. London: Dulwich Picture Gallery, n.d. 11–32.

——. 'Tamburlaine and Edward Alleyn's Ring'. *Shakespeare Survey* 47 (1994): 171–9.

——. 'Philip Henslowe, Simon Forman, and the Theatrical Community of the 1590s'. *Shakespeare Quarterly* 44 (1993): 145–59.

Chambers, E. K. 'The Date of Marlowe's *Tamburlaine'*. *The Times Literary Supplement* 28 August 1930: 684.

——. *The Elizabethan Stage*, vol. II. Oxford: The Clarendon Press, 1923.

Chaudhuri, Sukanta. 'Marlowe, Madrigals, and a New Elizabethan Poet'. *Review of English Studies* 39 (1988): 199–216.

Cheney, Patrick. *Marlowe's Counterfeit Profession*. Toronto: University of Toronto Press, 1997.

——. 'Introduction: Marlowe in the Twenty-first Century'. In *The Cambridge Companion to Christopher Marlowe*. Edited by Patrick Cheney. Cambridge: Cambridge University Press, 2004, pp. 1–23.

Connolly, Annaliese. 'Fruits of Fancy: Elizabeth I and the Rejection of the Panegyric Tradition in Marlowe's *Dido* and Shakespeare's *Dream'*. Forthcoming in *Goddesses and Queens: The Iconography of Elizabeth I*. Edited by Annaliese Connolly and Lisa Hopkins.

Crane, Nicholas. *Mercator: The Man who Mapped the Planet*. London: Phoenix, 2002.

Diehl, Huston. 'Inversion, Parody, and Irony: The Visual Rhetoric of Renaissance English Tragedy'. *Studies in English Literature* 22 (1982): 97–209.

Dodds, M. H. 'The Daughters of Thomas Percy, Seventh Earl of Northumberland'. *Notes and Queries* 169 (1935): 165–6.

Doran, Susan, 'The Politics of Renaissance Europe'. In *Shakespeare and Renaissance Europe*. Edited by Andrew Hadfield and Paul Hammond. London: Thomson Learning, 2005, 21–52.

Dutton, Richard. *Mastering the Revels: The Regulation and Censorship of English Renaissance Drama*. Basingstoke: Palgrave, 1991.

Eccles, Mark. 'Marlowe in Kentish Tradition'. *Notes and Queries* 169 (1935): 20–3, 39–41, 58–61, 134–5.

Empson, William. *Faustus and the Censor: The English Faust-book and Marlowe's Doctor Faustus*. Edited by John Henry Jones. New York: Basil Blackwell, 1987.

Farley-Hills, David. 'Tamburlaine and the Mad Priest of the Sun'. *Journal of Anglo-Italian Studies* 2 (1992): 36–49.

Fehrenbach, R. J. 'A Pre-1592 English Faust Book and the Date of Marlowe's *Doctor Faustus'*. *The Library*, 7th series, 2.4 (2001): 327–35.

Findlay, Alison. 'Heavenly Matters of Theology'. In her *A Feminist Perspective on Renaissance Drama*. Oxford: Blackwell, 1999.

Foister, Susan. 'Edward Alleyn's Collection of Paintings'. In *Edward Alleyn: Elizabethan Actor, Jacobean Gentleman*. Edited by Aileen Reed and Robert Maniura. London: Dulwich Picture Gallery, n.d. 33–62.

Frohnsdorff, Michael. *Christopher Marlowe: The Local Connection and New Research*. Faversham: The Faversham Society, 2003.

George, David. 'The Playhouse at Prescot and the 1592–1594 Plague'. In *Region, Religion and Patronage: Lancastrian Shakespeare*. Edited by Richard Dutton, Alison Findlay and Richard Wilson. Manchester: Manchester University Press, 2003, pp. 227–42.

Greenfield, Matthew. 'Christopher Marlowe's Wound Knowledge'. *PMLA* 119.2 (March 2004): 233–46.

Greg, W. W. 'The Bakings of Betsy'. *The Library*, 3rd series, II.7 (1911): 225–59.

Gristwood, Sarah. *Arbella: England's Lost Queen*. London: Bantam Press, 2003.

Hammer, Paul E. J. 'A Reckoning Reframed: the "Murder" of Christopher Marlowe Revisited'. *English Literary Renaissance* 26.2 (Spring 1996): 225–42.

Hendricks, Margo. 'Managing the Barbarian: *The Tragedy of Dido, Queen of Carthage*', *Renaissance Drama* 23 (1992): 165–88.

Hillman, Richard. *Shakespeare, Marlowe, and the Politics of France*. Basingstoke: Palgrave, 2002.

Holmes, Martin. 'An Unrecorded Portrait of Edward Alleyn'. *Theatre Notebook* (1950–2): 11–13.

Holmes, M. Morgan. 'Identity and the Dissidence it Makes: Homoerotic Nonsense in Kit Marlowe's *Hero and Leander*', *English Studies in Canada* 21.2 (1995): 151–69.

Hopkins, Lisa. *Christopher Marlowe: A Literary Life*. Basingstoke: Palgrave, 2000.

——. '*Doctor Faustus* and the Spanish Netherlands'. *Shakespeare Yearbook*, forthcoming.

——. 'New Light on Marlowe's Murderer'. *Notes and Queries* 249 (September 2004): 251–4.

Hoy, Cyrus. '"Ignorance in Knowledge": Marlowe's Faustus and Ford's Giovanni', *Modern Philology* 57 (1960): 145–54.

Jardine, Lisa. 'The Place of Dialectic Teaching in Sixteenth-Century Cambridge', *Studies in the Renaissance* 21 (1974): 31–62.

Johnson, Francis R. 'Marlowe's Astronomy and Renaissance Skepticism'. *ELH* 13 (1946): 241–54.

Jones, John Henry. *The English Faust Book: A Critical Edition Based on the Text of 1592*. Cambridge: Cambridge University Press, 1994.

Keefer, Michael H. 'Misreading Faustus Misreading: The Question of Context', *Dalhousie Review* 65 (1986): 511–33.

——. 'Right Eye and Left Heel: Ideological Origins of the Legend of Faustus', *Mosaic* 22.2 (1989): 79–94.

——. *Christopher Marlowe's Doctor Faustus: A 1604-Version Edition*. Peterborough, Ontario: Broadview Press, 1991.

Keenan, Siobhan. *Travelling Players in Shakespeare's England*. Basingstoke: Palgrave, 2002.

Kendall, Roy. 'Richard Baines and Christopher Marlowe's Milieu', *English Literary Renaissance* 24 (1994): 507–22.

——. *Christopher Marlowe and Richard Baines: Journeys through the Elizabethan Underground*. London: Associated University Presses, 2003.

Kocher, Paul H. 'The English *Faust Book* and the Date of Marlowe's *Faustus*', *Modern Language Notes* (February 1940): 95–101.

——. 'François Hotman and Marlowe's *The Massacre at Paris*', *PMLA* 56 (1941): 349–68.

——. 'Some Nashe Marginalia Concerning Marlowe', *Modern Language Notes* (January 1942): 45–9.

——. 'Nashe's Authorship of the Prose Scenes in *Faustus*', *Modern Language Quarterly* 2 (1942): 17–40.

——. 'Marlowe's Art of War'. *Studies in Philology* 39 (1942): 207–45.

Kuriyama, Constance B. 'Marlowe's Nemesis: The Identity of Richard Baines'. In *'A Poet and a filthy Play-maker': New Essays on Christopher Marlowe*. Edited by Kenneth Friedenreich, Roma Gill and Constance B. Kuriyama. New York: AMS Press, 1988, pp. 343–60.

——. 'Second Selves: Marlowe's Cambridge and London Friendships', *Medieval and Renaissance Drama in England* 14 (2001): 86–104.

——. *Christopher Marlowe: A Renaissance Life*. Ithaca, NY: Cornell University Press, 2002.

Lacey, Robert. *Sir Walter Ralegh*. London: Weidenfeld & Nicolson, 1973.

Loomie, Albert J., S. J. *The Spanish Elizabethans: The English Exiles at the Court of Philip II*. New York: Fordham University Press, 1963.

McMillin, Scott, and Sally-Beth MacLean. *The Queen's Men and their Plays*. Cambridge: Cambridge University Press, 1998.

Mills, L. J. 'The Meaning of *Edward II*', *Modern Philology* 32 (1934): 11–31.

Morey, Adrian. *The Catholic Subjects of Elizabeth I*. Totowa, NJ: Rowman and Littlefield, 1978.

Nashe, Thomas. *The Unfortunate Traveller and Other Works*. Ed. J. B. Steane. Harmondsworth: Penguin, 1972.

Nicholl, Charles. *A Cup of News: The Life of Thomas Nashe*. London: Routledge and Kegan Paul, 1984.

——. *The Reckoning: The Murder of Christopher Marlowe*. London: Jonathan Cape, 1992.

Norton, Jenny. 'Flags out for New Tamburlaine.' *The Guardian* (16 October 1996): 16.

Noyes, Alfred. *Tales of the Mermaid Tavern*. Edinburgh: William Blackwood & Sons, 1913.

Perry, Curtis. 'Yelverton, Buckingham, and the Story of Edward II in the 1620s'. *Review of English Studies* 54 (2003): 313–35.

Pinciss, G. M. 'Marlowe's Cambridge Years and the Writing of *Doctor Faustus*'. *Studies in English Literature 1500–1900* 33 (1993): 249–64.

Reid, Aileen, and Robert Maniura. *Edward Alleyn: Elizabethan Actor, Jacobean Gentleman*. London: Dulwich Picture Gallery, n.d.

Ribner, Irving. 'Marlowe and the Critics'. *Tulane Drama Review* 8 (1964): 211–24.

Riggs, David. *The World of Christopher Marlowe*. London: Faber and Faber, 2004.

Roth, Cecil. 'The Jews of Malta', *Transactions of the Jewish Historical Society of England*, 12 (1928–31): 187–251.

Rukeyser, Muriel. *The Traces of Thomas Hariot*. New York: Random House, 1970.

Rutter, Carol Chillington. *Documents of the Rose Playhouse* (revised edition). Manchester: Manchester University Press, 1999.

Sachs, Arieh. 'The Religious Despair of *Doctor Faustus*'. *Journal of English and Germanic Philology* 63 (1964): 625–47.

Scott, Margaret. 'Machiavelli and the Machiavel'. *Renaissance Drama* 15 (1984), 147–74.

Seaton, Ethel. 'Marlowe's Map', *Essays and Studies* 10 (1924): 13–35.

——. 'Marlowe, Robert Poley, and the Tippings', *Review of English Studies* 5 (1929): 273–87.

Stevens, Henry. *Thomas Hariot, the Mathematician, the Philosopher, and the Scholar*. New York: Lenox Hill, 1972 (rpt).

Stump, Donald. 'Marlowe's Travesty of Virgil: *Dido* and Elizabethan Dreams of Empire'. *Comparative Drama* 34.1 (1999): 79–107.

Tannenbaum, Samuel. *The Assassination of Christopher Marlowe*. Hamden, Conn.: The Shoe String Press, 1928.

Thomas, Vivien and William Tydeman. *Christopher Marlowe: The Plays and Their Sources*. London: Routledge, 1994.

Traister, Barbara Howard. *Heavenly Necromancers: The Magician in English Renaissance Drama*. Columbia: University of Missouri Press, 1984.

——. *The Notorious Astrological Physician of London: Works and Days of Simon Forman*. Chicago: University of Chicago Press, 2001.

Urry, William. *Christopher Marlowe in Canterbury*. London: Faber & Faber, 1988.

Vella Bonavita, Helen. 'Key to Christendom: The 1565 Siege of Malta, its Histories, and their Use in Reformation Polemic'. *Sixteenth Century Journal* 33.4 (2002): 1021–43.

Voss, Paul J. *Elizabethan News Pamphlets: Shakespeare, Spenser, Marlowe and the Birth of Journalism*. Pittsburgh: Duquesne University Press, 2001.

Waswo, Richard. 'Damnation, Protestant Style: Macbeth, Faustus, and Christian Tragedy', *Journal of Medieval and Renaissance Studies* 4.1 (1974): 63–99.

Wernham, R. B. 'Christopher Marlowe at Flushing', *English Historical Review* 91 (1976): 344.

West, Robert H. 'The Impatient Magic of Dr. Faustus', *English Literary Renaissance* 4:2 (1974): 218–40.

Wheeler, Richard P. *Creating Elizabethan Tragedy: The Theater of Marlowe and Kyd*. Chicago: University of Chicago Press, 1988.

Wilson, Richard. 'Visible Bullets. Tamburlaine the Great and Ivan the Terrible', *ELH* 62 (1995): 47–68.

——. 'Introduction: a Torturing Hour – Shakespeare and the Martyrs'. In *Theatre and Religion: Lancastrian Shakespeare*. Edited by Richard Dutton, Alison Findlay and Richard Wilson (Manchester: Manchester University Press, 2003), pp. 1–39.

——. 'Tragedy, Patronage, and Power', in *The Cambridge Companion to Christopher Marlowe*. Edited by Patrick Cheney (Cambridge: Cambridge University Press, 2004), pp. 207–30.

Woolley, Benjamin. *The Queen's Conjuror: The Life and Magic of Dr Dee* [2001]. London: Flamingo, 2002.

Wraight, A. D., and Virginia F. Stern. *In Search of Christopher Marlowe*, 2nd edition. Chichester: Adam Hart, 1993.

Wyckham, Glynne. *English Professional Theatre, 1530–1660: A Documentary History*. Cambridge: Cambridge University Press, 2001.

Zimansky, Curt A. 'Marlowe's *Faustus*: The Date Again'. *Philological Quarterly* 41:1 (January 1962): 181–7.

Index